CAHUILLA NATION ACTIVISM AND THE TRIBAL CASINO MOVEMENT

THE GAMBLING SERIES

Series Editor, David G. Schwartz (UNLV)

The Gambling series seeks to cultivate and encourage scholarly investigation of gambling across several disciplines, including history, sociology, economics, psychology, business, and political science. Gambling is both a growing global industry and a widespread pastime throughout the world. The ways that gamblers, governments, and businesses approach gambling are many and varied, and they are a treasure trove of source material for scholars in a variety of disciplines. The series encompasses all forms of gambling, including casinos, lotteries, racing, and sports betting, and will examine organizations owned by private companies, state and national governments, and tribal governments.

Gambling is always in the news—both in Nevada and throughout the world. At present, the major axes of study are problem gambling and the business of gambling. But as gambling continues to grow and become normalized, there will be an increased demand for scholarly work on normative gambling. This series fits that need by publishing books that continue the discourse on problem gambling and those that push the boundaries of what has traditionally been published.

New Politics of Indian Gaming: The Rise of Reservation Interest Groups
by Kenneth N. Hansen & Tracy A. Skopek

Macau and the Casino Complex
Edited by Stefan Al

All In: The Spread of Gambling in Twentieth-Century United States
Edited by Jonathan D. Cohen & David G. Schwartz

Cahuilla Nation Activism and the Tribal Casino Movement
by Theodor P. Gordon

CAHUILLA NATION ACTIVISM AND THE TRIBAL CASINO MOVEMENT

Theodor P. Gordon

UNIVERSITY OF NEVADA PRESS *Reno & Las Vegas*

University of Nevada Press | Reno, Nevada 89557 USA
www.unpress.nevada.edu
Cover photograph in the Carol M. Highsmith Archive, Library of Congress,
    Prints and Photographs Division.
Cover design by Louise OFarrell

LIBRARY OF CONGRESS CATALOGING-IN-PUBLICATION DATA
Names: Gordon, Theodor P., 1984– author.
Title: Cahuilla nation activism and the tribal casino movement / by Theodor P.
    Gordon.
Description: Reno : University of Nevada Press, 2018. | Series: The gambling series |
    Includes bibliographical references and index.
Identifiers: ISBN 978-1-943859-93-1 (pbk. : alk. paper) | ISBN 978-1-943859-81-8
    (cloth : alk. paper) | ISBN 978-1-943859-82-5 (e-book) | LCCN 2018004903 (print) |
    LCCN 2018007342 (e-book)
Subjects: LCSH: Cahuilla Indians—History. | Cahuilla Indians—Government
    relations. | Cahuilla Indians—Finance. | Gambling on Indian reservations. |
    Cabazon Reservation (Calif.)
Classification: LCC E99.C155 (e-book) | LCC E99.C155 G67 2018 (print) |
    DDC 979.4004/9745—dc23
LC record available at https://lccn.loc.gov/2018004903

The paper used in this book meets the requirements of American National Standard
for Information Sciences—Permanence of Paper for Printed Library Materials,
ANSI/NISO Z39.48-1992 (R2002).

FIRST PRINTING

Manufactured in the United States of America

To Christen

CONTENTS

ACKNOWLEDGMENTS

I am grateful for the many individuals and organizations who helped make this book possible. For their expertise, guidance, and help, I would like to thank Kate Spilde, David Schwartz, Hannah Nyala West, Caitlyn Marrs, David Kronenfeld, Yolanda Moses, Clifford Trafzer, Michael Kearney, Anthony Madrigal Sr., Elizabeth Wessells, Maija Glassier-Lawson, Melanie Spoo, Gene Anderson, Anna Norris, Katie Langer, and my parents, Charles and Beverly Gordon.

The following institutions provided invaluable resources in support of my research: the Malki Museum, the Agua Caliente Cultural Museum, the Twentynine Palms Historical Society, Joshua Tree National Park, the Joshua Tree National Park Association, the Center for Gaming Research at the University of Nevada Las Vegas, the California Digital Newspaper Collection, the National Archives and Records Administration, the Sycuan Institute on Tribal Gaming, the Institute for Research on Labor and Employment, the University of California Riverside, the College of Saint Benedict, and Saint John's University.

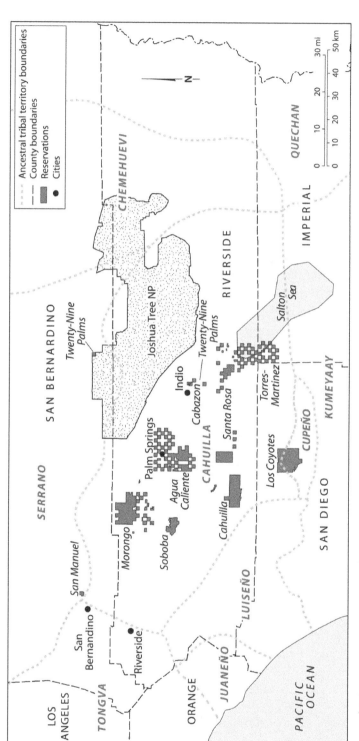

Map of Cahuilla ancestral territory (note: boundaries are approximate) by Bill Nelson

INTRODUCTION

ON OCTOBER 18, 1980, in an isolated stretch of California's low desert, the City of Indio Police Department raided a crowded room and arrested its occupants in hopes of shuttering their operation, a modest poker club. A federal judge threw out the case because the club was not in the city limits of Indio: it was on the reservation of the Cabazon Band of Mission Indians, one of the Cahuilla nations indigenous to inland Southern California.[1] The Cabazon Band reopened their club, only to be raided again on February 13, 1983, this time by the Riverside County sheriff. Certainly, the county sheriff reasoned, the Cabazon Reservation is inside Riverside County, and therefore subject to county laws prohibiting gambling. In 1987, seven years after first opening their gaming venture, this legal battle culminated with the U.S. Supreme Court deciding the landmark case *California v. Cabazon Band of Mission Indians* (480 U.S. 202). The Court agreed with Cabazon by finding that as a federally recognized native nation, Cabazon has civil and regulatory jurisdiction on its reservation.[2] Therefore, if an activity is regulated in the surrounding state (as gambling was in California when Cabazon first opened their casino), then native nations within that state can regulate that activity on their reservations as they see fit. With this decision, a vast new realm of possibility opened for native nations across the United States and set the course for new political and regulatory regimes, starting with Congress passing the Indian Gaming Regulatory Act (IGRA) in 1988 (Pub.L. 100-497, 25 U.S.C. 2701). Tribal gaming quickly grew into a nationwide movement, which became a legal and viable opportunity for many (though not all) impoverished tribes to raise much-needed revenue. At the same time, it also became a new arena to contest the rights of tribal governments.

Cabazon's successful defense of their gaming venture set the legal precedent for what is now a $30 billion industry that rivals the United

States' commercial (i.e., private or nontribal) casino industry (National Indian Gaming Commission 2017). While the growth of Indian gaming rapidly transformed native and nonnative communities across North America, the source of the Indian casino movement stems from the sovereignty (i.e., the capacity for self-reliance and self-determination) that native nations have practiced since time immemorial. Their practice of sovereignty flows, uninterrupted, from before European contact to today, when it significantly shapes the regional and national political-economy. In fact, the Cahuilla nations (which include the Cabazon Band) have continued their practice of sovereignty that persisted even during the California gold rush, when the early state pursued a policy that it referred to as extermination, and can rightfully be called genocide (Lindsay 2012).³ In the decades after the California gold rush many prominent settlers (i.e., North American non-Indians) assumed that all Indian communities would collapse due to their alleged inferiority (Fitzgerald 1878/1881; Trafzer and Hyer 1999).⁴ However, by the early twentieth century the Cahuilla nations, in partnership with other native nations, were lobbying Congress to recognize their rights (Thorne 2004; Trafzer 2002). Today, the growth of the tribal casino industry ensures that more and more settlers engage in economic and cultural activities initiated by native nations. Yet among the public there remains a dearth of knowledge about Indians in the past and present. Today, competing perspectives of native nations affect the political and cultural processes of revitalization (Darian-Smith 2004; Steinman 2006). From genocide to gaming, this book examines how the Cahuilla and other native nations have succeeded in challenging many non-Indians to rethink their assumptions about American Indians and, in doing so, their understanding of the United States as a democratic society.

It has never occurred to most Americans that the United States contains not only fifty states, but also multitudes of native sovereign nations. At the time of this writing the federal government recognizes 566 native nations. Since a Supreme Court ruling in 1831, *Cherokee Nation v. Georgia* (30 U.S. 1), the federal government has deemed these tribes to be "domestic dependent nations" that exist under the overarching sovereignty of the United States (2). In addition to these 566, there are many more native nations, some with state-level recognition and others still working toward recognition. Yet many institutions of public education teach a peculiarly incomplete and partial history of the United States that erases the existence and contributions of native nations, past and present. As demonstrated by Trafzer and Lorimer's (2014, 64) analysis of California's public-school curricula and textbooks, "The California State Department of Education denies the genocide [of California Indians] and textbook companies are silent of Indian genocide in spite of overwhelming evidence." Although recent reforms and a growing minority of individual school districts and teachers are working to provide students with a more complete understanding of native Californians, most Californians received little, if any, education about California's native nations. As a result, most Californians' knowledge of their native neighbors comes from simplistic and often crude representations of natives in the media. How then are nonnative Californians to make any sense of the emergence of tribal casinos that millions visit? How did American society reach a point where revitalized tribal sovereignty significantly impacts settler society while settlers themselves have no understanding of the history that led to this? With absent or fallacious knowledge, settlers have no means to understand their native neighbors. As will be shown, the stories settlers create to make sense of tribal casinos do not reflect the history of native nation activism. Instead, they reveal common assumptions about American society. By investigating the history of tribal self-determination and how settlers have attempted and often failed to understand it, this book reveals changes in how settlers understand nationhood and their identity as Americans. As will be shown, these changes may shape the future of self-determination in the land now known as the United States.

In this book I demonstrate how the Cahuilla's central role in the Indian casino movement is linked to their history of continuous political, economic, and cultural influence on the development of California settler society, dating to the first Spanish settlements. Furthermore, I argue that the Cahuilla and other native nations persevered through centuries of persecution in large part by waging a war of cultural knowledge wherein they understood settler society better than the settlers themselves. Again and again, when settler institutions attempted to annihilate native nations, native activists have intervened by working to educate the public, spurring cultural and political reforms. The Cahuilla and other native nations used this strategy from the California gold rush, through the termination era, and into the current Indian gaming movement. I build this argument from a case study of archival and ethnographic research conducted in the present-day communities now in the Cahuilla's ancestral territory, which today includes the metropolises of Palm Springs and Riverside in inland Southern California.

In *Mohawk Interruptus*, Audra Simpson (2014, 177) demonstrates how native nations' "insistence upon certain things—such as nationhood and sovereignty—fundamentally interrupts and casts into question the story that settler states tell themselves." Following Simpson, there may be no more visible symbol of native nation sovereignty than tribal casinos. Tribal casinos interrupt the story that the United States tells itself. The resilience of native nations overturns old assumptions and, in some cases, creates new assumptions. This book builds on Simpson by exploring how the Cahuilla have consistently used the strategy of challenging how settlers understand their own society. With the advent of tribal casinos, this strategy now has even broader impacts on the ways that nonnative Americans think about the United States.

In his insightful work *Indians in Unexpected Places*, Philip Deloria (2004) asked readers to consider why so many nonnatives act surprised at the sight of American Indians at a beauty parlor, on the field playing a football game, or behind the wheel of a modern automobile. He demonstrated how those moments when nonnatives are surprised to see American Indians engaged in the various trappings of modern life reveal what settler society has come to expect. Deloria (11) urged us to "think of [these] expectations in terms of the colonial and imperial relations of power and domination existing between Indian people and the United States." Moreover, these expectations do more than just reveal how colonialism led to the common assumption that American Indians were left behind, or incapable of taking part in, modernity. These expectations also provide opportunities to challenge these misconceptions. Deloria provided an invaluable framework for identifying when and where these assumptions might be challenged. According to this framework, in some cases Indians engaged in modern activities might be perceived by nonnatives as "anomalous, which reinforces [nonnative] expectations" (11). In other cases, Deloria goes on, they might be perceived by nonnatives as "unexpected, which resists categorization and, thereby, [cause nonnatives to question] the expectation itself" (11). Gambling is no less a modern activity than any of those described by Deloria, therefore Deloria's framework suggests that tribal casinos have the potential to reinforce or challenge settler expectations. Tribal casinos can disorient settlers who have come to assume that Indians exist only in the past or in communities isolated from modern life.

This book builds on the work of Deloria, Simpson, and other Native American studies scholars who chart the implications of settler colonialism for native communities. The interdisciplinary nature of Native American studies allows the field to grow by adopting and adapting tools from across academic disciplines. Cognitive anthropology seeks to understand how societies come to hold different assumptions about how the world works and how those assumptions can vary though time and across populations (see also Blount 2011; D'Andrade 1995; Kronenfeld 1996, 2008, 2018; Kronenfeld et al. 2011; Ross and Medin 2011; Weller and Romney 1988). It asks many of the same questions as are found in Native American studies, particularly because both are interested in how certain assumptions become widespread and how they can be challenged. However, these two fields have yet to benefit directly from each other even though they work independently toward similar goals. To this end, this book seeks to combine two strands of theory, from cognitive anthropology and Native American studies, to illustrate how the theories can benefit each other. Later in this introduction I will briefly introduce tools from cognitive anthropology and demonstrate how they can be integrated with Native American studies. But before drawing connections between these fields, it is important to define two of the concepts that are foundational to this book: nationhood and sovereignty.

Nationhood and Sovereignty

In his influential book *Imagined Communities*, Benedict Anderson (1983, 6) defined nationhood as "an imagined political community—and imagined as both inherently limited and sovereign.... It is *imagined* [emphasis in the original] because the members of even the smallest nation will never know most of their fellow-members, meet them, or even hear of them, yet in the minds of each lives the image of their communion.... In fact, all communities larger than primordial villages of face-to-face contact (and perhaps even these) are imagined." Anderson's research focused on nation-building, especially in Southeast Asia, but his contributions have implications for understanding the bonds within all communities, including those communities that many people may not even think of as nations. Anderson's work is especially relevant to native nations; he argues persuasively that nations are not made just from institutions—although institutions certainly can play a key role in nation building. Anderson argues that nations are formed, at least in part, in the imaginations of their members.

The concepts of nationhood and sovereignty emerged in a European context quite different from that of precontact North America. Like any other words from a foreign context, the terms "nationhood" and "sovereignty" can be only partially and imperfectly translated and applied to describe the precontact peoples of native North America. But there are many reasons why, however imperfect, this terminology might be among the best suited in the English language to begin discussions of native political organization. How can we use terms from the English language and Western political theory to describe native social organizations? However imperfectly, these terms can be used if we acknowledge their imperfections and adapt accordingly. Benedict Anderson's (1983, 6) note that perhaps even "primordial villages of face-to-face contact" are imagined communities is one possible starting point for describing native North American societies as nations. Imagination, after all, is a mental process. Any community capable of self-determination, regardless of its size or the structure of its institutions, has a population with a set of at least some shared experiences and shared knowledge. Anderson (13) argued that preindustrial self-governing communities imagined themselves "largely through the medium of a sacred language" based on their shared origin stories. Likewise, Cahuilla nations' origin stories underpin their desire for and capacity for self-determination, as well as their ties to their ancestral land. As will be shown, even though it is a Western concept, nationhood quickly became the terminology of choice for European colonizers encountering native peoples, and native peoples quickly picked up on nationhood as a way of describing their own societies to settlers.

Like nationhood, sovereignty originated from European political thought and can be applied to native nations, if its application comes with some important caveats. Observing the shortcomings of this term, Joanne Barker (2005a, 21) noted, "There is no fixed meaning for what *sovereignty* [emphasis in original] is—what it means by definition, what it implies in public debate, or how it has been conceptualized in international, national, or indigenous law. Sovereignty...is embedded within the specific social relations in which it is invoked and given meaning." This book uses the terms "sovereignty" and "self-determination" interchangeably because native nations and the U.S. political system frequently use these terms for describing the capacity for tribes to make decisions independently. The word "sovereignty" derives from European discourse. It originally referred to the absolute power of a monarch and the belief that a monarch's power came from a spiritual source, or god. No doubt this is quite different from the contexts and meanings in which the term is used by native nations. For this reason, Taiaiake Alfred (2005, 46–47) called for "people committed to transcending the imperialism of state sovereignty...to de-think the concept of sovereignty and replace it with a notion of power that has at its root a more appropriate premise." Following Barker and Alfred, this book pays close attention to the different meanings given to sovereignty by different actors, with a critical eye toward the differences in how Europeans and native nations conceptualize power. When I use the terms "sovereignty" and "self-determination," I am generally referring to the capacity for native nations to make decisions for themselves because this is the meaning most often ascribed to these terms by both native nations and the U.S. government.

Given that nationhood, as understood by Benedict Anderson, exists, at least in part, in the minds and imaginations of a nation's citizens and that sovereignty itself has been imbued with a wide variety of meanings, I find it useful to distinguish between cultural and political sovereignty as others have done before (Wilkins 2007). In other words, a nation's self-determination involves both cognitive and social processes. Nations exist both in individuals' minds as ideas and in the patterned interactions between individuals that create a nation's institutions. A nation does not exist without constituent members who identify as part of that nation. When I refer to the cultural dimension of sovereignty, I mean shared beliefs of members of community that want to exercise self-determination. This includes individual community members' beliefs that they are part of a community whose members have the right to determine the course of their future. It often also includes a shared belief among community members that they have an inherent connection to a specific place where they should exercise their self-determination. However, this cultural dimension by itself cannot provide a community with the capacity for self-determination. To act on its belief in sovereignty, a community needs political sovereignty, those institutions through which decisions are made and implemented. A shared belief among individuals that they constitute a nation is necessary but not sufficient for those individuals to act meaningfully as a nation. That belief must also be coupled with actions that seize and reproduce self-governance. The political and cultural dimensions of a polity strengthen each other, but these two dimensions should not be conflated. As will be shown, there are times when native nations, including the Cahuilla nations, had

TABLE 0.1. Dimensions of Sovereignty

	INTERNAL	EXTERNAL
POLITICAL	• Leadership roles • Decision-making councils or legislature • Constitution	• Intergovernmental relations, treaties, diplomacy, compacts
CULTURAL	• Origin stories • Shared beliefs about rights for one's own community to be autonomous	• Shared beliefs about a neighboring polity's rights, especially autonomy

severely limited political sovereignty. However, just because the United States constrains native nations' capacities for self-determination does not mean that the United States succeeded in extinguishing them. At different times the United States came close to eliminating native nations' political sovereignty, but despite policies such as forced attendance at boarding schools and relocation, attempts to assimilate native populations have instead only strengthened their cultural sovereignty. Therefore, it is not enough just to speak of the political and cultural dimensions of sovereignty. It is also helpful to think of sovereignty as strengthened through interdependencies and mutual recognition. Because nations are strengthened or hindered by their relations with other nations, it can be useful to think of sovereignty as having internal and external dimensions that crosscut the political and cultural dimensions outlined above.

No nations exist in isolation and no nation can thrive without recognition by other nations. All nations are (to varying ways and degrees) interdependent. Sovereignty entails internal and external processes that are both cultural and political. Internal processes encompass the beliefs and actions of individuals that affect the nation they belong to. External processes involve the beliefs and actions of outsiders that affect a nation. The internal/external and cultural/political dimensions embed each other such that a nation's internal cultural sovereignty emerges from its members' beliefs about their nation. A nation's external cultural sovereignty depends on outsiders' beliefs about that nation's right to self-determination (i.e., the members of one nation believing that a neighboring community could or should be autonomous). Governmental institutions (e.g., councils, constitutions, etc.) create internal political sovereignty. Diplomatic relations between governmental structures produce external political sovereignty.

Today, for most nation-states, the internal and external dimensions, and the cultural and political dimensions, support each other. In other words, most nation-states recognize each other, and themselves, through cultural and political practices. For example, an independent Canada and an independent Mexico on the northern and southern borders of the United States are not controversial. American citizens are largely in agreement with Canadian and Mexican citizens that each of the three nations should be independent, and the diplomatic relations between these nations follow suit, with each having embassies and an array of other institutions of formal diplomacy. But external sovereignty is not always so straightforward. Is Palestine part of Israel or a separate nation? Is Taiwan independent of China? In terms of external cultural sovereignty, it depends on whom you ask. I use the examples of Palestine and Taiwan not to take any particular stance on recognizing their sovereignty (which would be well beyond the scope of this book) but rather to highlight the importance of interdependence, of mutual recognition, for a polity to have the capacity for self-determination. Depending on where you ask, people can disagree quite vehemently on whether Palestine or Taiwan should be independent nations. Likewise, the external political sovereignty of Palestine and Taiwan can be very different depending on where you look. More than 130 nations formally recognize Palestine as an independent state (Tharoor 2014), but Israel and the United States do not. The Dominican Republic and the Solomon Islands, among a handful of other nations, have formal diplomatic relations with Taiwan (Ministry of Foreign Affairs, Republic of China [Taiwan] 2016), but, importantly, China and the United States do not recognize Taiwanese independence. I use these examples because their sovereignty is contentious and this contention limits their capacity for self-determination. Native nation sovereignty is also contentious, in that the federal government frequently changes the degree to which it attempts to terminate or recognize native nation self-determination. Likewise, the United States' settler population often has internal disagreements about relations with native nations, and settler perceptions of native nations can shift as often as federal policy. One key strategy used by the Cahuilla and other native nations is to educate the public to strengthen their external political sovereignty. As demonstrated throughout this book, time after time this strategy has provided real, though limited, success in leading policymakers to strengthen native nations' external political sovereignty.

From the time European nations began colonizing North America they recognized the sovereignty of native nations through the signing of treaties, although they rarely, if ever, respected the terms of those treaties. Historically, the United States has swung, repeatedly, between attempts to terminate native nation sovereignty and limited recognition of their sovereignty. Moreover, just because the United States officially recognizes 566 native nations does not mean that it recognizes those nations on their own terms. Glen Sean Coulthard (2014, 179) forcefully makes this point in *Red Skin, White Masks*, where he calls for a "shift in our attention away from the largely rights-based/recognition orientation that has emerged as hegemonic over the last four decades, to a resurgent politics of recognition that seeks to practice…alternative structures of law and sovereign authority grounded on a critical refashioning of the best of Indigenous legal and political traditions." At times, the United States has allowed native nations to practice a limited and constrained external political sovereignty. However, native nations may have little reason to be content with accepting such constraints on their capacity for self-governance. Indeed, the Cabazon Band's activism through direct action, specifically opening a gaming establishment that the band knew would bring legal challenges, can be seen as part of Coulthard's "resurgent politics of recognition" that reject complacency with status quo constraints on external political sovereignty.

Settler Colonialism

The external constraints on native nation sovereignty are the legacy and product of the ongoing colonization of North America. By enforcing its dominion over native people and their land, the expansion of the United States across western North America was and is an act of colonization. This colonization is not unlike that by other empires, especially settler colonies like Australia and Canada. In settler colonialism, the expanding nation encourages and facilitates settlers to replace the native occupants of the colonized territory. Patrick Wolfe noted, "Settler colonies were not primarily established to extract surplus value from indigenous labour. Rather, they are premised on displacing indigenes from (or replacing them on) the land" (Wolfe 1998, 1). Wolfe finds parallels between settler colonialism in Australia, the focus of his research, and North America, where "Native (North) Americans were cleared from their land rather than exploited for their labour, their place being taken by displaced Africans who provided the labour to be mixed with the expropriated land"

(1–2). Wolfe's definition of settler colonialism reflects most of the history of United States' federal Indian policies, but it is not the only form of colonialism to shape North America. California, perhaps more so than any other state, has a history that does not neatly fit Wolfe's definition of settler colonialism. California was first colonized by Spain, which used its network of missions to exploit the labor of California Indians without an intensive immigration of settlers. Among the first laws passed by California's legislature after it was annexed by the United States and it gained statehood was an act that legalized and regulated the buying and selling of California Indian children for the purpose of exploiting their labor well into adulthood. (See chapters 1 and 2, respectively, for more discussion of the missions and the enslavement of California Indians.) This history makes California somewhat of an exception, perhaps more than other states, to the general trajectory of settler colonialism in the land that is now called the United States of America. As will be shown in chapter 3, native labor helped usher in a wave of tribal activism because wages earned through their labor funded their efforts to restore tribal sovereignty. Aside from the exception of these and other instances of native labor exploitation, the focus of the United States' federal Indian policies has mainly been to remove native peoples from their land in order to replace them with a settler population and to exploit native natural resources. Because most of this book focuses on California, it is helpful to place California in the context of the overarching pattern of the settler colonial policies in the United States. The following section briefly traces the moments when settler colonialism in the United States increased in intensity. Contrasting the limited sovereignty of the fifty states with native nation sovereignty can be a useful way to begin an analysis of the ways in which native nations fit, and do not fit, into the wider political system of the United States.

Most nation-states, including the United States, subdivide aspects of internal political sovereignty into state and local governments. The Tenth Amendment (U.S. Const. amend. 10) of the Constitution of the United States recognizes that state governments have rights, often called states' rights: the powers not delegated to the federal government are reserved for states. Most divisive policy questions, such as abortion, civil rights, and slavery, entail some degree of conflict over the rights and limits of state and federal sovereignty. Can states legalize marijuana even if doing so violates federal law? Can they outlaw or restrict access to abortions if the U.S. Supreme Court has found that such a ban violates

individual rights? The boundaries of state government sovereignty ebb and flow as new political controversies emerge, forcing states and the federal government to renegotiate the line where state authority ends and federal authority begins. In other words, not even state governments have fixed boundaries for their capacities for self-determination. Though they appear relatively stable, states can have broader or narrower capacities for self-determination as determined by the federal government. One consistent theme that we will return to throughout this book is the question of what kinds of authority, if any, a state has over the native nations that reside within that state's geographic boundaries. Moreover, while the limits of state sovereignty may be open to negotiation, state governments themselves cannot be readily terminated by the federal government. This is where the external political sovereignty of native nations differs significantly from that of the fifty states. Tribal governments are vulnerable in that they are subject to potential termination by Congress. The federal government at times recognizes that native nations have certain rights. Sometimes it allows limited expansions of these rights and other times it seeks to terminate tribal sovereignty entirely. Federally recognized native nations are like state governments in that the federal government recognizes some form of their capacity for self-determination and they can at times conflict with the federal government over the limits of their self-determination. But the federal recognition of native nation sovereignty has been much more capricious than federal recognition of state rights. At times, federal Indian policies have been downright malicious. To be clear, the internal dimensions of tribal sovereignty are resilient. A native nation's belief in its right to self-determination and its own internal structures for decision-making can persist even when federal policies and settler perceptions of native nations want to eliminate native peoples.

Native nation internal cultural sovereignty flows from the nations' origin stories. For all the diversity of native nation spirituality, one common thread is an origin story that tells of the creation of their nation as an autonomous community with rights and obligations to a specific place, the nation's ancestral territory. The internal cultural sovereignty of native nations persists, even when external cultural sovereignty vacillates as settler perceptions sway between support and denial of tribal sovereignty. Likewise, native nation political structures, whether the precontact organizations of the past or the tribal governments of today, are hallmarks of internal political sovereignty. Native nation external political sovereignty lies in formal relations with other governments, especially the federal and state governments. Thus, in the 1890s and again in the 1950s when the federal government intensified efforts to advance settler colonialism by terminating native nation sovereignty through forced assimilation, it could succeed only in terminating native nation external political sovereignty. As will be seen throughout this book, the internal and external dimensions of sovereignty impinge on each other, but only rarely can one extinguish the other.

Since the first arrival of Europeans in North American, the Doctrine of Discovery guided colonial relations with natives. Often misconstrued to mean that colonizers conquered a territory and its people merely by discovering them, in practice the Doctrine of Discovery only provided colonial regimes with the exclusive right to preempt other colonizers from negotiating with native people (Wilkins and Lomawaima 2001, 26). The nations that colonized North America, primarily Spain, France, and Britain, largely agreed that whichever first "discovered" a territory had the right to negotiate with its inhabitants for the purchase of land. From the onset of colonization—and for most of the time since then— European governments and their people, as well as the United States and Americans, recognized native nations as sovereign. As Vine Deloria (1979, 23) noted, "Indigenous nations are constitutive of settler state sovereignty" because negotiating treaties with indigenous nations provided legitimacy for their colonizing efforts "in the eyes of other states and in the eyes of tribe nations." The settlers of North America did not give sovereignty to native nations. Instead, North American native nations already had the capacity for self-determination, which colonizers recognized through the process of treaty signing—even though colonizers consistently broke the terms of those treaties.

Under the statutes laid out in the Constitution of the United States, the federal government has discretion over Indian policies. Individual states generally do not have authority in tribal relations, but there are important exceptions (Rosen 2007; Wilkins 2007, 112). A Supreme Court decision in 1831 gave Congress the sole authority over relations with native nations, thus beginning a convoluted succession of often contradictory federal Indian policies. This decision, *Cherokee Nation v. Georgia,* declared that Indian peoples are "domestic dependent nations" whose "relations to the United States resemble that of a ward to his guardian." This decision only gave more power to the federal government, which just one year prior enacted one of its most egregious acts of settler colonialism, the Indian

Removal Act of 1830 (U.S.C. 21, 2, 148), which mandated the removal of native peoples from the Southeastern United States to the west, culminating in the forced march known as the Trail of Tears. Only within the lands reserved by Congress for tribes could tribal societies practice a degree of self-rule. Federal acknowledgment of tribal land rights further eroded in 1887 when Congress passed the Dawes Act. The Dawes Act (Pub.L. 49-119) divided tribal lands into individual parcels and assigned each to an American Indian family or individual, in an attempt to subvert communal property ownership, make tribal lands open for settlers to purchase, and assimilate tribal peoples. This policy failed in its goals and only further marginalized and impoverished native nations.

In 1934 Congress passed the Wheeler-Howard Act (Pub.L. 73-383), better known as the Indian Reorganization Act, to overturn the Dawes Act and allow tribes to practice limited self-governance on reservations under a corporate structure prescribed by the Bureau of Indian Affairs (BIA). However, this policy reform was quickly reversed. In the 1950s and 1960s Congress terminated tribal governments and relocated thousands of American Indians to cities (Fixico 1986). Termination devastated tribes, but it also spurred American Indian activism. In the early 1970s, in response to increasing pressure and highly visible campaigns by the American Indian activists, President Nixon ended the termination era and began restoring federal recognition to terminated tribes. In 1975 Congress passed a series of laws (including the Indian Self-Determination and Education Assistance Act, Pub.L. 93-638) to further support a limited revitalization of tribal sovereignty. Tribal gaming is, in part, a consequence of this revitalization.

When the federal government began to once again recognize a limited form of tribal sovereignty in the 1970s, though still overwhelmingly impoverished, many tribes generally began to experience relative increases in economic development because they were increasingly able to independently control tribal resources (Wilkins 2007). To further economic development, several tribal governments began developing and operating gaming enterprises. In 1976 the Oneida Indian Reservation in Wisconsin opened a bingo hall and advertised it to nonmembers (Hoeft 2014). Three years later the Seminole Indians of Florida opened their own high-stakes bingo parlor. State law allowed only charities in Florida to operate bingo and the state limited the size of the jackpot. The sheriff of Broward County attempted to shutter the Seminole's operation because, from his perspective, the Seminoles violated Florida law in that their tribal government is not a charity and their jackpot exceeded the state limit. In 1984 the tribe won a federal court case (*Seminole Tribe of Florida v. Butterworth*, 658 F2d. 310) that found the tribe could use its powers, as a sovereign government, to operate high-stakes bingo. The court reasoned that because the Seminoles have regulatory jurisdiction on their reservation, they could legalize and regulate any activity that is legal and regulated in Florida, including bingo. The *Cabazon* decision, described in detail in chapter 5, involved a similar dispute between state and tribal authorities. In 1987 Cabazon's fight to operate its poker and bingo enterprise succeeded at the Supreme Court, affirming the right of native nations across the United States to offer gaming as a means to gain economic self-sufficiency. The following year, the U.S. Congress passed the IGRA, which mandates that tribes that pursue Class 3 gaming (e.g., slot machines, most card games, and other Vegas-style games) must negotiate a compact with the surrounding state. These compacts provide state governments with the capacity to regulate and possibly constrain tribal casinos to the point of eliminating their feasibility. Thus, the IGRA created a new and unprecedented role for state governments, which, since the 1832 Supreme Court decision *Worcester v. Georgia* (31 U.S. 515), have not had any federally delegated power to intervene on noncriminal actions on tribal lands.

So where do native nations reside in the United States' political system? Kevin Bruyneel (2007, xvii) convincingly argued that they exist in what he calls a "'third space of sovereignty' that resides neither simply inside nor outside the American political system but rather exists on [the] boundaries, exposing both the practices and the contingencies of American colonial rule." The federal government affords a limited and partial allowance for native nation self-determination, but there is much more to their self-determination than just what the federal government allows. Bruyneel's argument that they exist in a third space of sovereignty illustrates how native nations can simultaneously draw on their constrained external sovereignty and on their own internal sovereignty, which lies outside the authority of the United States. Bruyneel showed how, by operating in this third space, native nations can make visible the contradictions that would otherwise be invisible to American settler society.

Investigating the origin and impacts of the tribal casino movement can further illuminate the cleavages between how Americans understand their society and the actions of the United States' political system. As federal Indian policy scholar Felix Cohen once observed, "The Indian plays much the same role in our American society that the Jews played in Germany. Like the miner's canary, the Indian marks shifts from fresh air to poison gas in our political atmosphere; and...reflects the rise and fall in our democratic faith" (Cohen 1953, 390). Changes in tribal external sovereignty not only reflect changing perceptions of American Indians, but also mark moments of growing and fading dedication to democratic values. Throughout its history, the U.S. government has advanced a settler colonialist agenda, which at times has intensified into genocide and forced assimilation. When it reaches these moments of brutality against its own people, the U.S. government has been, as Cohen noted, violating its self-proclaimed democratic faith. Thus, by examining the origin of the tribal gaming movement and its subsequent implications for tribal sovereignty, this book traces the United States' pursuit of settler colonialism, which has, at times, directly contradicted its adherence to its self-proclaimed democratic values.

Tribal Gaming Research

Despite its striking and diverse impacts on native and settler communities, tribal gaming receives little attention from scholars, including anthropologists. This blind spot might exist because tribal gaming lies at the intersection of two spheres that are often considered taboo by scholars and the public: gambling and indigeneity. Gaming scholarship is relatively new, despite the prehistoric roots of gambling and the staggering size and influences of its modern-day forms (Schwartz 2013). As described by Eadington and Schwartz (2012, 1), the emergence of gaming as an area of scholarly interest in the early 1970s was met with skepticism and contempt by "traditional academics...suspecting that the [gaming] researchers were themselves caught up in the thralls of gambling obsession; like studying prostitution or illicit drugs, such researchers must have impure ulterior motives if they are pursing such perverse undertakings." Likewise, anthropological research with native nations in North America is taboo, although for a different reason. At times anthropology has been complicit in settler colonialism. Vine Deloria (1969) rightly identified many of the field's so-called sins. Fortunately, tribal gaming is now a growing field of scholarly research, with more and more anthropologists and other scholars applying their expertise to the subject. This book rests on the work of others who have demonstrated that this area of research is not only possible but also necessary.

Katherine Spilde undertook the first intensive ethnographic inquiry on tribal gaming with her dissertation "Acts of Sovereignty" (1998). She worked with the White Earth Indian Reservation in Minnesota to demonstrate how tribal gaming makes native and settler economies increasingly interdependent and how it provides a counter-narrative to settler perspectives that assume the extinction or inauthenticity of native identities. Eve Darian-Smith (2004), with her ethnographic account of the sociopolitical conflicts associated with the development of Indian gaming at the Chumash Reservation in Santa Barbara, California, explored the implicit, and often explicit, counter-narratives embedded in the rise of tribal casinos. Darian-Smith's (81) interviews and observations of the communities neighboring the casino reveal that many concerns about the tribal casino development (including attracting questionable clientele, traffic, and other social problems in their community) are rooted in preexisting economic class divisions and settler misconceptions of native identity. Like Spilde, Darian-Smith found that the widely publicized success of several gaming tribes challenges settler preconceptions of American Indians while enabling tribes to pursue cultural revitalization (109–11). Jessica Cattelino's ethnography of the Seminole Tribe of Florida extends Spilde's analysis of tribal gaming as a marker of increasing tribal/settler interdependency by "illuminating [the] ways that sovereign polities…are produced and sustained interdependently" (Cattelino 2008, 200).

From these analyses of tribal and settler society interdependencies, it follows that sovereignty is not a zero-sum game. Sovereigns can use their self-determination to help their neighbors; neighboring nations can strengthen their own self-determination while strengthening the self-determination of others. The success of one political community does not necessarily come at the expense of others. One television advertisement sponsored by the San Manuel Band of Serrano Indians (2009) puts the concept this way: "Tribal self-reliance makes California self-reliant." This book further explores the ways in which interdependency can strengthen neighboring nations by adopting the framework (described above) that parses those internal and external dimensions of sovereignty. This framework allows for us to trace the different ways in which nations recognize (or fail to recognize) each other through cultural knowledge and political institutions.

However, despite this emerging strand of tribal gaming research led by Spilde, Darian-Smith, Cattelino, and others, there is an alternative perspective promoted by Comaroff and Comaroff (2009), who argue that native nations and for-profit corporations now co-opt each other. Comaroff and Comaroff claim that tribal casinos do not result in their greater inter-dependency but rather on the blending of the two into a new social institution, which they refer to as ethnocorporation. Unlike Spilde's and Cattelino's findings of interdependence, Comaroff and Comaroff (82) find that "once ethnically defined populations have their sovereignty officially recognized—itself the object of a great deal of political and economic exertion on their part—they tend to assert it *against* the state" (emphasis in the original). As is demonstrated throughout this book, native nation sovereignty emerges from within native actions and exists whether or not settler society acknowledges it (though that acknowledgment can certainly help native nations thrive). Furthermore, native nation sovereignty generally, and tribal gaming specifically, entail often-overlooked interdependencies between native and settler societies and economies. Even uses of tribal sovereignty that appear to be against the settler governments (local, state, and federal) may, in fact, only create further independencies between settler and tribal governments.

Recent studies on the impacts of tribal casinos demonstrate the range of economic and social benefits that both native and tribal communities can experience when native nations pursue self-determination. For example, Marks and Spilde Contrares (2007) found that, in the case of tribal gaming in California, the geopolitical constrictions on tribal gaming can contribute to its overall beneficial impact on local economies. Their statistical analysis of the socioeconomic effects of tribal gaming in California concluded that the development of tribal gaming is associated with a significant (approximately 40 percent) increase in per capita income on the reservation and in communities that neighbor gaming reservations compared to those ten miles or more away. Spilde Contrares' (2006) study of tribal gaming development on the Pechanga Reservation in Temecula, California, reported that increased political and public recognition of their sovereignty, when combined with increased revenue from tribal casino development, enabled the Pechanga nation to work with neighboring local governments to more effectively pursue collective goals.

Of course, while increased tribal self-determination can have significant benefits for settler society, the overarching goal of revitalizing tribal self-determination is to strengthen native nations. An emerging strand of research now shows how tribal gaming can have profound benefits for native nations even when a tribal casino yields only a modest increase in income. In their groundbreaking longitudinal study, Jane Costello and her colleagues (2010) examined the association between tribal casino income and the prevalence of mental illness among the youth of the Eastern Band of Cherokee Indians. By comparing tribal youth to their nontribal counterparts in the region, Costello et al. found that increased income from the tribe's casino, including increases up to $750 a month, may result in significant decreases in psychiatric and substance use disorders in reservation youth. Costello et al.'s longitudinal study found that as youths exposed to this increased household income age into adulthood, they suffer significantly less from mental illness and substance abuse. Their results suggest "whether or not individuals have a genetic vulnerability to a disorder, there are environmental interventions [such as increased income from tribal gaming] that can have long-term benefits" (1959). Tribal gaming can provide economic benefits, but those benefits should never be considered in isolation. Its economic benefits can significantly improve the mental health of tribal youth, helping them realize their potential as adults. Thus, even if native nations at times appear to assert their sovereignty against the state, by exercising their sovereignty to increase economic development native nations can provide their youths with something that settler society has often denied them: a better chance to grow up healthy.

This book expands the literature by examining the historical and contemporary assertions of tribal sovereignty in what is now the epicenter of the tribal gaming movement, the Cahuilla territory of inland Southern California. As an interdisciplinary field, Native American studies grows by adopting and adapting new theories and methods from a variety of academic disciplines. Cognitive anthropology has tools for investigating the assumptions people hold about the world around them. One goal of this book is to demonstrate how these tools might be valuable in Native American studies, especially as tribal gaming increasingly interrupts settlers' understandings about their own society.

Cultural Knowledge and Colonialism

Cognitive anthropology is founded on a pragmatic and knowledge-based view of culture (Blount 2011). Ward Goodenough (1957, 167), one of the early influences on cognitive anthropology, defined culture as "whatever it is one has to know or believe in order to operate" acceptably in a given society. One compelling advantage of this definition is that it opens the possibility of drawing on methodological and theoretical tools from psychology and the cognitive sciences. By framing culture as a kind of knowledge, often called cultural knowledge, cognitive anthropology can link anthropology's questions about culture to psychology's questions about the mental processes by which individuals make sense of the world around them. Developmental psychologist Jean Piaget (1953) laid the foundation for psychology's study of the ways that individuals acquire information and knowledge. He developed the idea that schemata are the basic units or building blocks of knowledge. Decades later, Piaget's research has been refined; the core of his work, however, remains foundational to psychology's understanding of how individuals acquire knowledge, assimilate new experiences, adapt their knowledge to fit new experiences, and draw on their knowledge as they interact with the world. Because it situates culture as an emergent property of shared knowledge, Goodenough's definition of culture allows anthropologists to incorporate concepts from psychology and the cognitive sciences into anthropological theory. Why might concepts from psychology, like schemata, be useful for studying tribal activism? As this book will show, schemata can help us understand how individuals acquire assumptions about their social worlds and how they react to new experiences.

Although he did not explicitly make this connection, Philip Deloria's (2004, 11) distinction "between the anomalous, which reinforces expectations, and the unexpected, which resists categorizations, and thereby questions expectations itself" parallels the assimilation and accommodation of schemata, as outlined by Piaget. In short, Piaget found that when a person encounters a new experience, that experience is sometimes close enough to the person's knowledge that she readily assimilates it into her existing schemata. In this case, akin to what Deloria called the anomalous, a new experience does not change a person's underlying assumptions. Piaget also found that at times new experiences can be so new and so different from a person's existing knowledge that his or her schemata change to accommodate the new experience. This, which Deloria called the unexpected, challenges underlying assumptions, forcing them to change. While Deloria's framework came from an indigenous perspective within Native American studies, his observations about the different ways non-Indians react to new experiences dovetails with Piaget's major contribution to the field of psychology: people make assumptions based on their previous experiences and these assumptions shape responses to new experiences. Throughout this book, I use terms such as "cultural knowledge," "expectations," and "shared assumptions" interchangeably to refer to schemata that are (or once were) widely shared.

One trait of schemata has great relevance to the study of settler colonialism. As bundles of shared assumptions, schemata can sometimes contradict each other, causing what psychologists call cognitive dissonance. Psychologist Leon Festinger (1957) first defined cognitive dissonance as the simultaneous processing of two contradictory ideas or schemata. It is the uneasy feeling someone has when trying to accept two ideas that contradict each other. Festinger found that we all want to have beliefs and actions that are consistent with each other, even though our beliefs and actions are often at odds. In the decades following Festinger's work, psychology and the cognitive sciences have continued to refine our knowledge of the different strategies we all use to alleviate cognitive dissonance (Harmon-Jones and Mills 1999). We use rationalizations and avoidance to prevent feeling as if our beliefs and actions are in conflict. As will be seen, many of the peculiar ways in which United States' settler society understands itself result from a collective cognitive dissonance between the nation's commitments to democracy and justice and its legacies of injustice. The contradictions between what North American settler society would like to believe about itself (e.g., its commitment to democracy and justice) and its unjust settler colonial practices have led to a collective form of cognitive dissonance, which I refer to as historical dissonance (see chapter 3 for further discussion). From this historical dissonance springs settlers' shared desires to rationalize colonialism and resist or ignore any evidence that could challenge the belief that the United States is a just democracy that would never attempt to exterminate its own people.

By defining culture as a kind of knowledge and using that definition as a bridge to adopt ideas from psychology and the cognitive sciences, cognitive anthropology, as described by Blount (2011), D'Andrade (1995), Kronenfeld (1996, 2008, 2018), Kronenfeld et al. (2011), Wassman, Klug, and Albrecht (2011), and others, provides theoretical and methodological tools for describing the diversity of thought within a society and explaining how different segments of society can develop different understandings about any given matter. According to this approach, every individual's working knowledge of the world is as unique to that individual as that person's experiences. Therefore, knowledge held by members of any given population share commonalities to the extent that they have had common experiences. Meaningful communication between individuals and cooperation among groups is possible only because of this shared common knowledge, also known as cultural knowledge. It is whatever people believe to be true. Because it focuses on the structure and distribution of cultural knowledge, cognitive anthropology uses methods such as surveys, interviews, and ethnography to illicit patterns in the different ways members of a society understand the world around them (Handwerker 2011). This book both advances knowledge of the historical interactions of populations in inland Southern California and examines the structure and distribution of the settler population's cultural knowledge of its native nation neighbors. Cognitive anthropology has primarily focused on synchronic studies of contemporary communities. This book takes up Chrisomalis's (2016) suggestion to develop methods for applying cognitive anthropology to historical questions. To this end, I use concepts from cognitive anthropology to analyze historical documents in order to better understand why different kinds of cultural knowledge became popular at different times and in different communities. This historical approach prevails in chapters 1–5, while survey and interview methods developed from cognitive anthropology prevail in chapter 6. By applying cognitive anthropology to understand changes in the content and distribution of cultural knowledge, we see that changes in settlers' knowledge of their native neighbors reflect political and economic changes. Native activists often target settler institutions with the goal of interrupting the assumptions settlers hold about their own society. In fact, the very experience of marginalization may provide native activists with unique tools for changing settler society.

When used to study the cultural knowledge of marginalized communities, cognitive anthropology aligns, in part, with feminist standpoint theory. In defining feminist standpoint theory, Sandra Harding (2004, 7) asserted, "To the extent that an oppressed group's situation is different from that of the dominant group, its dominated situation enables the production of distinctive kinds of knowledge.... Thus standpoint theories map how a social and political disadvantage can be turned into an epistemological, scientific, and political advantage." Indeed, native nations, such as the Cahuilla nations, have been particularly adept at influencing cultural knowledge in order to strengthen their external cultural sovereignty and to pressure policymakers to recognize their political sovereignty. By enduring the injustices wrought by colonialism, native peoples have both knowledge of U.S. settler society that settlers do not have as well as an especially strong motivation to learn about settler institutions to change them. On the other hand, with its lack of rich and nuanced experience with native societies, settler society has had only limited and flawed understandings of native nations. The failures and contradictions in federal Indian policy may be in part a result of this limited and flawed understanding.

From Cognitive to Cultural Boundaries

One common yet flawed assumption people often make about culture is that all members of a given culture must share a specific set of traits. Often these traits may be thought of as innate, based on DNA or blood, or some other assumed underlying, essentialized nature. Our species may even be predisposed to make these problematic and essentialist assumptions about cultures. (See Gelman 2005 for further discussion.) In 1969 anthropologist Fredrick Barth proposed a constructionist approach that avoids the pitfalls of these essentialist understandings of culture. Barth argued that cultural groups, like ethnicities, are defined through their relations with each other. While the boundaries of ethnic groups may appear fixed, Barth found that in fact they are defined through a process of self-ascription and ascription by others. By ascription, Barth was referring to a process of recognition, where ethnic groups recognize their own members and members of other groups by applying culturally established criteria. Language, dress, religion, phenotype, and other physical and behavioral characteristics are all traits by which individuals recognize who is a member of which group. By highlighting the interplay of self-ascription and ascription by others, Barth's insight was that ethnic categories are defined not by some absolute or intrinsic quality, but rather by their positions relative to each other. Cognitive anthropology links with Barth's approach because the ascriptive processes of boundary formation occurs through shared recognition of identity markers. What shapes how one recognizes another, or one's self, as a member of an ethnic group? The answer, provided by cognitive anthropology and Barth's constructive approach, is that the processes that demarcate ethnic boundaries rest on cultural knowledge. Therefore, ethnic boundaries are constructed by shared knowledge.

Swiss linguist Ferdinand de Saussure developed a metaphor that can illuminate the implications of Barth's insight that ethnic groups are defined in relation to each other. Saussure (1916/1998) proposed that all signs and symbols are constellations in the sense that their meanings are defined only by their differences relative to each other. Because ethnic labels (like other words) are linguistic symbols, his analogy illustrates how ethnicities may appear fixed, but in fact have no intrinsic or absolute meaning. In an astronomical constellation a group of stars appears to take a shape that has meaning to a particular community. That shape appears only when viewed from one perspective (i.e., from the Earth). The constellation emerges from the position of stars relative each other. Only when taken as constellation and seen from a certain perspective do these points gain their shape and meaning. The perceived movement of one star can disrupt the shape of the constellation, while potentially forming a new one. It may be worth extending Saussure's analogy to ethnic groups. For example, consider that in the night sky, some stars are light-years apart but from our perspective on Earth they appear so close together that we perceive only one star where, in fact, there are many. Likewise, an outsider might see two ethnic groups as very similar, even when those groups see themselves as strikingly different. Even if they speak different languages, any outsider population unfamiliar with or distant enough from those languages might not distinguish between the two. Yet, from a perspective within one of those two groups, their differences are not only vast but also help to define group identity. For native nations the settlers' inability or refusal to distinguish between their unique identities has had devastating results. (Chapter 2 describes how in the 1860s many settlers failed to distinguish between different tribes, with deadly results for many Serrano and other native nations.) Looking at social groups as constellations, we can trace how specific phenomena, like native activism, can change how settlers perceive native nations and, in turn, can change how they see their own society.

One premise that cognitive anthropology adopts from psychology is that we make sense of new phenomena through our schemata, our knowledge, of similar phenomena. But what if we have no prior knowledge of similar phenomena? In cases where individuals are confronted with something new that is unlike anything else they know, they might construct an understanding that reveals little about the actual phenomena but plenty about the assumed knowledge underlying the individuals' worldview. Tribal gaming is one such phenomenon: most settlers have no frame of reference for understanding it, but, especially in locations like Southern California, it is ubiquitous and controversial. Therefore, tribal gaming offers an opportunity to study settler assumptions about their own society. As settlers struggle to make sense of tribal gaming, they create stories to explain its origin. As will be demonstrated in chapter 6, settlers' attempts to explain tribal gaming often have no historical basis, but they can reveal the foundational assumptions of settler society. By examining how settler assumptions about native nations evolve across time and space, this book traces ongoing changes in the settler assumptions of what it means to be an American.

Chapter 1, "Cahuilla Lifeways and the Spanish Conquest," provides an analysis of the social organization and worldview of the Cahuilla prior to the arrival of the Spanish, and the rapid changes that took place as New Spain began its conquest of the territory that it called Alta California (which stretched north to the Pacific Northwest and east toward present-day New Mexico). This includes an examination of the religious and political processes that organized Cahuilla lifeways and their relations with native nations across the Southwest. This chapter describes indigenous cultural and governing practices of the Cahuilla and the strategies used by Cahuilla communities to maintain these practices in spite of missionary attempts to forcibly "civilize" this population.

Chapter 2, "Genocide in California," examines the arrival of American settlers in California and the impact of the California gold rush on the state's indigenous population. Building on the work of James Rawls (1984) and an analysis of primary historical documents, especially newspaper articles and BIA records, this chapter identifies different California settler perceptions of natives and the links between these perceptions and divergent state policies, including the legalized enslavement and attempted extermination of native peoples. It demonstrates how the economic growth of California depended on resources extracted from natives, especially native labor and land. It concludes by examining Cahuilla strategies for survival during this period of history, including their role in the war between the United States and Mexico.

Chapter 3, "Activism and Dissonance," builds on the concept of cognitive dissonance to develop what I refer to as historical dissonance. It argues that historical dissonance can help explain how settlers increasingly came to believe that native nations had disappeared at a time when natives continued to play significant roles in settler society. This chapter begins with a case study of oral histories from the land now known as Joshua Tree National Park (JTNP). This case study demonstrates how settlers relied on Cahuilla labor and how those who worked closely with natives developed working, though flawed, understandings of Cahuilla society. This reliance of settlers on native labor came at a time when media began representing native nations as extinct. Far from extinct, in the first half of the twentieth century the Cahuilla's and other native's labor played important roles in the settler economy. Moreover, tribal labor provided the resources to form activist groups, such as the Mission Indian Federation, which successfully lobbied Congress to lay the groundwork for future revitalization.

Chapter 4, "Termination and Revitalization," explains how native nations, including the Cahuilla, responded to the crises of the termination era. After World War II Congress feared that tribal land ownership was a kind of insidious communism lurking within the United States. Motivated by this fear and a desire to extract more native resources, Congress and private businesses conspired to revoke federal recognition for native nations and to open their land to private development. This and other injustices led to widespread resistance, including the formation of the American Indian Movement (AIM) and many other activist organizations. This chapter follows the role of the Cahuilla nations in resisting termination by forming organizations such as Spokesmen and Committee and the American Indian Historical Society. The Cahuilla also collaborated with a local newspaper to expose what would become known as the Agua Caliente Guardianship scandal. Cahuilla resistance efforts maintained their sovereignty while helping return federal policy back to its limited recognition of tribal sovereignty. This return to limited recognition set the stage for the emerging Indian casino movement.

Chapter 5, "The *Cabazon* Decision and Its Aftermath," describes the origin of the Indian casino movement as well as its political and economic impacts for native nations across North America and in the Cahuilla nations. This chapter provides a brief account of the events that precipitated *California v. Cabazon,* in which the Supreme Court recognized that the sovereignty of federally recognized tribes provides their right to regulate gambling. This chapter examines legislative records, court rulings, election results, and economic impact data to demonstrate how the political and economic revitalization of native nations, especially casino development, impacts both tribes and neighboring communities through increased employment, traffic, purchases of goods and services from local vendors, and charity, as well as other economic partnerships. The chapter concludes by analyzing the role of Cahuilla and their neighboring nations in organizing statewide ballot measures that secured and expanded tribal casino operations in California.

Chapter 6, "Contested Knowledge," examines the contemporary sources, structure, and distribution of settlers' cultural knowledge of native nations. It is divided into two parts. The first part addresses how the Cahuilla and other native nations increasingly take advantage of new opportunities (e.g., powwows, ads, educational displays, etc.) to represent themselves to the public and to challenge common misconceptions about their identities. This part also examines media content created by opponents of tribal casinos, especially political advertisements that present contrasting explanations of the Indian casino movement and its impacts. The second part of chapter 6 synthesizes interview and survey data from segments of the population of present-day Cahuilla territory, especially tribal casino employees and clientele, as well as residents who live near Indian casinos. This analysis demonstrates how the impacts of tribal revitalization, in addition to the increasing visibility of tribal representations of self, shape the structure and distribution of settler cultural knowledge. It finds the emergence of a new perception that equates native nations with private corporations; this has prompted new challenges for tribes.

The concluding chapter asserts that while the Indian gaming movement is shaped by indigenous traditions, especially self-determination, North American settler society lacks the knowledge necessary to comprehend the historical relations that provided the impetus for the movement. Without this knowledge, settlers construct ad hoc understandings of native nations (e.g., the conflation of native nations and corporations) in response to the resurgence of native political and economic power. These new understandings could directly impinge on the capacity for native nations to self-govern. By briefly reviewing the key events in the historical and contemporary relations between the Cahuilla and settlers discussed throughout the book, this chapter demonstrates how theories from cognitive anthropology and Native American studies can be combined to explain the evolution of settler perspectives over time and the impacts of these perceptions on tribal communities. This chapter concludes the book by showing how, in order to preserve their sovereignty, the Cahuilla nations have consistently challenged settler cultural knowledge. Ultimately, the Cahuilla's strategy has succeeded and settler attempts to annihilate them have failed because native nations often understand settler society better than settlers understand themselves.

Before proceeding I want to provide both a caution and an invitation. I caution readers from assuming that this book is, or attempts to be, a definitive and complete history of Cahuilla and settler society relations. There is much more to this history than could ever be included in any single analysis. One of my goals is to provoke more research. I hope any limitations or shortcomings of this book invite such future research.

Notes

1. Cahuilla is pronounced Ka-wee-yah. The double el (l) is pronounced like the letter why (y). "Mission Indians" is a term that has often been applied by both the federal government and tribes themselves to refer to native peoples in Southern California to refer to their past relationships with the missions of New Spain. As explained in chapter 2, the term is a bit of a misnomer: the missions had a profound impact on tribes along the coast but had minimal impact on those located farther inland, like many of the Cahuilla nations, including Cabazon.

2. This book uses the terms "native nation" and "tribe" interchangeably because both native nations themselves and the federal government use nation and tribe to describe historical and contemporary American Indian polities.

3. This book applies the United Nations' definition of genocide. In 1948 the United Nations adopted General Assembly Resolution 260, "Convention on the Prevention and Punishment of the Crime of Genocide," which defines genocide as "any of the following acts committed with the intent to destroy, in whole or in part, a national, ethnical, racial or religious group, as such: a) Killing members of the group; b) Causing serious bodily or mental harm to members of the group; c) Deliberately inflicting on the group conditions of life calculated to bring about its physical destruction in whole or in part; d) Imposing measures intended to prevent births within the group; e) Forcibly transferring children of the group to another group." In 1988 the United States ratified the UN Convention on Genocide when President Reagan signed the Genocide Convention Implementation Act of 1987 (commonly known as the Proxmire Act; 8 U.S.C. 1101). All five acts in this definition clearly apply to the repeated federal and state actions intended to destroy native nations. Acts a, b, c, and e are described in chapter 2's discussion of the state-funded militias sent to exterminate native people, the removal of California Indians to barren reservations, and the transfer (often by force or coercion) of native children from their parents to boarding schools. Jane Lawrence's (2000, 410) review found part d was widespread: "Various studies reveal that the Indian Health Services sterilized between 25 and 50 percent of Native American women between 1970 and 1976" without their consent.

4. I use the term "settler" to refer to the non-Indian population of North America, from initial contact through the present. The term "settler" is not synonymous with white or Anglo American, although the overwhelming majority of settlers discussed in the book are white.

CAHUILLA LIFEWAYS
AND THE SPANISH CONQUEST

ARGUABLY ONE OF THE most ecologically diverse indigenous territories in North America, the Cahuilla nations' ancestral land includes vast expanses of low, dry desert punctuated by steep mountains with artic peaks. Between the harsh desert below and the alpine tundra above, forest plateaus provide moist and shaded relief. Ranging from the low Colorado Desert, one of the hottest and driest in North America, to alpine tundra above ten thousand feet, and nearly every ecological niche in between, the Cahuilla's ancestral territory was no match for European colonists until late in the nineteenth century. With knowledge and traditions passed from generation to generation, though, the Cahuilla thrived in the diverse and extreme environments of inland Southern California. In 1769, when the Spanish constructed the first permanent European settlements in the land now known as California, they brought their own Spanish traditions and institutions. For centuries prior to their arrival in California, Spain's military and religious officials pursued the conquest and conscription of native people in the region that is now Central Mexico. The two societies transformed each other when they collided. Most Californians are aware of the Spanish influence on California, but Native Californians' knowledge and traditions shape today's California in ways that often escape settler imagination. Understanding present-day settler societies, including California, is not possible without first considering the interactions between enduring indigenous traditions and intervening European regimes. This chapter offers a brief description of what we know about the Cahuilla nations before Europeans arrived, and how the arrival of New Spain altered life for both the Cahuilla and the Spanish settlers. As will be shown, the Cahuilla's cultural knowledge and practices enabled their survival during the Spanish conquest and the brutality yet to come from the growing migrant Anglo population. (I use the term "Anglo" throughout to refer specifically to English-speaking settlers.)

Cahuilla Lifeways

Many of the Cahuilla's core beliefs and practices continue to be practiced today. Unfortunately, some of their knowledge and traditions have not survived settler attempts at native genocide and forced assimilation. What we know about Cahuilla lifeways prior to contact comes from oral histories of living and past Cahuilla elders, ethnographers who visited the nations in the early and middle twentieth century, written settler accounts and archives, and the archaeological record. By knowing the perspectives of each source and seeking the points where different lines of evidence converge, we can create a more complete picture of what life might have been like for the Cahuilla before Europeans arrived. Prior to contact the Cahuilla nations were, most likely, never united as a single nation, but instead were a federation of sovereigns, held together by language, culture, and a worldview that united them with each other and with their ancestral territory. However, the Cahuilla, like most native nations, do not share the creedal, dogmatic spirituality of Western religions. There is no single, official origin story. Multiple versions of their creation story exist, though the central themes remain the same. The following is a brief retelling of the Cahuilla origin story adapted from a compilation published by the Agua Caliente Cultural Museum (2014), followed by a description of how key themes from the origin story shaped both precontact social organization and Cahuilla strategies for continuing self-determination in the face of settler colonialism.

According to the Cahuilla origin story, in the beginning the cosmos was a dark void, filled only with the sounds of humming and thunder. Then the darkness became lighter, with different colors that combined to form a single point. Two embryos formed at this point but were stillborn. They developed again and eventually became the first two beings, the twins Mūkat and Temaīyauit. The twins could not see in the darkness but they could talk and quarrel with each other. Both created tobacco and pipes. Mūkat created the sun to light their pipes. To entertain each other, the two created a guessing game, where one would try to guess where the other hid his pipe. The two fought over the game. Then the twins chose to create the world. At first their work was unstable; they made repeated attempts until they eventually bound the world together with animals, oceans, and rivers. After they created the world, they looked down to see smoke. Mūkat explained to Temaīyauit that the smoke came from "the place where we were lying and comes from our afterbirth. It is black blood, red blood, fresh blood, smallpox, colds and sore throat, cramps in the back, boils, mumps, hives and itches, inflamed and sore eyes, blindness, acute body pains, palsy and twitching, consumption, venereal disease, rheumatism, emaciations, swelling of the body, and all other sickness" (Agua Caliente Cultural Museum 2014, 17). Mūkat decided that if their world were ever to be inhabited they would need to endow their creations with the ability to heal. To populate the Earth, the twins created beings. First, Temaīyauit created coyote and Mūkat created horned owl. Then the twins drew mud from their hearts to form human bodies. Mūkat worked slowly and deliberately to produce the human form that we have now. Temaīyauit rushed, creating monstrous forms. Coyote took the completed bodies and put Temaīyauit's on one side of the Earth and Mūkat's on the other. Mūkat and Temaīyauit began to fight, disagreeing on what form humans should take and whether they should be mortal. Mūkat insisted that death must exist and that the dead cannot return to the living. Upset and feeling that he always lost arguments with his twin, Temaīyauit went to the bottom of the Earth, taking all of his creatures with him.

Mūkat's people came alive. They all spoke different languages but one individual, Kiathwasimut, spoke a language that Mūkat could understand. This was the language of Cahuilla, thus Kiathwasimut was the first person to speak Cahuilla, and Cahuilla is the language of Mūkat. Mūkat kept Kiathwasimut nearby, while the other humans scattered. All Mūkat's creations were male except Menily, the moon maiden. Menily divided the humans into two groups, the wildcats and the coyotes. She divided each into smaller groups and instructed each group to choose one leader. This became the basis for the Cahuilla's social organization, described later in this chapter. Menily also turned some of the humans into women. She was the first woman and established the Cahuilla's expectations for female gender roles.

Mūkat instructed his creations to make bows and arrows. Then he asked them to fire at each other. The people were scared, but *takwic*, a fireball demon and shaman who resides atop Mount San Jacinto, convinced the others that there was nothing to be afraid of. The people fired arrows, striking and killing each other, and nearly all died. Mūkat had deceived them for his own amusement. His creations no longer trusted him. Then Mūkat sexually assaulted Menily. Menily fled Mūkat and left the Earth for the sky. She was and still is beloved by the Cahuilla. She promised them that even though she would live in the sky, she would visit her people nightly. According to the Cahuilla worldview, to this day Menily continues her nightly visits: she is the moon.

The Cahuilla began to fear Mūkat. He had tricked them into fighting each other and he had abused Menily, forcing her to leave. Mūkat's creations developed a plan to poison him with his own excrement. The plan succeeded: Mūkat died and his creations cremated him. Unknown plants began to grow on Mūkat's burial mound. At first the Cahuilla feared the plants. A shaman was able to communicate with Mūkat's spirit to ask about the plants. Mūkat's spirit told the shaman to make use of the plants that grew from his buried ashes. They were tobacco, corn, squash, watermelons, and mesquite beans. The shaman learned how to take advantage of these crops and went on to teach the rest of Mūkat's people to gather them each year to give thanks.

The specific events of the creation story vary by version, and the story as told here is far from complete. But it does illustrate central components of the Cahuilla worldview that inform their precontact social structure and their adaptations to their environment and settler colonialism. First, as illustrated in the stillborn embryos of the first twins and in the unsteadiness of the primal world, the cosmos is inherently unstable. Disorder predominates and order, while possible, is always tenuous. As described by Bean (1972, 160), in the Cahuilla worldview the universe is divided into phenomena with and without the power or will to act. The Cahuilla's story of the origin of the universe illustrates the central role of this power to act. Mūkat created the universe through exercising this power. Bean (163) highlighted how Mūkat's misuse of his power shaped the Cahuilla's political structure: "There was conflict between Mūkat and his creations.... The Creator himself was unpredictable and unstable because he tricked people into performing acts which were harmful to them. He also violated basic moral principles by molesting Menily, 'moon maiden' who was a mother symbol, and caused her to leave the people.... This cosmological precedent justified replacing unstable or unpredictable political leaders when they behaved as Mūkat did." This is a worldview where the cosmos is inherently unstable. Power can corrupt. The creator Mūkat was killed by his own creations who had learned to fear him. Leaders who act selfishly, as Mūkat did, are subject to exile no matter what they have created in the past. Conflict within a family may cause a group to fission, such as what happened to the twin brothers. Plants and animals hold the world together. Without them chaos would tear everything apart. The creation of the world also saw the origin of illness, but the twins created medicine men with healing power. According to their origin story, Cahuilla is the language of the creator. We also see the origin of wagering on games of chance. Guessing the position of an object held by a competitor is the basis of the game *peon. Peon* played a significant role in the Supreme Court's ruling in the *Cabezon* decision; it is still played today.

Cahuilla Ecology

To European settlers and their descendants, the Colorado Desert is an unforgiving, harsh environment with the only relief up impenetrable mountain slopes, which include some of the steepest mountain faces in North America. For the Cahuilla nations, cultural knowledge and traditions can unlock bountiful harvests of acorns, deer, fruit, and plants that they used as medicine. Prior to European contact, the Cahuilla could be roughly divided into three interdependent populations: the Desert, Mountain, and Pass Cahuilla, each with its own dialect and each partially conscribed by an ecological niche. The Desert Cahuilla resided in the hot, dry low desert, much of which is around sea level but one hundred miles inland, separated from the coast by mountains that block the cool, moist sea air. At a few places geothermal energy heats underground water to produce hot springs and mud volcanoes. In the low desert, women gathered cacti, agaves, yucca, fan palms, berries, succulents, and other produce to provide a nutritious diet for their families. The Desert Cahuilla men hunted large game and, when the winter solstice approached, in some locations planted corn, beans, and squash. By maintaining irrigation ditches, the Desert Cahuilla channeled water from underground springs and mountain runoff to their crops (Bean 1972, 48; Lawton and Bean 1968). High up in the San Jacinto Mountains, the Mountain Cahuilla resided in the cool, moist terrain shaded by ancient stands of oak trees. Every two or three years each oak tree yields several hundred pounds of acorns. Men, women, and children worked together in the acorn harvest, crushing and straining them to leach out tannins. Once processed, an acorn harvest would be preserved for years, providing sustenance in times of scarcity. The Mountain Cahuilla men hunted large game, including deer and sheep. Elders specialized in hunting small game such as rabbits, rats, and squirrels (Bean 1972, 58). The Pass Cahuilla thrived in the San Gorgonio Pass, with a microclimate between the extremes of the mountains and the desert. The pass was marked by the ever-present wind channeled from the coast through the pass. The Pass Cahuilla thrived with access to the resources of both the mountains and the desert. The Mountain and Pass Cahuilla knew of the agriculture practiced by the Desert Cahuilla, but with ample resources available through foraging, they had no need to plant crops.

The ability to make group decisions (what I refer to as internal political sovereignty) was distributed across territorially based kin groups, which anthropologists (e.g., Bean 1972) identify as sibs or clans. Each sib further divided the obligations of self-determination among three to ten lineages. As established by the Cahuilla origin story (described above), all lineages were classified as one of two groups, wildcat or coyote, in what is known as a moiety structure (a partition of a society's members into two overarching kin groups). This moiety system stretched across the land now known as the American Southwest: their neighbors all participated in this system. Marriage between the Cahuilla sibs was valued but marriage outside of the moiety was culturally mandated. Wildcats and coyotes needed to marry each other and any marriage that involved only wildcats or only coyotes was strictly taboo. While the Cahuilla preferred to marry other Cahuilla, this was not as important as the need for coyotes and wildcats to marry each other. Thus, it was not uncommon for Cahuilla to marry members of neighboring native nations including the Serrano, Mojave (or Mohave), and Chemehuevi peoples. These marriages were permitted as long as they ensured a marriage between a wildcat and a coyote. After marriage each woman moved to her husband's village. Their children would become a part of the husband's lineage, but the wife would always remain in her lineage of birth. Thus, members of one sib predominantly inhabited each village, though there was always a significant population of married women from outside sibs. This patrilineal, patrilocal moiety structure ensured that links between lineages and sibs were continuously maintained and replenished through marriage. Through trading and reciprocal gift exchanges along these extensive kinship networks each sib had access to the resources of the Cahuilla territory's diverse ecological niches. When one sib's territory had a surplus harvest, it distributed its harvest through kin networks to those who suffered from scarcity. At times climatic variations could provide any given lineage's territory with an abundance of resources, or a devastating drought. The complex network of marriage and trade alliances provided security by redistributing resources from lineages with ample food to those who were lacking. Cahuilla cultural knowledge and social structure sustained them in this manner for countless generations.

Sibs worked together not only to distribute resources but also to fulfill all social and spiritual obligations. Within each sib, individual lineages held roles for managing different spheres of social relations. The *net* was the highest position in the sib social structure. Typically, the first son of a *net* became the next *net*. Thus, this status was inherited through the patriliny, from father to son, although exceptions could be made. The *net*'s obligations included maintaining ceremonial practices, the ceremonial house, and the sacred bundle. The *net* counseled with *nets* from different sibs to discuss issues and disputes regarding boundaries, marriage, war, and the timing and location of hunting (Bean 1972, 105). The *net* presided over ritual gift exchanges that operated through networks established through kin relations and that typically occurred at ceremonies. Assisting the *net*, the *paxaa* was an inherited position responsible for ceremonial and administrative protocol. The *paxaa* provided counsel to the *net* for important decisions (106).

While the *net* held political authority, a spiritual leader, known as a *puul*, was an intermediary between the sib and the higher spiritual authorities of the overarching nonphysical cosmos. The *puul*, collectively known as the *puvalam*, inherited spiritual power through birth, received it from another *puul*, or achieved it through dreaming. Park (1938, 48) wrote of the source of the supernatural power: "Cahuilla shamans are supposed to derive their powers from Mūkat, the creator, but power is conferred through the medium of guardian spirits. These are probably the animals such as owl, fox, coyote, bear, and others that act as messengers to shamans." If contacted by a guardian spirit, a young man would tell his father and *net* of the experience. Bean (1972, 110) explains, "If he felt the candidacy was legitimate, the *net* contacted the *paxaa* and various *puvalam*, who talked with the boy and came to a final decision" before beginning the initiation rites. The guardian spirit gave the *puul* the power to create bountiful harvests, to control the weather, and to cure disease. However, the inherited powers of the *puvalam* and *nets* were not absolute. Abuse of this power was often met with the appointment of a new *net* or the fission of a sib or lineage. Sib and lineage fission was sanctioned by their worldview and served as a mechanism for mitigating conflict and restoring order when social or ecological factors stressed the unity of a sib or lineage. Cahuilla leadership was diffused among sibs and lineages, and by the separation of political, administrative, and spiritual powers by the *net, paxaa,* and *puul,* with each leadership position determined by a combination of inheritance and consensus.

While the ancestral territory of the Cahuilla included extreme desert and alpine environments, and today many settlers might assume much of this area is devoid of sustenance, the lifeways of the Cahuilla allowed them to thrive. Sibs had self-determination and their sovereignty was further partitioned among constituent lineages, thereby establishing the mutual independence and interdependence of each lineage. A network of kin alliances ensured that lineages could rely on each other when resources were low. Their worldview obliged this reciprocity and justified the inevitable fissions among lineages experiencing social and environmental stresses. Thus, before European contact, sovereignty in the Cahuilla nations was distributed and federated. Individual sibs and lineages cooperated in political and ritual affairs, and kinship further linked disparate villages. As shown below, while European contact radically altered life for the Cahuilla, the flexible structure of their political and cultural organization underpinned alliances that shaped, and continue to shape, society in Southern California. Their sovereignty today remains diffuse across many nations, with separated leadership roles structured by familial and democratic relations, reflecting their precontact power dynamics. As will be seen, the primary organizational structures of aboriginal organization of Cahuilla lifeways underpin their strategies for responding to colonization and continue to serve as the dominant governing processes in their actions through the era of the Indian casino movement.

The Spanish Conquest

The Cahuilla knew about the Spanish long before contact. Beginning in the sixteenth century, Spanish voyagers set sail north from colonial New Spain to explore the coastline of what is now called California. These explorers saw native people on the shore. Some of their ships capsized, drowning the sailors; their remains washed ashore and were found by natives. By way of their extensive kinship and trade networks, news of the arrival of the Europeans to the south likely spread to the north, alerting the Cahuilla. By 1769, when New Spain established its first permanent settlement on the Pacific Coast of present-day California, the Spanish empire had almost three centuries of experience colonizing and converting indigenous peoples in the New World. A strict religious mandate for conquest and caste propelled New Spain's elites to prosperity. The Requerimento, a mandate written by the Spanish in 1513, required indigenous peoples to submit to Spanish authority and Catholic proselytizing. Under Spanish law natives could not be enslaved. Isabella I of Castile, queen of Spain, declared that native peoples were free vassals of the crown, saving slavery for only the imported African population. However, although this distinction existed in the realm of law and language, it was not always followed in practice. Spanish law offered multiple opportunities for settlers to exploit native labor, including the mission system.

In 1769 the Spanish military and missionaries expanded north to establish the first mission in what was called Alta California (in contrast to Baja California, located to the south), and we know now as California. The first mission was in present-day San Diego and was accompanied by a *presidio*, or fort, to protect the mission and to aid in gathering and maintaining a population of native residents, who the Spanish called neophytes. The expressed goal of the missions was to convert Indians to Catholicism and to the Spanish language and customs, which the colonial regime considered the hallmarks of European civilization. Missions also served a vital economic function for New Spain: the missionaries, with the aid of the Spanish military, forced Indians to farm and raise cattle, which provided the colony with resources essential for expansion. Florence Shipek's (1987) analysis of mission documents demonstrates how forced labor and food shortages at the missions resulted in a significant decline of all indigenous populations subjected to the mission experience. Frequently, Indians escaped from the missions; Spanish soldiers found and captured and, often, executed the escapees (Phillips 1997, 23). Moreover, the arrival of the Spanish brought devastating diseases, including tuberculosis, influenza, and syphilis, that traveled ahead of the colonizers, decimating many native communities before the arrival of the settlers. When native communities along the coast began to decline, the Spanish missionaries and military looked toward inland California to find new recruits for the dwindling mission populations.

Cahuilla in the Missions

In 1772 Pedro Fages led the first European expedition across Cahuilla territory. His journey took him through the San Jacinto Mountains, San Jacinto Valley, San Bernardino Valley, and finally through the San Bernardino Mountains. Two years later Captain Juan Bautista de Anza led the first expedition to enter present-day California from the east by crossing the Colorado River. These first visits into inland Alta California were peaceful. As part of their custom, native nations provided the expeditions with gifts of food and shells (Trafzer 2002, 47–48). As they explored the territory, Bautista and his men accepted the offerings of its native inhabitants, while he claimed the land for Spain. Many Cahuilla villages, especially those farther inland, remained outside Spanish control, but others were raided by the Spanish military that sought to capture neophytes to labor at the San Gabriel and San Fernando Missions. At the missions, cattle herds often complicated Spanish agricultural pursuits, including gardens and vineyards. As a result, the Spanish established *asistencias* to raise cattle in the interior of California, farther into Serrano and Cahuilla territory (45). The *asistencias* performed many of the economic functions of the missions deep in Cahuilla territory. Although they did not include the missions' religious and cultural indoctrination, they were marked by the exploitation of native labor and resources that underpinned the mission system.

The increased kidnapping of native men, women, and children did not take place without retaliation. In 1810 a coalition of an estimated eight hundred Indians, including Tongva-Gabrieleno, Serrano, and Mojave, raided Mission San Gabriel. In 1819 Mission San Gabriel established an *asistencia*, known as Rancho San Bernardino, near present-day Redlands, at the frontiers of Cahuilla and Serrano territories. Before the Spanish arrived, a Serrano village known as Guachama, with a population near 200, occupied the site of the future *asistencia* (Trafzer 2002, 49–51). From 1834 to 1835, as the *asistencia* increasingly held indigenous captives, native coalitions engaged in multiple raids to free the neophytes. The Cahuilla communities that remained outside the direct influence of the mission system retained their political and economic independence in addition to their cultural practices. Those residing in Mission San Gabriel and elsewhere in the mission system entered what Phillips (2010, 140–141) called a "foreign social environment" where they lived with others from a wide range of linguistic and cultural groups. Between some of these groups, such as the Serrano and Tongva, longstanding disputes remained. Phillips (141) found that "to maintain order among the disparate groups, Father Zalvidea (of Mission San Gabriel) and the other missionaries divided the Indians into distinct categories based on age, gender and marital status, all of which ran counter to traditional culture, especially the practice of housing young unmarried men and women in different quarters." The indigenous individuals who found themselves within the mission system experienced a radical restructuring of their social organization in which the missionaries attempted to alter the native social institutions and boundaries to fit the colonial agenda of New Spain.

Conquest Interrupted

Because Alta California was on the then-remote frontier of New Spain, far from Mexico City and other colonial cities, the Cahuilla and their neighbors were relatively sheltered from the turmoil of Mexico's long war for independence. In 1821, after more than a decade of violence, Mexico gained independence from Spain. The war's greatest impact on the native nations of Alta California was creation of a secular Mexico that severed its ties to the Catholic Church, bringing an end to the mission system. Passed in 1833 by Mexico's congress, the Secularization Act privatized the missions and their resources. It confiscated property from the Church and converted it to pueblos and private ranchos. It also granted citizenship to the former neophytes. Many freed neophytes remained working the fields and ranches of the former missions to earn a living by using their agricultural skills acquired from the Spanish missionaries. Other neophytes returned to their native communities, or whatever remnants of those communities they could find. While in certain respects the Secularization Act freed the neophytes, many became indebted to one of a few wealthy Mexican families. When the missions became privatized, a few wealthy families came to own their farm and ranchlands, and converted them into private haciendas, or plantations. Many former neophytes worked at these haciendas as indentured servants, in many ways reproducing the missions' labor structure (Rawls 1984, 21). The mixing of diverse native nations in the missions continued in the Mexican economy. For those who labored in the haciendas, marriages between members of different nations became increasingly common (Trafzer 2002, 54). While the moiety structure had permitted Cahuilla to marry outside their linguistic and cultural group, marrying inside one's moiety became increasingly common, breaking the longstanding tradition of marrying outside one's moiety.

Relative to their neighbors closer to the coast, the Cahuilla experienced fewer direct impacts from the missions. The desert was far too hot and dry to suit Spanish agriculture, and the mountains too steep and remote for easy access. Some Cahuilla did labor in the system; the very presence of the missions disrupted the Cahuilla's access to and relations with their resources and neighbors at the western edges of their territory, but most of Cahuilla territory remained outside the missions' direct influence. Mission San Gabriel was the only mission founded on the frontier of Cahuilla territory, and it operated for only fourteen years before secularization. Today the assimilative impacts of the missions on the Cahuilla, and across California native nations generally, are often exaggerated (as further discussed in chapter 6). Challenged by the missions' spread of disease and disorder, California Indian nations continued to exercise political autonomy, albeit in a new cultural and political climate.

In this new environment Mexican and native communities grew interdependent, allowing for new political alliances and economic opportunities. These new relations began in earnest in 1842, when Antonio Maria Lugo, a wealthy rancher, purchased 37,700 acres overlapping Cahuilla and Serrano territories in what is now San Bernardino County (Hoffman 1862). On his purchase, Lugo founded Rancho San Bernardino and hired Serrano, Cahuilla, and other natives to farm his land. Parties from along the Colorado River, including Chemehuevi and Mojave, raided Rancho San Bernardino to steal cattle. To protect his property, Lugo hired Juan Antonio, a Cahuilla leader from the San Jacinto Mountains. Antonio and Lugo's trust in each other grew as Antonio contracted for Cahuilla men to secure Rancho San Bernardino. Though the short-lived relationship came to an end after the war between Mexico and the United States, their partnership demonstrates the capacity for post–mission era Cahuilla leaders to engage in diplomacy with colonizers when necessary in order to preserve their independence.

California did not experience the full brunt of the war between the United States and Mexico, but several smaller battles in the territory illustrate how the warring empires depended on native populations, which acted independently of each other, as the Cahuilla and Luiseño did. On December 6, 1846, Andres Pico led a band of Mexican troops to attack American troops and their Luiseño allies in northern present-day San Diego County. In the attack, which became known as the Battle of San Pasqual, twenty American soldiers died and Pico's forces stole horses from the Pauma band of Luiseño Indians. In retaliation, a band of Luiseño attacked Pico's troops, killing eleven soldiers. This attack became known as the Pauma Massacre. The Mexican army responded to the Pauma Massacre by sending José del Carmen Lugo, from Rancho San Bernardino, to lead a force including Juan Antonio and other Cahuilla, against the Luiseño. Lugo and Antonio traveled to the village of Temecula to ambush Luiseño forces. In the confrontation, known as the Temecula Massacre, the Cahuilla forces killed between thirty and forty Luiseño. Ultimately, the impact of the Cahuilla's victory over the Luiseño did little to support their Mexican allies, who surrendered to the United States in

1848 with the Treaty of Guadalupe Hidalgo (9 Stat. 922). In 1851, with the power of Mexican elites in decline, the Lugo family sold Rancho San Bernardino to settlers from the Church of Jesus Christ of Latter-day Saints, which established the first Anglo settlement in San Bernardino County.

The Eve of American Occupation

Prior to European contact, the Cahuilla maintained self-reliant networks of sovereign polities rooted in their origin story. The initial contacts with Spanish expeditions were peaceful. Violence began as Spanish missions raided villages and kidnapped Indians. Coalitions of Indians raided the Spanish missions and *asistencias,* but this era ended abruptly when Mexico gained independence. The brief Mexican period was marked by a relative degree of integration, with many former neophytes finding work by using skills they had learned in the mission. For some, their work included indentured servitude. With these economic relations came further social integration, as many Indians and Mexicans intermarried. This integration, however, was uneven. Many Cahuilla living farther inland remained largely isolated from the Spanish-speaking settlers.

With the American invasion, the Cahuilla and their neighbors became independent actors in the larger war; their knowledge of the land and military skill made them powerful allies coveted by the warring empires. The Lugos distinguished between the Cahuilla and the natives that came from the east to raid their rancho. Juan Antonio and his men ensured the rancho's safety. Unlike the forced labor in the missions, Antonio and his men freely worked for Lugo. Through Antonio's alliance with the Lugos, the Cahuilla fought alongside the Mexicans against the Americans. The next chapter shows how Antonio made certain to not just maintain peaceful relations with Americans but also to adopt a hybrid identity as both an Indian and an American.

The practice of decentralized sovereignty continued, playing a significant role in shaping the Californian political economy, especially during the onset of the war between the United States and Mexico. Political alliances often set Indian against Indian, as independent native sovereign nations became entangled in disputes between settlers and, even more so, during the war between the Mexican and American empires. As demonstrated in this chapter and illustrated throughout this book, European settlement in the land known as California has always depended on indigenous resources, labor, and knowledge. Moreover, the structure of native nations before contact continues to underpin the dynamics of settler–native relations.

GENOCIDE IN CALIFORNIA

WHEN THE UNITED STATES took possession of the land along the Pacific Coast in 1848 the exploitation of local Indians not only continued but also intensified and diversified, leading to the near collapse of the indigenous populations. With the acquisition and rapid settlement of the Pacific Coast, the United States' previous policy of removing natives to the west became obsolete. Indians could not be removed farther west because the United States had completed its march across North America. This impasse drove policymakers to devise solutions to the so-called Indian problem, including the creation of the reservation system. However, what would have become the first reservations were never implemented. As described in this chapter, congressional representatives, backed by wealthy settlers, successfully derailed the creation of the original reservations in California. In the vacuum left by the absence of federal action, competing factions of settlers swayed the California state government to support two divergent and exploitive practices: the virtual enslavement of California Indians on private ranches that perpetuated the missions' labor system, and the genocide of native populations residing in the state's mountainous gold-bearing regions. By the late nineteenth century these practices gave way to policies of assimilation and settler perceptions of natives marked by both romanticism and fatalism. This chapter analyzes the evolving policies and cultural knowledge of the settler population and examines how the growing Anglo settler population and the deteriorating yet resilient native populations engaged each other during the first five decades of California statehood. In the face of settlers who were intent on exterminating or enslaving California Indians, the Cahuilla and other native nations developed strategies to maintain their capacity for self-determination. The two types of native exploitation, extermination and enslavement, served different political and economic purposes and reflected different settler worldviews.

Before the California Conquest

The American regime inherited a tradition of settler colonialism from the British that significantly differed from the colonial strategies implemented by New Spain. Because of these differences in colonization, the annexation of the Southwest thrust the indigenous nations of this territory into a vastly different political terrain. Unlike the Spanish colonizers, whose primary goals included the use of missions to convert natives to Christianity and who exploited native labor, the first British colonial efforts focused on establishing and populating permanent settlements. The first British settlements in North America maintained distinct boundaries between native and settler communities. While individual conversions and intermarriage did occur, the British made no systematic attempt to assimilate the indigenous populations. Instead, the British recognized native communities as sovereign nations and sought to displace those native nations through the same means the British used in territorial conflicts with European nations: war and treaty. This chapter begins with a brief discussion of British and American settler colonial practices before the conquest of California to demonstrate how the annexation of California forced the United States to develop new strategies, especially reservations, for removing native peoples from their land.

In 1763, in the wake of the Seven Years War, increasing conflict between natives and British settlements led the British Crown to issue a proclamation that prohibited all settlers from residing west of the Appalachian Mountains. Many of the colonists resisted this and the resulting dispute further inspired many colonists to reject the Crown and seek independence. Likewise, during the Revolutionary War many tribes allied with the British, since they preferred the British attempts to limit westward expansion. Signed in 1783, the Treaty of Paris ended the Revolutionary War, declaring the thirteen colonies independent from Britain. This ended the British proclamation, thus allowing settlers to move west. However, the newly independent United States faced the same challenges as the British and responded with the same prohibition. Shortly after achieving independence, George Washington, then commander of the Continental Army, wrote,

> But as we prefer Peace to a State of Warfare, as we consider them [native nations] as a deluded People; as we perswade ourselves that they are convinced, from experience, of their error in taking up the Hatchet against us, and that their true interest and safety must now depend upon our friendship. As the Country, is large enough to con-

tain us all; as we are disposed to be kind to them and to partake of their Trade, we will from these considerations and from motives of Compn [compassion], draw a veil over what is past and establish a boundary line between them and use beyond which we will endeavor to restrain our People from Hunting or Settling. (Washington 1783)

The leadership of the early United States certainly wanted to expand westward free from consequence, but, recognizing the military might and commercial potential of native nations, they quickly established boundaries to separate settler and native communities. Likewise, the United States continued in the British tradition of signing treaties with native nations that recognized indigenous sovereignty. The formal recognition of native nation sovereignty and land rights proved invaluable to the United States because tribal alliances were necessary for fighting the British in the Revolutionary War and again in the War of 1812.

As the newly independent United States expanded westward, it imposed a policy of removal that recognized native nation sovereignty as it sought to remove these nations to the west. The policies of the removal era were unwavering in their recognition of tribal sovereignty even as they became tools to further settler colonialism, as illustrated in 1832 when the Supreme Court ruled in the landmark case *Worcester v. Georgia*:

The Indian nations have always been considered as distinct, independent political communities retaining their original national rights as the undisputed possessors of the soil, from time immemorial, with the single exception of that imposed by irresistible power, which excluded them from intercourse with any other European potentate than the first discoverer of the coast of the particular region claimed.... The very term "nation," so generally applied to them, means "a people distinct from others." The Constitution, by declaring treaties already made, as well as those to be made, to be the supreme law of the land, has adopted and sanctioned the previous treaties with the Indian nations, and consequently admits their rank among the powers who are capable of making treaties. The words "treaty" and "nation" are words of our own language, selected in our diplomatic and legislative proceedings by ourselves, having each a definite and well understood meaning. We have applied them to Indians as we have applied them to other nations of the earth. They are applied to all in the same sense. (*Worcester v. Georgia* 1832)

The Supreme Court unequivocally asserted that the word "nation" accurately describes native polities and that treaties with these nations are no different from treaties with any other nation. *Worcester v. Georgia* found that only the federal government could engage in diplomatic relations with native nations because the Constitution prohibits state governments, such as Georgia, from foreign relations. Georgia cannot negotiate directly with European nations nor can it establish its own policies governing native nations. President Andrew Jackson's Indian Removal Act, which enshrined the long-practiced removal policies into a singular federal law, sought to remove native nations but not to completely extinguish their sovereignty. The act ensured the forced expulsion of native nations west of the Mississippi River and, like *Worcester v. Georgia*, recognized a limited amount of native nation self-determination: removed tribes could not determine where they lived, but once removed they could govern themselves. The act's primary goal was not to exterminate or assimilate native nations: it was to remove them. No doubt this imposed significant constraints on native nations' external political sovereignty, but it did not extinguish it. The United States' conquest of California was a turning point in the federal government's removal policy. At this point, there was no place farther west to remove tribes to, and the discovery of gold prompted rapid settlement. The United States' expansion to the West Coast, combined with pressures from the California gold rush, led the federal government to shift away from removal. As the federal government worked to implement a new approach, the state of California (statehood was granted September 9, 1850) pursued its own policies of extermination and enslavement.

Mission Labor in California

In 1846 Commodore John B. Montgomery, the commander of American forces in San Francisco, issued the first American order governing California native nations. In his "Proclamation to the Inhabitants of California" (published in the Monterey newspaper *Californian* on November 7, 1846) he declared, "The Indian population must not be regarded in the light of slaves," and "all Indians must be required to obtain service [and] it is…necessary that the Indians within the settlement shall have employment." The proclamation's doublespeak is as apparent as the economic purpose it served. While on the surface the proclamation claims to reject slavery, in effect it mandated the arrest of all unemployed natives, with a sentence of forced labor. Natives who did not work for settlers were arrested and forced to work in the settler economy. This was not the chattel slavery endured by African Americans in the American Southeast, but it was state-sponsored forced labor. It was involuntary servitude, which is a type of slavery. Yet the Proclamation enabled California to claim itself as a free state when it sought statehood during a time of increasing tension between free and slave states. Commodore Montgomery sidestepped this conflict simply by claiming the practice was not slavery, but something else. In doing so, he provided a legal avenue for and supply of free labor to settlers. Soon after gaining statehood, California's legislature enacted laws further entrenching forced labor. California remained a free state in name only. As Rawls (1984, 86) pointed out, "They were to remain essentially what they had been under the previous regime: a subservient class of laborers. Although the delegates voted unanimously to prohibit slavery in California, their attention was on black slavery not on Indian slavery." This position enabled the legislature to avoid antebellum disputes over free and slave states and territories, while exploiting native labor. These policies quickly expanded to promote practices of forced child labor and sexual exploitation that can only be properly described as slavery.

Worcester v. Georgia prohibited states from establishing their own policies for governing native nations, but that did not quell the desire for California's first state policymakers to enact legislation that exploited the native population. The Act for the Government and Protection of Indians (Chap. 133, Cal. Stats., April 22), passed in 1850, provided the state's first definition of the legal status of California Indians and continued the tradition of exploitation that had been started by the Spanish missions. This act extended the policy first put forth under the Proclamation to the Inhabitants of California. Under the act, white settlers could not directly enslave native people because that would contradict California's status as a free state. However, the act required that all unemployed or "vagrant" Indians be arrested and jailed. Those Indians who could not afford to pay their own bail, which was most of them, could have their bail paid for by a white man. When a white man paid an Indian's bail the law required "the Indian shall be compelled to work for the person so bailing, until he has discharged or cancelled the fine assessed against him" (Rawls 1984, 87). This created a system of indentured servitude that legalized a cycle of forced labor. When natives completed enough time as an indentured servant to repay their debt, they could leave, only to then be subject again to arrest for being unemployed. However, even this cycle of arrest and servitude was not the most egregious part of the act.

Known as Indian apprenticeships, a provision of the 1850 act created a structure through which white persons could purchase Indian children for labor, provided that the child was an orphan or was obtained with permission from an adult who claimed to be the child's parent or guardian (Statutes of California, 1st sess., chap 133, p. 408). An apprenticeship in name only, the intent of this act was no different from those laws that enshrined slavery in the Southeast: generations of natives would live their entire lives experiencing only forced labor at white-owned farms. These apprenticeships were only a thinly veiled guise for slavery, as noted by an 1860 editorial in the *Sacramento Standard* (quoted in "The Standard on Indians" 1860) that argued, "The most humane disposition that could be made of them [Indians], is, probably, to reduce them to a mild system of servitude. Call them slaves, coolies or apprentices—it is all the same; supply them with Christian masters and make them Christian servants." At first the act allowed so-called apprentices who reached adulthood to seek freedom, but in 1860 the state legislature passed an amendment to include adult Indians, precluding any opportunity for them to leave their "Christian masters." Held as apprentices through adulthood, this system had little to do with any of the training that its title might suggest. The apprenticeship system extended to adult natives the status of perpetual child, needing adoptive parents throughout adulthood, thereby allowing the continued practice of enslavement while keeping California out of the coalition of slave states on the eve of the Civil War. Passed at the conclusion of the Civil War, the Thirteenth Amendment (U.S. Const. amend. 13) prohibited slavery and indentured servitude, effectively ending California's so-called apprenticeship system. The Cahuilla and other native California nations did not idly accept these apprenticeships and other forms of exploitation.

Juan Antonio and the Garra Uprising

In 1851 local officials in Southern California, acting independently of both federal and state authorities, devised a scheme to tax Indian villages. Many villages paid reluctantly, while others simply refused. After San Diego County sheriff Agoston Haraszthy ordered the Cupeño Indians working at Warner's Ranch to pay the taxes or he would confiscate their property, Cupeño allied with neighboring native nations, including some Cahuilla, to organize a revolt against white settlers.

Rumor of the revolt spread, with newspapers claiming that Antonio Garra, a Cupeño and former neophyte from the San Luis Rey Mission, was leading the revolt. As rumor of the revolt spread, fear and hostility increased among the then-outnumbered but increasing Anglo population. Forty-seven years later, on March 1, 1898, Judge B. S. Eaton gave a talk to the Pioneer Society about the uprising. The next day the *Los Angeles Herald* printed the following:

> Judge B. S. Eaton gave an account of the Indian campaign of 1851. It was rumored that the Cahuilla Indians of the mountains had conspired to massacre all of the whites of San Diego, Los Angeles and San Bernardino counties. A company of volunteers was raised in Los Angeles.
>
> At San Bernardino the people were so frightened that they had built a fort.... An Indian runner came into their camp at Chino and reported that the leaders of the insurrection were prisoners, held by the old chief, Juan Antonio of San Gorgonia. Antonio Gara [*sic*], the leader, and four of his men were shot.
>
> The Indians at that time destroyed Warner's ranch and it was reported killed eleven men. Warner killed several of the Indian assailants before he could make his escape. ("Pioneer Society" 1898)

The settlers' response to hearing of Garra's plans reveals their insecurity in the face of the perceived threat from the Cahuilla. Gripped by the spread of disease and food insecurity, Mark Rifkin noted that the Cahuilla and Cupeño did not have the military capacity to "massacre all of the whites of San Diego, Los Angeles and San Bernardino counties," and that newspapers' "focus on Garra [as the purported organizer of the revolt] indexes a broader discursive formation in which native peoples are cast as lacking political intelligence and initiative" (Rifkin 2009, 182). In other words, not only were settlers inflating fear about the military potential of native nations, but also, as Rifkin argued, by attributing the revolt to Garra, newspaper accounts portrayed natives as blindly following a political leader. Of course, to the extent that Garra was a leader of the revolt, he was only directing the ire of natives who held deep and legitimate grievances against settlers. Moreover, even the Cahuilla and Cupeño were themselves divided on whether to revolt violently or to peacefully, but firmly, negotiate with settler society. Juan Antonio, who had fought against American forces in the war with Mexico, was one Cahuilla leader who worked to build rapport with American settlers after

Mexico ceded territory to the United States. Juan Antonio recognized that violent revolt against settlers would only intensify settler hostility toward natives. He intervened in the revolt by arresting and then executing Garra. In doing so, Antonio demonstrated to the settlers the potential that some natives could be allies.

Juan Antonio did not protect settlers because he hoped to assimilate the Cahuilla into settler society. Rather, he did it to maintain Cahuilla sovereignty by building interdependency with settler society. For Antonio, maintaining a dual Cahuilla and American identity, while cooperating and negotiating with settler society, was the best way to preserve self-determination. Antonio's strategy is exemplified in a speech he gave. In November 1861 the San Bernardino County sheriff arrested a Cahuilla for the murder of another Indian. Antonio agreed that the Indian was guilty of murder, but he found that the sheriff acted outside his authority by arresting an Indian for a crime against another Indian. Antonio, followed by forty to fifty of his supporters, traveled to the private residence of the county judge to demand the Indian's release. Antonio argued that only the Cahuilla should have jurisdiction of crimes committed within their community. Through an interpreter, Antonio said,

> I come because my people asked me; they sent for me.... They came and told me that murders were being charged upon my people. I took some of my old men...and came a long way to meet you. On our way we caught an Indian who murdered a Sonoranian named Antonio. But...last night he made his escape. But my Indians are on his trail, and he cannot escape if he remains in the Indian country. He is a bad Indian and should be hung. I am an American—my people are all Americans, although we are Indians. If we should hear of armed men in these mountains, we should come and tell you, and help fight with you. This is our country, and it is yours. We are your friends; we want you to be ours.
>
> Some of my people are bad men and commit crimes. But all are not bad.... If the [president] of the United States should say my people are all bad, and must be killed, then you should kill us. But the [president] does not say so, and he never will.... My people come here to the white people...and white men give them whiskey, and then they try to get their squaws, and then they fight. My people are buried all around, killed by white men. I shall take my people away from this place, and then there will be no more of

this. When white men want Indians to work, they can come and get a recommend from our village, and then they will get good men.... I will deliver up any white man who commits crime to be dealt with by his people, and I wish to punish my people my own way.... If a white man deserves hanging, let the white men hang him. (Antonio 1861 cited in Philips 1975, 158)

Upon hearing Antonio's speech, the judge released the Indian, dropping the murder charge so that Antonio could punish him. This speech illustrates Antonio's philosophy and a strategy that has proven useful throughout the Cahuilla's history. Unlike Garra and others who sought to defend their people with violence, Antonio sought to cooperate with settlers and to urge them not to indiscriminately categorize all Indians as hostile and violent. Similar to Antonio's defense of Rancho San Bernardino against Indian raids, his speech to the judge confronted settlers with the divisions within native nations. In both cases, Antonio urged settlers to understand that some Indians might be violent criminals, but most are not. Antonio worked to help settlers realize that when they acknowledge that "all [Indians] are not bad" then settlers and Indians can live side by side and forge mutually beneficial relationships. In his speech, the cooperation Antonio envisions is both political and economic. He offered help to settlers hoping to secure Indian employees and to capture and turn over white criminals on Indian land. Moreover, his statement, "I am an American—my people are all Americans, although we are Indians.... This is our country, and it is yours" posited a hybrid identity, where the Cahuilla are just as American as any settler. For Antonio, the two identities were not mutually exclusive. Antonio's strategy is repeated throughout the Cahuilla's relations with settlers. During the first years of California's statehood, it appeared that the federal government was posed to provide limited protections for native nation self-determination. However, settlers who coveted native resources worked to block these limited federal protections. In the absence of these protections, the exploitation of Californian native nations was limitless.

The Eighteen Treaties

In 1851 the federal government sent agents to California to negotiate treaties with California native nations for the purpose of establishing substantial reservations where California's native nations could maintain their independence. To the chagrin of many California settlers and politicians, *Worcester v. Georgia* forbid California from establishing any policies governing relations with native nations within state boundaries or directly interfering with the treaty process. In order to halt the treaty process, policymakers in California would have to urge the U.S. Congress to block the ratifications of the treaties. Ultimately, they were successful, and the reservations, as outlined in the treaties, never came to fruition. However, the process by which the treaties were drafted and eventually rendered ineffective illustrates how the transformation of the removal policy was not just a change in policy but also was a fundamental restructuring of how white settlers envisioned the future of their society from one that negotiated, albeit on quite unequal terms, with native nations to one that utterly disregarded native cultural and political sovereignty.

The federal agents and native nations signed eighteen treaties, which reserved approximately 7.5 percent of California for native nations to exercise self-determination. These reservations were to be east of the coast in territories that at the time had little settler development. In the Treaty of Temecula (or Unratified California Treaty K 1852), tribal leaders, including Juan Antonio, agreed to acknowledge the authority of the federal government and cede certain territories in exchange for a protected land for themselves. The original text of the treaty provides a rich example of the extent to which the federal government recognized the political sovereignty of California's native nations:

ARTICLE 1. The several nations [Luiseño and Cahuilla] above mentioned do acknowledge the United States to be the sole and absolute sovereign of all the soil and territory ceded to them by a treaty of peace made between them and the republic of Mexico. ART. 2. The said nations of Indians acknowledge themselves... under the exclusive jurisdiction, authority and protection of the United States, and hereby bind themselves...to refrain from...all acts of hostility and aggression towards the government or citizens thereof, and to live on terms of peace and friendship among themselves, and with all other Indian tribes which are now or may come under the protection of the United States; and furthermore bind themselves to conform to and be governed by the laws and regulations of the Indian bureau. (Unratified California Treaty K 1852)

The repeated use of the term "nation" follows the argument in *Worcester v. Georgia* that the federal government has always recognized native polities as nations. By requiring these nations to cease "all acts of hostility and aggression towards the government or citizens," the treaty tacitly acknowledged the native nations' military potential. Much like the earlier treaties signed between the British and American regimes, the federal agents in California sought to acknowledge the settlers' desire for land and to prevent the native nations' military aggression against the encroaching settler society.

Why had the U.S. Congress rejected the same treaties it funded agents to negotiate? They rejected the treaties they commissioned because of the intensifying settler demands for native resources, especially labor and land. In 1852 California's legislature identified the proposed reservations as encompassing "extensive tracts of valuable mineral and agricultural lands, embracing populous mining towns, larger portions of which are already in possession of, and improved by, American citizens" (Senate of California 1852, 44). In agreement that the proposed reservations would impede development, California's legislature instructed its delegation to the U.S. Congress to block the treaties. In the absence of the protections that the treaties would have provided, the California legislature urged the development of twin policies of extermination and enslavement. Regarding the Mission Indians, the legislature concluded, "They will resume to their former occupation, and supply, to a great extent, what is so much needed, that labor, without which, it will be long before California can feed herself" (598). As Rawls observed (1984), while the legislature anticipated that the former neophyte population would continue to provide the forced agricultural labor necessary for the continued growth of settler society, it cast the non-Mission Indians, those remaining so-called wild Indians, as obstacles to accessing the state's mineral wealth, especially gold. From the legislature's perspective, these wild Indians needed to be removed from the land, either by forced relocation or by extermination.

In 1852 Congress sympathized with the California delegation's objections and rejected the treaties, leaving a vacuum of federal authority. The state of California then implemented its own agenda. Whereas the treaties would have provided the tribes with annuities and reservations in exchange for ceding territory, California took all of the land without any exchange. Moreover, the reservations that were to be created through the treaties were never created. As discussed later in this chapter and in chapter 3, the reservations that exist today were created decades later by executive order. And the present-day reservations are much smaller and more isolated than those that would have been created by the treaties. Thus, the decades after the United States annexed Alta California saw a vast increase in the exploitation of California Indians, with their rights even more severely restricted. Although the Treaty of Guadalupe Hidalgo promised U.S. citizenship to all Mexican citizens in the territory ceded to the United States, the American Indians who lived in this territory were denied U.S. citizenship, even though they had been citizens of Mexico. The federal government denied native people basic rights, including the right to vote and the right to testify as a witness in court (Goodrich 1926, 10–11).

Under the direction of superintendent Edward Fitzgerald Beale, the federal Office of Indian Affairs (the precursor to the BIA) proposed a new model for reservations, one that began in California and was later adopted throughout the United States at the end of the removal era. Unlike the Indian lands demarcated through removal policies, the new lands were military posts administering the education and organizing the labor of native communities. Beale suggested smaller reservations on lands owned and controlled by the federal government and established unilaterally without treaty negotiations. According to Rawls (1984, 149), Beale's proposal was "a distinctively California product in several respects," including its creation in response to the end of the removal era with the settlement of the West Coast and Beale's hope to recreate the assimilative and labor practices of the Spanish missions. Seeing potential in Beale's vision, Congress funded the creation of military post reservations in Northern California. However, the reservations were inadequately funded and existed only in the north. Many native nations in the north and all of them in the south found themselves without any protected land in the decades after the gold rush.

California native nations were not the only population to lose land at the conclusion of the war between the United States and Mexico. Under the Treaty of Guadalupe Hidalgo, land-owning Mexicans were to retain their land after cession to the United States. The U.S. Land Act of 1851 made this nearly impossible. Under the act the burden of proof was on landowners to affirm their ownership of land. Land-owning former citizens of Mexico had to bear the costs of attorneys and travel to San Francisco for their Mexican titles to be recognized by the United States. Often these expenses forced the sale or forfeiture of their land. In the years after the Treaty of Guadalupe Hidalgo, the Mexican ranchos increasingly came under Anglo control, while the exploitation of native labor continued to fuel the state's growth (Rifkin 2009).

However, as Phillips (2010, 290–91) pointed out, the legislature's proposed reliance on Indian labor came under increased scrutiny. An editorial in the *Los Angeles Daily News* entitled "Labor the Great Necessity of Los Angeles" explains the perceived shortcomings of native labor:

The problem: The great necessity of any agricultural county is labor—active, intelligent laborers who invest the savings from their earnings in farms and lots, and build houses that identify them with the permanent interests of the county.... In this portion of the State and particularly in this county, the great bulk of labor has been performed by Indians, who are at best but inferior laborers, totally void of that interest in the welfare of the community.... They build no houses, own no lands, pay no taxes, and encourage no branch of industry; their scanty earnings at the end of the week being spent for rum in the lowest purlieus of the city, where scenes of violence occur.... During eighteen years...nothing has been added to the county by them save the debt and public expenditure in punishing them by the courts for murders and robberies committed in their drunken and phrenzied debauches. They have filled our jails, have contributed largely to the filling of our State prison, and are fast filling our graveyards, where they must either be buried at public expense or be permitted to rot in the streets and highways.

The solution: It is time that the men of wealth and influence in this county should take some steps to encourage a different and more useful class of laborers, who will combine the qualities of good and useful citizens to that of good laborers. By consulting the census returns of 1860, we find that this country contained a population of two thousand and fourteen Indians, male and female, who subsists (their living is a bare subsistence) by their daily labor.... If they had been sent to reservations and their places supplied, ten years ago, with two thousand intelligent white laborers, at least two-thirds of that number would to-day be land owners; their numbers would have doubled, and a large and valuable accession of the population made to the independent yeomanry of the county; farms and hamlets would have covered the now barren plains, schools, churches and other evidences of high order of civilization, would have occupied the sites of gainly *Rancherias*; and peace, intelligence and happiness would dwell where now misery and squalor reign supreme.

The Blame: The Indian being constantly brought into competition with that class of labor that would be most beneficial to the country, checks immigration and retards the prosperity of the county. It is of no use for our leading farmers to say they took Indian labor from necessity; that other labor could not be had, &c.; they have made no effort to induce other labor to come to their assistance, as the absence of labor exchanges, agricultural societies and other means of encouraging laborers abundantly proves, but have yet contented themselves to use the county jail for nearly twenty years as an intelligence office from which to gather information concerning the class of laborers mostly employed by them. ("Labor the Great Necessity of Los Angeles" 1869)

The editorial bluntly described the role of imprisonment in creating a system of indentured servitude, while blindly attributing the perpetuation of this system to the perceived inferiority of the California Indians and not to the exploitive structures of the system itself. The author suggested that instead of acquiring native labor through the prison system, the best solution would be to remove native people to reservations where the government could require them to assimilate into the dominant religion and culture.

Gold and Genocide

In *Murder State,* Brendan Lindsay (2012) provided a detailed account of the genocide in California, arguing that the term is aptly applied in this case because of the systematic and intentional attempts by the state government to exterminate native nations. California's first governor, Peter Burnett, could not have been more explicit in his call for genocide. In his January 6, 1851, State of the State Address, Burnett openly called to continue "a war of extermination...waged between the races until the Indian race becomes extinct" (California State Library 2017). This genocide occurred at the same time as the enslavement of Indians in the state's more developed regions. Rawls (1984, 144) suggested that if the Mission Indians were "useful" to the settlers, then the "wild" Indians, those not integrated into the settler society and economy, were "obstacles" to the state's wealth of gold and other mineral resources. Many settlers did not perceive the federal government's policy of removing native populations as a valid option. Newspapers openly advocated the genocide of California Indians. On August 7, 1853, the *Yreka Herald* proclaimed, "Now that the general hostilities against the Indians have commenced we hope that the Government will render such aid as will enable the citizens of the north to carry on *a war of extermination* until the last Redskin of these tribes has been killed" (emphasis added; cited by Rawls 1984).

Rawls's (1984) analysis of newspaper accounts from this time found that many settlers during the gold rush accepted the erroneous notion that the California Indians hibernated underground, like animals. I suggest that the perception that California Indians were obstacles operated in tandem with settler knowledge that categorized California Indians as animals. In other words, if the obstacle is an animal, its removal or extermination can be justified. These different and abhorrent ways that settlers thought of California Indians served a specific psychological function. Dehumanizing labels, such as these, can diminish the cognitive dissonance of those who exploited native peoples. These labels provided language to rationalize murder as a sport that served the greater good. In place of the child metaphor for useful Indians, the wild Indians became animals, deprived of their humanity and rationalized for genocide. To describe a population as animals is to deny their humanity and, subsequently, to ignore their religion, music, art, and other qualities that are uniquely human. "Buck," a common settler label for a male Indian in early settler California, is a metaphor that compares the male Indian to a male deer. From the hostile and myopic perspective of these settlers, hunting Indians is comparable to hunting deer.

In the gold-rich mountains settlers viewed the wild Indians as subhuman pests and obstacles to an otherwise unhindered pursuit of precious metals. This perception of natives contrasted with the stereotype of useful Indians. In the agricultural fields of California's fertile valleys, settler assumptions that Indian culture is childlike rationalized apprenticeships and indentured servitude. The wild Indians in the mountains, however, could not, in the minds of gold miners, ever become useful. Settlers' economic goals of agriculture and mining created divergent stereotypes of native and conflicting state policies. At the same time that the state supported the training of Indians through servitude and apprenticeships, it funded militias to exterminate the remaining wild Indians. Those who engaged in this genocide did not use language that described natives as children in need of training. If Indians are children, then, following this metaphor, they may be disciplined, though certainly not murdered. Even a childlike adult is a human. But if Indians are animals, as settlers in California's mountains and frontier often called them, then hunting Indians is no different from hunting any other animal.

Reflecting on his experiences with California gold miners, Fitzgerald provides a description of his encounter with a settler, who bragged of the "bucks" he has killed:

> In we galloped at full speed, and as the Injuns come out to see what was up, we let 'em have it. We shot forty bucks—about a dozen got away by swimmin' the river.... A few [women] were knocked over. You can't be particular when you are in a hurry; and a squaw, when her blood is up, will fight equal to a buck." The fellow spoke with evident pride, feeling that he was detailing a heroic affair, having no idea that he had done any thing wrong in merely killing "bucks." I noticed that this same man was very kind to an old lady who took the stage for Bloomfield—helping her into the vehicle, and looking after her baggage. (Fitzgerald 1878/1881, 25)

Fitzgerald's account of the settler illustrates the capacity for those who commit genocide to describe the atrocities they commit in mundane terms as they use language to suppress their cognitive dissonance. It also demonstrates how those who committed these atrocities could appear kind in other contexts, reserving their violence only for those who they deemed nonhuman.

The Digger Indian and Other Settler Labels for Indians

Settler classifications in no way reflected the diversity of natives. Instead, these distinctions reveal shared settler assumptions, including the belief that native Californians differed from those elsewhere in North America. Settlers commonly referred to the natives of this region as Diggers. For example, Samuel Upham, an Anglo who visited California tribes in 1849, wrote that the "Digger... burrows in the earth like a prairie dog, and emerges from his den in the spring as fat as a grizzly" (Upham 1878, 240). In this passage, and others like it, the California or Digger Indian is dirtied and dehumanized, by comparison to deer, prairie dogs, and other wild animals. A frequent assumption among settlers was that all native people were inferior and that Digger Indians were the lowest type of native.

In 1848 Adam Johnston, a United States subagent for California Indians, claimed, "[The California Indians] are in general stupid, indolent, and ignorant, and in intellect far inferior to any of the tribes east of the Rocky Mountains. This does not perhaps apply to the pure Indians inhabiting the more mountainous part of the country, but to those residing at or near to either a mission or a rancho" (Senate of the United States 1853, 35). Johnston's description directly compares California Indians to eastern tribes and posits a distinction between the "pure" Indians of the mountains and the (implicitly) "impure" Indians of the missions and ranchos. This corresponds to the wild/useful distinction applied by the state legislature, where the pure Indians are wild and the impure are useful. Johnston's account parallels the child metaphor because he found the difference between the intellect of Mission Indians and pure Indians to be the result of historical processes (e.g., the Spanish and Mexican missions and ranchos) and not a reflection of inferior biology. According to Johnston, the Mission Indians were especially ignorant and lazy when compared to other California Indians. His characterization is especially ironic given the settlers' dependence on the labor of natives trained by the missions. However, these perceptions may be understood in light of the ideologies underpinning the 1850 Act for the Government and Protection of Indians and Apprenticeship System, in which the purported laziness of California Indians justified forced labor in the name of advancing the Anglo population.

Perhaps the most elaborate written description of the stereotype comes from the former superintendent of education for California and Regent of the University of California, O. P. Fitzgerald. His book *California Sketches* (1878/1881) devoted an entire chapter to speculating about the alleged inferiority of California's Digger Indians, placing Indians at the bottom of humanity and Digger Indians at the bottom of the Indian category. He listed several points of contrast that distinguish Diggers from other Indians and presents the same etymology for Digger as found in the *Oxford English Dictionary*: digger refers to the digging for roots, in implicit contrast with the nobler "hunting" of unmarked Indians. Fitzgerald (15) wrote, "The Digger Indian holds a low place in the scale of humanity. He is not intelligent; he is not handsome; he is not very brave. He stands near the foot of his class.... It is not because he is an agriculturist that he is called a Digger, but because he grabbles for wild roots, and has a general fondness for dirt." Again, like Samuel Upham's characterization of California Indians hibernating in dirt, Fitzgerald notes that this "general fondness for dirt" along with other perceived attributes— less intelligence, less attractive, and less brave than the rest of the native population—sets the Digger below other native North Americans.

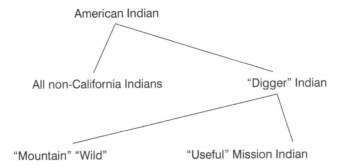

American Indian

All non-California Indians   "Digger" Indian

"Mountain" "Wild"   "Useful" Mission Indian

Figure 2.1. Taxonomy of Settler Categories of California Indians

By unpacking the meaning of the Digger label, one can uncover the knowledge assumed by settlers. The label marks a contrast between the Digger Indians of California and unmarked, or default, Indians who were native to the rest of North America. In other words, we can understand descriptions of Digger Indians are implicit comparison between Diggers and the rest of the native population. This settler classification further separated the Diggers into pure, mountain, and wild on the one hand, and mission and useful on the other; these names represent the perceived difference between neophyte descendants and the rest of the population. The typology in figure 2.1 illustrates the settler classification.

After the Gold Rush: "Sympathetic" Policies and Perspectives

Both the apprenticeship system and state-sponsored militias ended abruptly in 1865 when the Thirteenth Amendment outlawed forced labor in addition to slavery, and miners had excavated most of the state's easily accessible gold. Diseases (e.g., tuberculosis, smallpox, measles, influenza, syphilis, and cholera) and acts of violence decimated California's native population, which had an estimated population of about 30,000 at the end of the nineteenth century, at least one-tenth the size of their population before European contact (Cook 1976). While their population was at its nadir, though, California Indians formed political alliances with each other and sympathetic non-Indians lobbied Congress to establish reservations across the state. The indigenous population no longer posed a threat to gold mining and no longer provided a valuable labor resource, especially as immigrants from China and Mexico had arrived in California seeking work. This changing political economy coincided with new images of California Indians in both public education and popular media as a vanished race. But far from being extinct in the second half of the nineteenth century, California's native nations were just beginning to lay the foundation for the future expansion of their capacities for self-determination. It is ironic that, when these tribes began successfully advancing their sovereignty, the public largely viewed them as extinct.

The Doomed Humans: Fatalism and Genocide

While not delivered with the concrete violence of extermination or forced labor, fatalism can, in itself, serve to further genocide. Whether explicitly stated or implied, social Darwinism and related ideologies increasingly informed emerging settler knowledge of the indigenous population and often justified inaction in the face of the humanitarian crises endured by California Indians at this time. O. P. Fitzgerald, at the time an architect of California's public-school system and one of the first regents of the University of California, expressed his fatalism in his description of Digger Indians:

> There is one thing a Digger cannot bear, and that is the comforts and luxuries of civilized life. A number of my friends, who had taken Digger children to raise, found that as they approached maturity they fell into a decline and died, in most cases of some pulmonary affection [sic]. The only way to save them was to let them rough it, avoiding warm bedrooms and too much clothing. A Digger girl belonged to my church at Santa Rosa, and was a gentle, kind-hearted, grateful creature. She was a domestic in the family of Colonel H—. In that pleasant Christian household she developed into a pretty fair specimen of brunette young womanhood, but to the last she had an aversion to wearing shoes.
>
> The Digger seems to be doomed. Civilization kills him; and if he sticks to his savagery, he will go down before the bullets, whisky, and vices of his white fellow-sinners (Fitzgerald 1878/1881, 28–29).

In this revealing passage Fitzgerald recognizes Diggers as humans and ascribes the savage category to them based on his purported knowledge of their physiology. Though we now know that natives fell victim to diseases spawned by the filthy conditions of European livestock husbandry, Fitzgerald saw their demise as markers of inferior biology. For Fitzgerald, Diggers and civilization were physiologically incompatible. Attempts by natives to adopt any aspect of white lifestyle would result in illness followed by death. In his view, the moral inferiority of Diggers matched their biological inferiority, such that their minds, like their bodies, are readily poisoned by civilization. In this ideology, assimilation is a lost cause: Indians are human and their death is tragic, but nothing can stop their death. According to this fatalistic perspective, Christianity may be able to save the souls of Diggers, but Anglo Californians are incapable of saving them from certain destruction. Assimilation will cause disease, while "stick[ing] to his savagery" will only further provoke genocide.

Fitzgerald was not alone in his view that the extinction of California Indians is both tragic and inevitable. As early as 1855 an editorial in the *Sacramento Daily Union* opined, "The fate of the Indian is fixed. He must be annihilated by the advance of the white man; by the disease, and, to them, the evils of civilization. But the work should not have been commenced so early a day by the deadly rifle" (Anonymous 1855). Like Fitzgerald, the author condemned the way that the California Indian population was being decimated, but he saw their annihilation as fixed, or inevitable. The attitude expressed by this author and Fitzgerald does not call for an end to the decimation of California Indians; from their perspective it is impossible for Diggers to coexist with civilization. According to these settler understandings about California Indians, no reservation system or government intervention could prevent their demise. These beliefs about California Indians are fatalistic because, according to this knowledge system, nothing could be done to stop their annihilation. They were doomed.

Sympathy and Discipline for California's "Children"

In 1851, when the federal government sent agents to negotiate treaties with and establish reservations for the California Indians, three agents wrote that most Mission Indians had "some knowledge of letters, of stock-raising, and agriculture. We think they will therefore make rapid improvement when schools, &c., shall be established among them" (McKee, Barbour, and Wozencraft 1851). They believed that extinction was not inevitable for California Indians. They argued that education would be critical for their survival and well-being. Those believing that education, not biology, was the barrier to Indians succeeding in the society that had overtaken them may have been in the minority in early settler California, but advocates of Indian education and assimilation grew more vocal through the turn of the century. This settler construction of

California Indian identity categorized Indians as neither racially inferior nor superior to Anglos. This knowledge is sometimes accompanied by metaphors and language that compares Indians to children, yet it differs from the childlike metaphors evoked by Indian apprenticeships in that education, along with (presumably unforced) labor, were seen as necessary for both saving the native population and integrating them into wider society.

Cornelia Taber's book *California and Her Indian Children* (1911) argued for her audience to have greater awareness of the California Indian population's history and present state, and for the government to protect and educate the native population. It is one example of the integration-by-education approach, instead of the forced labor perspective that became increasingly popular around the turn of the century. In a chapter titled "Present Conditions, Our Responsibility and Our Opportunity," Taber (1911, 11, 17–18) wrote,

> It is for no dying race that these efforts are put forth. With the help of even what has already been done, California Indians are now holding their own numerically.... (11)
>
> Every dweller in California lives where once an Indian lived.... (17)
>
> The white race found the Indians numerous, free, self-supporting, well fed, in good health, with, in many bands, a moral code and religious belief.... Shall we, can we, sit down in our luxurious, happy homes, heedless of their claims? No specious reasoning that claims the vesting of the rights of ownership in the man who can best develop the soil will cover the case. In that light, we Anglo-Saxons must give way before the children of the Dragon and the Sunrise, for they make a living where we but plant a flower garden. (17–18)

Taber asserted that the decimation of the California Indians is the fault of the settler population, and that natives are resilient and will thrive when given the opportunity. She directly countered arguments that settlers can claim ownership of Indian land based on the premise that Europeans "can best develop the soil." As Taber pointed out, if that were the case, then whites "must give way" to immigrants from China (i.e., the Dragon) and Japan (i.e., the Sunrise) because of their superior agricultural abilities.

Taber believed that Californians had a moral obligation to help California Indians. Her prescriptions for improving the lives of natives share many attributes of both the mission and the apprenticeship attempts at assimilation—namely Christianization and labor—but they are marked by a shift away from the thinly veiled exploitation of the past and toward a more empathetic, though paternalistic, approach. Taber outlined the following steps for integrating natives into settler society. Here are a few:

> We can study the Indians, their story, their possibilities and their needs.
>
> Among the latter we shall find *a better public sentiment*. Race prejudice is perhaps the worst disability against which our Indians have to contend...
>
> *Christian Teaching*. Fully 10,000 Indians in Northern California have never had a chance to hear the Gospel...
>
> *Medical Aid*.
>
> *Labor*.... The California Indian has a very good reputation for honesty.... There is no class of labor in California so reliable as Indian labor.
>
> *Christmas Boxes*. One of the very best ways to help is by means of a good Christmas box.... Clothing...books, pictures, Sunday School rolls... [and] toys for the children and candy for all, will bring smiles to sad faces and cheer to the hearts of the lonely workers. (Taber 1911, 18–20, emphasis in original)

While nothing in her writing suggests anything other than the condemnation of forced labor, she notes, as many others have, "There is no class of labor in California so reliable as Indian labor." Thus, her plea to protect California Indians is still framed toward political and economic leaders in terms of the economic benefit of protecting, educating, and employing this population. By focusing on the trustworthiness of natives instead of on their strength or endurance, Taber offers that the value of native labor is in the natives' humanity, an implicit plea for potential employers to consider the character of natives, and not just to consider their exploitable physical attributes. However, her Christianizing agenda leaves no room for the maintenance, let alone respect, of California Indian worldviews. Again here, as in previous regimes, the worldview of California Indians is seen as an obstacle that must be overcome in order for this population to survive. For Taber, knowledge about California Indian culture is not just an end in itself but is also a means by which public opinion will improve. Prayer, Christian teaching, and the Christmas boxes provide both moral and material support for California Indians as the settlers seek to Christianize the population. The title of Taber's (1911) book, *California and Her Indian Children,* implies that California Indians are originally (and intimately) connected to the land, and that they are somehow like children. The label "children" posits a paternalistic approach to Indians. From her perspective only education and Christianity can help them, by making them assimilate into settler society.

Empathy among Settlers

Critiques of the predominant and hostile perceptions of California Indians began with the first settlers. The settler population was far from monolithic in their perceptions of natives. These critiques came from a relatively powerless minority of settlers, yet they illuminate divergences among settler thought and demonstrate how the predominant settler knowledge of California Indians extended the child, animal, and other metaphors to the point that the faults in these logics became apparent, even to a number of those working to advance the development of California. For example, in January 1851 John McDougall (then governor of California) sent J. Neely Johnson (later elected governor of California) to Mariposa County to organize the Mariposa Battalion and to negotiate with the local tribes. Bunnell reported that before meeting with the tribes Johnson explained,

> While I do not hesitate to denounce the Indians for the murders and robberies committed by them, we should not forget that there may perhaps be circumstances which, if taken into consideration, might to some extent excuse their hostility to the whites. They probably feel that they themselves are the aggrieved party, looking upon us as trespassers upon their territory, invaders of their country, and seeking to dispossess them of their homes. It may be, they class us with the Spanish invaders of Mexico and California, whose cruelties in civilizing and Christianizing them are still traditionally fresh in their memories. (Bunnell 1880, 35)

Johnson asked for others to imagine the perspective of California Indians. He compared Anglo violence against natives to that of the Spanish, a politically dangerous step given the commonly held moral justification for conquering the Southwest from Mexico. He suggested that in the minds of the Indians the Americans are like the Spanish and Mexicans. Underpinning the request for Americans to imagine the Indian's perspective is the assumption that Indians and Anglos share the same emotional capacities.

Echoing Johnson's perspective, the article "Indian Curiosity," published in 1872, challenged the predominant racial hierarchy of the gold
rush by describing a commonality between Indians and Anglos:

It is the fashion to believe in the impertubality of the "noble red
men,"—that he can look on unmoved at anything, suppressing
all emotion, no mater how much he may be affected; but, as they
say on the street, when this is investigated it "won't wash;" they
are just as susceptible as other races; and wish as ardently to
have their curiosity gratified. When the Apache and other Indian
chiefs were sitting for their photographs in Bradley & Rulofson's
gallery, Max Bachert had the greatest difficulty in keeping them
quiet—they wanted to look in the instrument, and followed the
artist whenever he turned his back on them for an instant. The
usual grunt of satisfaction was given when the negative was
shown to them, though even then they wanted to put their fingers
on the glass. In this instance, at least, the noble scalper exhibited
as much curiosity as his pale face brethren. (Anonymous 1872, 1)

Here the author critiques the label and stereotype of "noble red men,"
and offers examples of the Indian chiefs' curiosity as a point of commonality between the "noble scalper" and "his pale face brethren." The
author of "Indian Curiosity" and Johnson challenged the predominant
racial taxonomies of their time by critiquing the notion that Indians are
innately inferior. This chapter's emphasis on the predominant settler
understandings of California Indians as animals to be exterminated or
children to be exploited should not be generalized to all settlers. Though
settler accounts that empathize with natives are not nearly as common
as mid- to late-nineteenth-century settler animosity toward natives,
their existence demonstrates that settlers held a variety of views and
many wanted to end the exploitation of natives, even if they lacked the
capacity to do so.

Cahuilla Survival During and After the Gold Rush

After settlers excavated the most-accessible gold from California's mountains, and the Thirteenth Amendment prohibited the exploitation of
Indian indentured servants, the federal government again took up the
issue of the plight of California native nations that lacked protected
land. From 1875 to 1876 President Ulysses S. Grant established seventeen
reservations in Southern California for the settlement of approximately

three thousand native Californians, including those from the Cahuilla, Serrano, Luiseño, and Kumeyaay nations. The administration of these reservations fell under the authority of the newly created Mission Indian Agency (MIA). While charged with improving the conditions of these native communities, the MIA lead agent S. S. Lawson had no prior experience with natives or any fluency in Spanish, a common language among Southern California native nations at that time (Thorne 2005, 147). Though unfamiliar with the region and its native people, Lawson advocated for providing the native nations under his supervision with adequate access to water and protection from settlers. With much of the arable land held by large ranches, a new wave of migrants arriving from the east to take advantage of the Homestead Act, and newly constructed railways through the region, settlers increasingly encroached on tribal land, seeking to evict its inhabitants. Lawson toured the region's native communities and observed the growing homelessness. Advocating for increasing and defining the size of the Potrero Reservation in San Gorgonio Pass, which later became the Morongo Reservation, Lawson wrote to Washington, "Given these *three sections* [emphasis in original] [that he proposed adding to the reservation], and the boundaries marked, so that they might know where is their limit, there would be no future disputes, and they would be provided for amply. In which case I would gather [the] wandering [desert] Indians upon it, keep them there with the few hundred now on it, and set them all to work to improve it and make their living" (Lawson 1878). Like so many other settlers who advocated for protecting California Indians, Lawson's efforts rest on his assumption that the inhabitants of this will work to improve—meaning to farm—the land.

During their first few decades, the populations of many of these reservations declined, but populations of others grew. The MIA conducted a yearly census to record the names and ages of each reservation resident in Southern California. My review of these census records at the National Archives and Records Administration found some had significant population declines. For example, over a thirty-year period starting in 1885 the Cahuilla Reservation declined from a population of two hundred seventy-five to one hundred fifteen. However, from 1908 to 1911 the population of the La Jolla Reservation grew from fewer than two hundred to almost three hundred residents. From 1899 to 1900 Pala grew from forty-three to sixty-four. In other words, there was not an across-the-board decline in reservation populations, but instead a combination of shrinking and growing populations. This may reflect a pattern observed by Strong (1929) that some reservations maintained ceremonial practice and spiritual leaders that attracted natives from native communities that were in decline. Future research could investigate whether these changes in population size reflects migrations from some locations to others.

San Manuel and the Smiley Commission

The injustices that the Cahuilla suffered during and after the gold rush laid the foundation for their eventual reorganization and revitalization. Details about the activities of these groups during this time are sparse. However, those who lived near the growing Anglo settlements were subject to the forced labor and apprenticeship policies of the early California state, while those residing in the mountains fell victim to assaults by militias seeking to exterminate the area's native populations. The events following the United States' conquest of the Southwest dramatically shaped the future of the Cahuilla nations. This section focuses on processes that led to the limited federal recognition of the San Manuel Band of Serrano Indians, which originated under Serrano leadership and today has a mixture of Serrano and Cahuilla members. The history of this native nation exemplifies the challenges faced by others in the region for whom federal recognition provoked outrage by local settlers who coveted the tribes' resources.

After the secularization of the Spanish missions, many neophytes returned to their ancestral homes. However, not long after their return, a settlers' militia intent on exterminating all natives in the mountains embroiled them in a conflict between settlers and the Chemehuevi that culminated in a month-long occupation of the San Bernardino Mountains. The conflict began in 1865 when the children of two settler families went hunting with four Chemehuevi boys who had been "adopted," by the settlers' families. The word "adopted," as Trafzer (2002, 63) pointed out, was a euphemism for enslaved native children. A fight broke out between the boys. A Chemehuevi boy shot a settler child in self-defense. When relatives of the settler boy led an expedition to ostensibly return the Chemehuevi boys to their families, one of the Chemehuevi boys escaped. The settlers murdered the other three boys. Then the settlers put the native children's heads on stakes at the Las Flores Ranch in Summit Valley as a clear signal to neighboring native people that settlers would murder any native person, including children, who interfered with settler expansion (63). In retaliation, a band of Chemehuevi attacked settlers operating a toll road through Cajon Pass, a major route connecting the San Bernardino Valley to northern and eastern portions of the state. Later, groups of Chemehuevi moved into the San Bernardino Mountains, where many Serrano resided peacefully separate from the settlers in the valley below. From the mountains the Chemehuevi staged raids on settler ranches, stealing livestock; these raids resulted in the deaths of four cowboys and caused settlers to flee the area of Summit Valley (64). The Chemehuevi then focused their attacks on settlers and sawmills in the San Bernardino Mountains. These raids fomented a hysteria that swept the San Bernardino Valley and settlers united to form a militia intent on ridding the San Bernardino Mountains of all Indians.

In 1866, in an offensive that lasted thirty-two days, settler militias swept through the San Bernardino Mountains, targeting all Indians, regardless of age, gender, or cultural affiliation. Thus, the Serrano, who had resided in the mountains and were not involved in the Chemehuevi raids on settlers, suffered immensely as the militia sought to exterminate all natives who lived in the mountains (Trafzer 2002, 66). While the number of Serrano killed during the onslaught is unknown, their population is estimated to have dropped from three thousand precontact to one hundred fifty or two hundred by the end of the nineteenth century because of a combination of the spread of new diseases and violent persecution. Seeking to escape the settler militia, a band of Serrano led by Santos Manuel moved out of the mountains to the foothills north of San Bernardino. At first this move to the outskirts of settler society appears counterintuitive. Moving out of the mountains removed the Serrano from the militia's assault on natives living there, but why move to live closer to the settlers when a move to the north or east would have both removed the Serrano from the mountains and placed them farther from the settlers that sought to exterminate them? A few Serrano did move north and east, but many followed Santos Manuel into the floor of the San Bernardino Valley. Based on his research with the San Manuel Band, Trafzer (69) suggests that moving into the valley allowed the Serrano to "demonstrate their peaceful intentions toward whites" while also being closer to potential employment. Living on the outskirts of San Bernardino, many members of Santos Manuel's band found work in the homes, orchards, and ranches owned by local settlers, while the Serrano women earned additional cash by making and selling baskets. Eventually their village became known as San Manuel, named after their leader. Located at the southern edge of the San Bernardino Mountains, the village was on the frontier of Cahuilla territory. Prior to European contact, the Serrano and Cahuilla connected with each other via kinship networks established through the moiety system. Forced to flee their homelands in the mountains and take up residence closer to Cahuilla nations, the connections between the Serrano and Cahuilla became even stronger. While the village of San Manuel was founded by Serrano, it has grown to incorporate a mixture of Cahuilla members as Serrano continued to form alliances and families with neighboring Cahuilla nations.

In 1877 the federal government established MIA to govern and administer to the native peoples in Southern California. In 1879 MIA was tasked with locating land suitable for Indian reservations. However, the processes of creating reservations was slow and disjointed, resulting in some tribes receiving reservations years before others, most reservations restricted to the poorest lands, and many native communities receiving no recognition at all (Trafzer 2002, 73). At this time, native alliances with sympathetic settlers proved vital to the federal government's creation of a reservation for the people of San Manuel. In 1890, under pressure from these settlers, including Helen Hunt Jackson's monograph *A Century of Dishonor* (1883), President Benjamin Harrison signed "An Act for the Relief of Mission Indians in the State of California." The act established a board of commissioners to designate reservation lands for San Manuel and other Mission Indians. The commission became known as the Smiley Commission, after its head, Albert K. Smiley, a Quaker and wealthy resort owner from New York, who had lived part time in Redlands, California, near San Manuel and other Serrano and Cahuilla nations. Without money to purchase land or power to remove non-Indians from proposed lands, in 1891 the Smiley Commission began surveying lands for a potential reservation for the San Manuel Band.

On its first visit to San Manuel, the commission identified a total of eight families and forty individuals living in the band, on land that Smiley had described as "worthless dry hills" (Trafzer 2002, 77). While their land bordered a large fertile valley, settlers had claimed that land, leaving for San Manuel the steep non-arable hills to the north of the San Bernardino Valley. A small spring enabled the band to develop a modest orchard that, in addition to wage labor for nearby businesses, provided food and resources for the village. The commission found an area of land, known as Section 20, that included most of the village and that would be suitable for a reservation. They submitted their recommendation to the commissioner of Indian Affairs in December 1891. In

1893 President Grover Cleveland signed into law the formal recognition of the San Manuel Reservation (80), although many settlers challenged the precise boundaries of the reservation for decades to come. In total the reservation was 640 acres, although only five to twenty were suitable for farming and could be irrigated from a small spring that the band retained the rights to. The MIA encouraged San Manuel to pursue agriculture in order to become self-sufficient. However, the dry, rocky land they received was grossly insufficient for agriculture.

It is important to note the success of Santos Manuel's strategy of moving his band toward the settlers who persecuted them. Living in the mountains to avoid settlers kept them out of harm's way until the settler militia sought the indiscriminate extermination of all Indians. By living close to the settlers and working for them, those who lived at San Manuel were able to make visible their peaceful intentions and to build alliances with sympathetic settlers. Santos Manuel's strategy paralleled the work of Juan Antonio. Both strengthened tribal self-determination by challenging settler perceptions. Albert Smiley's efforts to protect reservation boundaries came from his experiences living near San Manuel, a direct consequence of Santos Manuel moving his people to the edge of San Bernardino. Smiley is just one example, of many to follow, of a settler who worked to preserve tribal sovereignty because of his direct experience with native communities. As argued throughout this book, increased visibility can challenge simplistic cultural assumptions. The stereotype of lazy Indians and violent savages becomes increasingly untenable for those who live next to and employ Indians. However, the majority of settlers never have this kind of exposure to native people and therefore never have their own assumptions challenged.

Assimilation at Boarding Schools
In the late nineteenth century the federal government began a new approach to seize native resources—forced assimilation. Two policies in particular ushered in this new approach: the Dawes Act and Indian boarding schools. The Dawes Act of 1887 sought to end tribal collective ownership of reservation land; it ostensibly encouraged natives to adopt American forms of land ownership and agriculture. Under the act reservations across the United States were divided into separate allotments (often forty acres), with each tribal member receiving an allotment or a single family receiving a larger allotment, where, in theory (but rarely in practice) tribal members were to begin farming and were ultimately to shed their tribal identity. In practice, allotments often resulted in vast

amounts of tribal lands left unassigned to natives and subject to private purchase by settlers. In other words, rather than encourage natives to farm, the Dawes Act furthered the goals of settler colonialism by making additional native land available for settlers to exploit.

Indian boarding schools attempted to further the agenda of the Dawes Act by removing native children from their homes to be educated in American culture, farming, and domestic service. Captain Richard H. Pratt, founder of the first boarding school in Carlisle, Pennsylvania, infamously described the mission of these schools in his speech, "Kill the Indian, and Save the Man":

> A great general has said that the only good Indian is a dead one, and that high sanction of his destruction has been an enormous factor in promoting Indian massacres. In a sense, I agree with the sentiment, but only in this: that all the Indian there is in the race should be dead. Kill the Indian in him, and save the man…
>
> It is a great mistake to think that the Indian is born an inevitable savage. He is born a blank, like all the rest of us. Left in the surroundings of savagery, he grows to possess a savage language, superstition, and life. We, left in the surroundings of civilization, grow to possess a civilized language, life, and purpose. Transfer the infant white [*sic*] to the savage surroundings, he will grow to possess a savage language, superstition, and habit. Transfer the savage-born infant to the surroundings of civilization, and he will grow to possess a civilized language and habit. (Pratt 1892, 46–59)

Pratt believed this approach to be an improvement on previous federal policies that often resulted in wars of extermination with native nations. Relative to some of the policies and perceptions at the time, Pratt offered a less physically violent approach in that he saw native culture, not biology, as the problem. (Unfortunately, many native children experienced violence and abuse at these schools, although this violence was different from the previous military conquests.) Pratt foresaw a future in which the descendants of American Indians would have opportunities equal to those offered to other Americans willing to give up their identity. Like the Dawes Act, the boarding schools did not achieve their goal of assimilation, but instead devastated families. Native parents had no role in deciding how their children would be educated. Federal policies mandated that their children attend a school with assimilative curricula sponsored by the government. Some parents gave up their children voluntarily. Government agents took other children through force or deception. Note that, like the war of extermination waged against California Indians, these boarding schools fit the definition of genocide, as defined by the United Nations' (1948) "Convention on the Prevention and Punishment of the Crime of Genocide." Aside from fomenting resistance and unity among their students (discussed further in chapter 5), the schools' focus on agricultural and domestic work ensured that native students received an education inferior to their white contemporaries. Worse yet, many schools were sites of frequent physical and sexual abuse (Hirshberg and Sharp 2005; Irwin and Roll 1995).

With support from the federal government, boarding schools (some government sponsored and others church operated) opened up across the United States at the turn of the century. In 1892 the Perris Indian School opened in Perris, California, in order to draw students from nearby native communities, including the Cahuilla, Luiseño, and Serrano. In 1903 the school moved to Riverside and changed its name to The Sherman Institute. A November 1905 article from the *Los Angeles Herald* provided this description of the Sherman Institute:

The picturesque Indian maiden, attired in bead-trimmed buckskin costume or gaudy blanket, and feeding on jerked venison, corn bread and wild berries does not exist at Sherman. Indeed, she is fast becoming extinct under Uncle Sam's spreading educational system.

The modern Indian girl, as seen at the Riverside industrial school, is strong, deep chested and athletic. She is also possessed of a native dignity and a modesty of a manner that might well be the envy of many society girls.

Her time there is so systematically divided that she is trained in the dainty feminine accomplishments as well as the more substantial work of practical housekeeping and home making. Half of each day is devoted to the regular school work, leaving the other half for instructions in domestic science....

[Students frequently sing the] Cooking Class Song (Air: "Solomon Levi")
We are happy domestic science girls of Sherman Institute.
We've learned the art of cookery well and now we mean to cook
For sturdy, brave young Indian boys who are manly and true
Whom we know are on the lookout for just such girls as we.
O Sherman Institute, Class of 1905
O Sherman Institute, Hurrah for the purple and gold!
(Emboy 1905, 3)

These boarding schools never had their intended effect of complete assimilation, but they did tear families apart and ensure a supply of agricultural and domestic workers. Articles such as the one above also gave settlers comfort in the perception that Indian culture would vanish quietly.

Throughout this chapter primary texts reveal the different ways that settlers categorized California Indians. Settler perceptions varied across the population and through time. At the dawn of the American occupation some settlers advocated that natives were merely pests, while others claimed that adult natives were developmentally no different from children, and therefore should be relegated to abusive "apprenticeships" and "adoptions," forms of bondage that held natives from childhood to adulthood. By exploiting California Indians, as had the missions and ranchos before them, and by implementing the Indian apprenticeship system, the California legislature created a system of legal forced labor in a nominally free state as the country veered toward a civil war fought over the future of slavery. When Mexico ceded the Southwest to the United States, both the systematic exploitation of Indian labor and the cultural assumption that forced labor somehow educates or uplifts neophytes or apprentices endured. But, as the nineteenth century progressed, the metaphor that Indians are children took on a new meaning and significance. Cornelia Taber and others mobilized settler taxonomies that humanized California Indians and condemned the genocide of California Indians but also urged their assimilation. The metaphor that Indians are children was transformed from a justification of forced labor to a rationale for Christianizing, educating, and otherwise assimilating Indians. There were outspoken critics of the genocide of California Indians during the gold rush who pointed out obvious examples of the Indian's humanity, although these voices were in the minority. Juan Antonio and Santo Manuel took the courageous steps of confronting settlers with the realities and complexities of native communities. Their efforts changed how some settlers perceived tribes. These changes in perception led to relative increases in tribal self-determination even though these increases were limited. At the end of the century a shift in federal policy toward assimilation increased the threat posed by settler colonialism. In the twentieth century the Cahuilla and other allied native nations began work to change perceptions at a national scale and to secure measured but important victories for self-determination.

ACTIVISM AND DISSONANCE

MICHEL-ROLPH TROUILLOT (1995, 152) wrote, "Narratives are made of silences, not all of which are deliberate or even perceptible as such within the time of their production." For the Cahuilla, a striking paradox marked the early twentieth century. At the same time that the Cahuilla and other native nations began to recover from the violence and disease of the previous centuries and to pursue the revitalization of their sovereignty, the settler population began forgetting its awareness of neighboring native nations as they developed narratives about their own history, complete with the silences described by Trouillot. By the early twentieth century the fatalism of the previous decades had grown into the widespread assumptions that California's indigenous population was either gone or in the process of disappearing. How could settlers become increasingly unaware of their native neighbors at precisely the same time nearby native activists sparked national reforms in federal Indian policies? This chapter addresses this question and others by investigating the processes that underpinned both the early stages of native nation revitalization (that later propelled the tribal casino movement) and the settlers' growing ignorance of the surviving native peoples in their midst.

Cognitive anthropology investigates how assumptions become shared across a population and how different assumptions can become more common in different segments of a population. While this subfield is primarily concerned with the distribution of cultural knowledge, this chapter explores the dissipation of cultural knowledge. Because cognitive anthropology builds connections with psychology and the cognitive sciences, it provides tools for exploring how widespread forgetting can emerge, in part, from individual psychological processes. In this chapter I argue that cognitive dissonance, that uncomfortable feeling of trying to hold two contradictory thoughts at once, can play a significant role in a community forgetting parts of its past. In early-twentieth-century California the thought of the recent extermination and enslavement of native people could have caused cognitive dissonance for settlers who believed that the state of California could have never endorsed such atrocities. I use the term "historical dissonance" to refer to the widespread cognitive dissonance that could emerge when a community's history lies in direct contradiction with its perception of itself. Historical dissonance is one fact, among others, that led to the decreasing awareness that settlers had of their native neighbors. Another factor in this widespread cultural forgetting was a shift away from perceived utility of knowledge about California Indians. In this case, cultural forgetting can be seen as operating like the distribution of cultural knowledge (discussed in the Introduction's discussion of cognitive anthropology) but in reverse. Instead of more experience leading to more knowledge, less experience leads to less knowledge. When a population no longer has direct contact with a neighboring population, that population may not have the personal experiences necessary to know that their public schools and media are propagating an especially partial and pernicious history. In the case of settler knowledge of California native nations in the early twentieth century, an entire domain of knowledge faded from discourse, and settler society focused its attention elsewhere. Cultural elites, such as those who control the media or public education curricula, can play an important role in cultural forgetting by choosing which historical narratives are to be propagated and which are to be omitted. Although these elites can expedite and reinforce the forgetting process, they cannot create the conditions for forgetting. But collective cognitive dissonance and decreased direct experience can create an environment where certain myths, like the demise or assimilation of native peoples, can thrive.

Historical dissonance provides a framework for understanding the radical shifts in settler assumptions about native nations from the beginning of the twentieth century through contemporary revitalization. During this time, media, education, and other information sources paid decreasing attention to Californians' native neighbors. Unlike before the turn of the century, when the Cahuilla and other California native nations regularly made headlines in local newspapers, the visibility of natives to most settlers was significantly lower during the early through middle twentieth century. Even though many natives integrated into local economies through wage labor, this integration did not increase their visibility beyond their employers. Even those settlers who employed Indians often held simplistic, static understandings of natives. Unlike the first decades of California statehood when most agricultural pursuits depended on indigenous labor, the influx of immigrants from Mexico and Asia at the turn of the twentieth century decreased the proportion of Indians in the workforce. The number of natives working for settlers did not diminish, but their percentage of the overall workforce did. This decreased their visibility to the settler majority, which was also seeing an influx of settlers from the east. For the majority of the settler population that had no contact with natives, the native population of Southern California became increasingly invisible.

When considering the potential for widespread cognitive dissonance in California, it is important to recall that California entered the union ostensibly as a free state. It was not supposed to endorse any practices as morally corrupt as slavery. Though the Indian apprenticeships were well known among the farming and ranching communities of early California, memories of this travesty would directly challenge California's legacy as a state that opposed slavery. Equally, a government that claims to be a democracy while attacking its own people can stir cognitive dissonance among its residents (see Buchowski et al. 1994 for further discussion). After extermination efforts removed California natives from the lands most suited for development, forgetting these injustices would alleviate the dissonance between settler values and the policies that enable settlement. Not only was the visibility of Indians declining, but also any settler who thought of the surviving native populations and the injustices they endured would have evoked the overwhelming contradiction between the values that justified settlement and the practices that enabled it. With the native population interacting, on the whole, less with settlers than they had previously, forgetting that their native neighbors existed would reduce cognitive dissonance within the settler population. By forgetting that their neighbors existed they could avoid having two contradictory beliefs: that their native neighbors continued to endure injustice and that their nation is committed to justice for all.

Finally, the influx of new settlers, including immigrants from China and Mexico, further diminished general non-Indian awareness of native nations. New arrivals from China would have lacked historical knowledge of North American native nations generally, much less those in California. Mexico has its own tragic history of indigenous conflict and romanticized historical narrative of the mestizo (someone of mixed race). But immigrants fleeing the Mexican Revolution would have little knowledge of California's Indian apprenticeships or genocide. Moreover, Anglo migrants arriving from the eastern United States at this time would have simplistic knowledge about the Indian wars of the Great Plains, but likely no previous knowledge of native California's uniquely tragic history. The combination of settlers streaming in, the pressure of cognitive dissonance, and the decreasing perceived utility of knowledge of neighboring natives created an environment where the growing settler population would have little reason to contemplate or discuss the state's native nations, let alone challenge media accounts that native people had vanished.

This chapter begins with a case study from the area now known as Joshua Tree National Park (JTNP). This case study illustrates the structure and implications of native labor for settlers during the early twentieth century and the different ways that interactions with natives shaped settler perspectives. This case study is followed by an examination of the Mission Indian Federation (MIF), an activist coalition of native nations in Southern California who laid the foundation for future revitalization of native nation sovereignty. While the Cahuilla and other native nations worked closely with some settlers as they fought for their sovereignty, the media increasingly represented natives as a vanishing people. This chapter analyzes two exemplary representations that fed into this settler narrative: Helen Hunt Jackson's novel *Ramona* (1884) and a *Los Angeles Herald* article (Dudley 1908) that prematurely lamented the demise of the San Manuel Band of Serrano Indians. This chapter concludes by using the framework of historical dissonance to illustrate the political, economic, and cognitive processes at play in the systematic forgetting of knowledge and its implications for the future of native and settler relations.

Cooperation and Conflict in Joshua Tree National Park

The land now known as JTNP was home to native nations, including the Cahuilla, Serrano, Mojave, and Chemehuevi, who provided resources and knowledge critical to the success of early settlers. Presently, JTNP is slightly larger than the state of Rhode Island with almost 800,000 acres across Riverside and San Bernardino Counties. The park includes two desert ecosystems, the Mojave and the Colorado (Bean and Vane 2002). Beginning in the late 1860s when miners and ranchers began to settle the land that was to become JTNP, tribal communities were present and contributing knowledge and resources necessary for settlers to survive and, for a handful, to prosper. While much of their assistance to settlers led directly and indirectly to the destruction of land the natives held sacred, it also provided much-needed cash for the Cahuilla and neighboring native nations to establish a network of activists.

The first Anglo Americans to make contact with the land that is now part of the JTNP were in a survey team led by Colonel Henry Washington in 1855. When he encountered the Serrano village at the Oasis of Mara, he called the area Twenty-nine Palms (now spelled Twentynine Palms). Growth in this area was slow over the following decade. Incoming settlers met tribal communities at a time of rapid population decline caused by disease and displacement (Greene 1983, 6). The Oasis of Mara was the only permanent source of water for miles and enabled the Serrano to pursue agriculture for generations prior to contact. However, the Serrano fled the area during the 1862–63 smallpox epidemic, after which a band of Chemehuevi moved to the Oasis and shared it with the Serrano upon their return. This community, containing two native cultural groups, lived with an increasing presence of settlers in adjacent Twentynine Palms (Bean and Vane 2002). Beginning in 1865 the prospect of gold mining and cattle ranching, subsidized by the Homestead Act's provision of free land to settlers, brought a steady wave of settlers migrating to the land of JTNP. Mining began in the park area, with the first mining claim filed in 1865. Cattle ranching began in the 1870s, peaking in the 1920s. At the turn of the century, when California Indian populations were at their nadir, tribal communities supplied the knowledge and labor that fueled significant mining and ranching operations. In 1936 the shift to U.S. National Monument status shut down the mines within the monument's borders and closed the land to homesteaders. Little has been written about the tribes living on this land during the postcontact, pre-Monument period (Greene 1983 23–28). However, as demonstrated below, multiple lines of evidence reveal two strands of these relations: the diversity of settler attitudes about their indigenous neighbors, and the ways in which the settlers' livelihood depended on their indigenous neighbors.

Lost Horse Mine

Beginning operations in 1894, Lost Horse Mine went on to produce and mill more than 10,500 ounces of gold, garnering a fortune for its owners. The mill and mine employed as many as fifty Cahuilla from the Torres-Martinez Reservation. One of the most prosperous mines in Southern

California, its success would not have been possible without intensive indigenous labor. For its first and most successful decade, the water pumps and boilers that powered the operation ran on locally harvested wood (Greene 1983, 204). The volume of wood necessary to generate the necessary steam power was massive, yet the remote location rendered transporting the necessary wood too expensive. Today, visitors to the park might be surprised to know that pinyon and juniper trees once dotted the landscape. JTNP's Historic American Engineering Record (HAER) report on Lost Horse Mine does not address the role of Indian labor, but it does describe the evidence of the extensive harvesting of wood from the land around the mine. The HAER report explains, "Archaeological reconnaissance of the mining site and surrounding four-square mine area located numerous cut timbers of pinyon pine and juniper, as well as the ax-cut stumps and trunks of very large trees. Presently, pinyon and juniper trees are extremely small and are more properly described as bushes, except in well-protected and isolated canyons. It appears that before the initiation of mining in the 1890s, a mature pinyon-juniper stand existed in the Lost Horse Mountains. Requiring mine timber and wood fuel, miners scoured the local mountains for suitable wood" (HAER 1992, 47–48).

The HAER report indicates that harvesting firewood for Lost Horse Mine was extremely labor intensive and forever altered the landscape. The affected area is estimated to be at least four square miles and involved whole trees being removed with the assistance of horses and vehicles, while trees in harder-to-access areas were harvested by hand and ax.

To the mine owners, these trees were an ideal source of fuel for the isolated operating. All they needed was a supply of labor for the harvest. Multiple sources suggest that owners relied on longstanding relations with Desert Cahuilla to harvest the wood. Maud Russell (c. 1920, 7), a frequent visitor to Twentynine Palms who later retired to the area, wrote in her memoir *Yesterdays of Twenty-Nine Palms,* "Chief Fig Tree John was the chief of the tribe that cut the wood for both the Desert Queen and Lost Horse Mines. For the two mines, they employed about fifty men for that work, keeping the boilers running. The Indians did nothing but chop wood, for it took a lot, and it was from very large trees." This passage not only illustrates the intensity of labor involved to chop and haul large trees for the boilers but also names the native nation that provided the laborers. Chief Fig Tree John was leader of the Torrez-Martinez, a nation of Desert Cahuilla whose territory spanned the Southwestern portion of the Coachella Valley, including present-day Mecca and the Salton Sea. Later, a gas engine replaced the steam boilers as the land was stripped of trees.

One of the mine owners, Jim Fife, had ongoing trade and friendly relations with Torrez-Martinez. The HAER report for Lost Horse Mine found that Fife traded with the Indians near Mecca before he became a partner at Lost Horse Mine: "In Mecca...he [Fife] opened a trading post that served local agricultural and mining operations.... He also drove a 20 mule team monthly to Los Angeles for supplies, which he then traded for crafts, blankets, baskets and firewood stockpiled for him by local Indians" (HAER 1992, 7). As found in the HAER report, Fife's trade with this native community included firewood. This suggests Torrez-Martinez had experience in supplying firewood to Fife before he began work at Lost Horse Mine.

An article written by Fife's sons, Edward and Donald Fife (1982), and published by the South Coast Geological Society, provides additional details of his partnership with Fig Tree John to harvest firewood at Torrez-Martinez. Fife and Fife (458) explained, "A 20-mule team with the standard jerk line was driven monthly, or as often as necessary, into Los Angeles for supplies. Indian crafts, blankets, baskets and firewood (iron-wood) were traded for goods in Los Angeles. Ironwood was picked up along the route to Banning Pass. Jim made an arrangement with Figtree John and his tribe to stockpile the ironwood between trips." Through Fife and possibly through other settlers, Fig Tree John organized a network to trade Indian-made goods with communities as far away as Los Angeles. Of particular relevance here is the inclusion of firewood in this trade and the involvement of Banning Pass tribal communities in addition to Torrez-Martinez. Thus, an arrangement to hire a crew of Indians to harvest firewood at Lost Horse Mine could have been an extension of previous trade agreements between Fife and Fig Tree John. However, Lost Horse Mine is more than fifty miles away and thousands of feet higher in elevation than both Torrez-Martinez territory and the Banning Pass. Without an easily accessible route to transport the volume of firewood needed for the boilers, the laborers from the Torrez-Martinez nation had to relocate to the mine to harvest wood at the site.

Linda Greene's history of JTNP provides a further, although brief, description of the Indians' involvement. Greene (1983, 257) cites an early miner in the area, Chester Pinkham, as the source for her claim that "a crew of Mexicans and Indians was kept busy chopping juniper and pinyon pine for fuel to run the mills, hoist ore, and pump water. Supplies came from Banning, Sixty-five miles away." In addition to noting how firewood powered key parts of the mining and milling processes, Greene's report further suggests that Mexicans (or Mexican Americans) labored alongside natives. Patricia Parker's (1980, 49) history of the mine corroborates Greene's inclusion of Mexicans as workers harvesting wood for the mine. Parker (49) also quotes Chester Pinkham, who explained that "a crew of Mexicans and Indians cut juniper, cedar, and pinyon pine from the adjoining hills."

Another source, a 1975 interview with local cowboy Jim Hester by Park Ranger Reino Clark, includes suspect exaggerations. In the interview (JTNP n.d.), when asked about Fife and his partner Ryan's role at Lost Horse, Hester replied, "I couldn't get on the witness stand and say, yes, I know he killed so and so, but the gossip was that they had the killing up there and the gossip also was that Ryan would get these Indians and Mexicans up there and work the devil out of them and then when he got ready to pay them off, he'd kill them and bury them instead of paying them off. Now that was the gossip among the cowboys. But I couldn't testify to anything like that. It may be a lot of hooey." The only aspect of Hester's claims that is corroborated by other sources is that Lost Horse Mine employed Indians and Mexicans. There are no known mass burials in the vicinity of Ryan Ranch or Lost Horse Mine, or any other evidence that the miners murdered their own employees. Yet, when taken with the evidence presented above, Hester's account does further corroborate that labor provided by Indians as well as Mexicans was both intensive and crucial for the success of the mining operation. Later in this case study I will return to Hester's interview where he reveals his hatred for natives despite the assistance he received from them.

Currently there is scant archaeological evidence of Indian labor at Lost Horse Mine. However, at one site (Riv-350/H), not far from the Lost Horse Mine, archeologists found a metal hatchet at a rock shelter fortified with masonry. The site record's interpretation suggests the area was a prehistoric short-term habitation site that continued to be occupied into the historic period, potentially when Lost Horse Mine was in operation. Thus, this site is consistent with the evidence that Indians lived close to settlers and that they possessed tools that could have been used to process firewood or pursue other work for settlers.

While the data presented above do not present a clear image of the labor conditions for those Indians who worked at Lost Horse Mine, multiple independent sources corroborate not only the presence of Indian labor at the mine, but also the intensity of that labor and its necessity for the success of the mine. The gold strike at Lost Horse Mine was powered, first and foremost, by Indian labor. Again, the trees they harvested were sacred to the Cahuilla. However, by the turn of the century, the Cahuilla had lost access to their ancestral hunting and gathering grounds. With few avenues for procuring food and an increasing need for income as they became enveloped in the settler economy, destroying trees sacred to them would have been a last resort. While the harvesting of these juniper and pinyon trees led to irreversible environmental damage, the cash Indian laborers earned from their work combined with wage labor performed by Cahuilla across Southern California provided resources necessary for activism. This activism laid the foundation for the future revitalization of their sovereignty. The next section explores further examples of oral histories that illustrate the complex relations between settlers and Indians at JTNP and the different assumptions settlers held about natives.

Relations at the Oasis

The Oasis of Mara, being the only permanent native settlement and source of water for miles, was a center of native life before contact and a site of contention as settlers arrived. When settlers began herding cattle in the area they depleted the game that had sustained the Indians, forcing them to work for wage labor in order to provide for themselves. The plight of the Indians became even more severe in the 1870s when the Southern Pacific Railroad Company, which sought ownership of significant sections of land in the area, claimed ownership of the Oasis of Mara and denied the Indians access (Trafzer, Madrigal, and Madrigal 1997, 44). Pressure mounted as settlers began to build squatter settlements around the Oasis and to draw on its limited water supply. Because of their remote location away from other tribes that the Smiley Commission worked with, the commission did not focus its attention on the Oasis until 1890. In 1895 the commission registered the patent establishing the reservation at Twentynine Palms. However, the reservation did not include the Oasis or Indian village site. Instead, it included only a barren expanse of desert immediately to the south. Despite the fact that their reservation did not include the Oasis of Mara, they continued to live there and to rely on it as a necessary source of water.

Oral history and documentary sources indicate that while settlers continued to encroach on the land and draw on the limited water supply, many acknowledged its use by Indians. Mission Indian Agency (MIA) records indicate that in 1899 the reservation had twenty-seven residents (Greene 1983, 44). Beginning in 1908 the Office of Indian Affairs began forcibly enrolling many of the children at the Twentynine Palms Reservation in boarding schools. These children moved to the Morongo Reservation where they attended the St. Boniface Indian Industrial School. Elders, including Jim and Matilda Pine, stayed behind at the Oasis (Trafzer, Madrigal, and Madrigal 1997, 85). In 1910, as part of an effort to bring the Twentynine Palms Band closer to other reservations and thereby to give the MIA greater access to the Band, the federal government decided that the Twentynine Palms Band needed to relocate. MIA added 640 acres to the Cabazon Reservation, located in the Coachella Valley below, near Indio, and encouraged the Twentynine Palms Band to relocate there (95). By 1912 the Twentynine Palms Band had vacated the reservation near the Oasis and settled on the Cabazon Reservation. However, they remained in close contact with the Oasis and with the land that is now part of JTNP.

Written and oral histories provide a glimpse into the sources of strife and how such conflicts played out as settlers began encroaching on the Oasis of Mara. For example, a 1972 article in an edition of local newspaper *Desert Trails* tells the story of Phil Sullivan who came to the area in 1898. The passage from that article that follows illustrates the dynamics of Sullivan's relations with the tribal community at Twentynine Palms. While the article itself was written decades later and its veracity is uncertain, it is from a local source that highlights the possibility for settlers to have different levels of animosity and trust in the native population.

He [Phil Sullivan] was well acquainted with the Indians, he found that they knew a good deal about agriculture.... Phil got along well with them for the most part, because he could speak Spanish, a language they used besides their Indian tongue. Captain Jim Boniface, the early Chief, was a close friend of Phil's, but his successor, Jim Pine, proved another matter. As Chief, Pine declared, "todo tierra es Indio"—all the land belongs to the Indians—and kept sneaking down while Phil was away, and pouring dirt down his well. One day Phil hid out to watch him, after pretending to leave his place. He caught the Chief in the act, and promptly sent the hard toe of his boot into the Indian's rear. There was no more trouble after that. Shortly afterwards, the Indians left the Oasis.

Sullivan knew all about the waterholes and underground streams, from having lived among the Indians. (Anonymous 1972)

This passage is notable because it attributes Sullivan's knowledge of area waterholes and underground streams, resources that he and other settlers would have depended on for survival, to his acquaintance with the Indians at the Oasis. Sullivan's good relations with the Indians is attributed to his knowledge of Spanish, and the passage implies that language was a barrier for communication between most settlers and the Indian community.

Maud Russell, a resident of Twentynine Palms in the early 1900s, wrote of the friendship that developed between one of the earliest settlers to arrive in the area, Bill McHaney, and Jim Waterman, a leader of the tribal community at the Oasis of Mara: "One day when they were working at the Desert Queen Mine Bill McHaney showed Jim Waterman (Indian) some of the ore, and he, Jim, said 'I show you ore like this, enough too, for many white men.' Apparently he thought it took a lot of ore to satisfy a white man. The Indian, Jim Waterman, took Bill McHaney to the place where this gold was supposed to be, showed him a hill, and Bill dug there for thirty-five years but never found it. The trenches he dug may still be seen" (Russell c. 1920). Russell's story indicates the intensity of Bill McHaney's trust of Jim Waterman in his pursuit of the gold. McHaney may have had good reason to have faith in Jim Waterman's advice on locating gold, because sometime in the late 1880s Indians at the Oasis showed him the location of a nearby spring at Pinyon Well (Greene 1983, 44).

Bill Keys

In 1910 an assayer named Bill Keys moved to the Desert Queen Mine, which is inside the current JTNP boundaries. His interviews, conducted by park rangers in the 1950s and 1960s, are as colorful as they are perplexing. Keys came to know many Indians at the Oasis and in the wider area well, though his accounts could reflect more of his imagination than reality. Yet his interviews, especially when contrasted with other accounts, illustrate the diversity among settler perspectives of the surrounding native communities. One interview conducted in 1960, excerpted next, shows some of his perspective and reported experiences. In the interview records the Park Service interviewer is identified only as SS (JTNP n.d.).

SS: Were the Indians up around in here, when you first came? Up around this area or just the Oasis?

BK: Yup, they were the Paiutes and the Shoshone's came here and on rare occasions the Chemehuevis came from the Colorado River to trade with the Indians in the Coachella Valley here. This was only a hunting ground for meat, mountain sheep, pinyon nuts and acorns. They gathered that, and when the cold came, they went down into the Coachella Valley and they lived on the Mesquite beans then, grinding them and making flour, making bread. So as I claim, this was the Garden of Eden and the people here were Adam and Eve and they got along, as we may take it now. Who provided for them? We didn't, it must have been the God Almighty....

SS: Well, they didn't hang around here very long after you were here.

BK: No, they used to come up from Coachella Valley and come then when I was running the stamp mill here.... Well, the Indians would come here and shoot the sheep, you know, and load their ponies and go back to Coachella. Yeah, and those were the only Indians that came here when I first came in 1910.... Just past Ship Rock back there, I dug up that Indian there that was wrapped in palm leaves. Right in that cave there.... And that Indian was buried there, two feet deep and wrapped in palm leaves, and he was doubled up and tied, chucked into a little hole about 2 feet deep. But I saw the palm leaves sticking there and I dug in there and dug him out.... So I put him back in and covered him up but somebody dug it up later.

Keys's characterization of the Indians as Adam and Eve in the Garden of Eden is an example of the noble savage myth. He reported frequent contact with Indians who regularly traveled around his homestead, well inside the current park boundaries, to hunt and collect food. His account of finding an Indian burial site, digging it up, and reburying it might be as an example of his self-reported curiosity and reverence of Indians. In a separate interview, conducted in 1966, Keys told of finding spirit sticks, which he refers to as witch sticks, placed on mines to ward off settlers (JTNP n.d.):

BK: They had their witch sticks on the mine, and the gold was showing plainly there. Free gold. And it was almost turned red by the rays of the sun.

INTERVIEWER: They had their spirit sticks on there before.

BK: Before the white man, yea. And they knew what it was.... So the Indians knew all about that. But they had no particular use for it. Except they put that [spirit stick] there to keep the evil spirit away and that meant the White Man.

Here, Keys's statements suggest not only the presence of natives in the vicinity of mines well into the early twentieth century but also the actions they might have taken to use spiritual powers to keep miners from operating as they continued to inhabit and mark the landscape. Perhaps unable to repel the settlers through physical might they used spirit sticks in a manner similar to accounts of spirit stick use described by Bean (1972, 54). While Keys's accounts portray himself as an admirer of Indians who was aware of their concerns of the growing settler population, other settler accounts indicate a contemptuous view.

Jim Hester

One employee of the Swarthout Cattle Company, Jim Hester, in his 1975 interview with Park Ranger Reino Clark, reveals stark indifference and racialized hatred of Indians, despite his acknowledgment that he depended on water acquired through an agreement with the Indians at the Oasis of Mara. Below is Hester's response in his interview with Reino Clark from an interview recorded on February 8, 1975 (JTNP n.d.):

JH: Of course, water was our main object. Our headquarters or stopping points, whatever you want to call them was only where there was water. Of course at Twenty-Nine Palms now there was water. Now Black and Kimball had an agreement there with the Indians.... That was the old Swarthout corral. Now there were a couple of squaws there.... One of them was a Kitchen.... This was 1910 to 1914 we're talking about.... Now the Kitchens was from the Morongo tribe. Her name was Maria and...a couple of brothers...were the main stems at this point.... They had information on all the water in that Monument and through them, we—that is the cattle company, was able to graze that country, and find out where the water holes were.

In the above excerpt Hester identified the Indians who taught his company the location of waterholes across the land now in the park as boys from the Kitchen family at Morongo and Pine, from the Twentynine Palms Band. Later in the interview Hester described his animosity toward Indians by using a racist slur for African Americans. Despite his contempt for Indians, Hester confirmed that his company could operate in the area only because of the knowledge they received from natives.

RC: Okay, coming back to these Indians again. Did you know any of them personally?

JH: Oh hell, yes. I knew all of them.... I never slept with them or ate with them, because you didn't do those things in those days. In those days—well, when I was a kid, even when I was your age, you didn't associate with niggers, you see.... We didn't have anything to do with Mexicans, nor we didn't have anything to do with Indians. If they wanted something, "What the hell you want, you son of a bitch? Beat it. Vamoose." That's about as close as you can come to them....

RC: Do you know the name of the tribe? What they called themselves?

JH: I think they were part of the Morongos.

RC: They seem to have close contact, right?

JH: ...This Maria Kitchen was a Morongo. She belonged to the Morongo tribes. Course this was all the Shoshone nation, you know. All these tribes here are the Shoshone nation. You know that, don't you?

RC: Yes.

JH: Even the Missions and the Indians around Palm Springs, that's all the Shoshone nation. I'm sure they were all Morongos. I could be in error on that....

RC: Did they ever bother the cattle or anything like that? The Indians?

JH: Well, I don't remember any trouble with them.

Hester's interview shows his white supremacist and settler colonial worldview. He immediately turned to a racist slur for African Americans when Clark asked about Indians. His indifference and hatred of Indians and other minorities is both repugnant and revealing. He claims to have known all the Indians who lived and traveled through the area, to have depended on their knowledge for locating much-needed water in the desert, and to have never had any trouble with them. Yet he says he would not help them in any way. Despite his antipathy for natives, Hester indicated that the Kitchen family from Morongo directed them to the water sources. His claim that the Morongo nation is Shoshone further reveals his ignorance of native culture.

The contrast in settler relations with Indians, especially between Keys and Hester, shows the settlers were far from monolithic. Bill Keys's description of the local native population as Adam and Eve in the Garden of Eden lies in stark contrast to Jim Hester's quip, "What the hell you want, you son of a bitch? Beat it" if asked for anything by an Indian. What could account for such wide variations in settler views? The cognitive approach taken in this book suggests that their different views come from their different life experiences, although there is too little biographical information about these settlers to discern exactly how they developed such different views. However, there are some clues in some cases. For example, the *Desert Trails* story about Phil Sullivan becoming well acquainted with the Indians at the Oasis of Mara, due in part to his ability to speak with them in Spanish, highlights the potential problems many settlers could have had in communicating with the natives. As the article tells the story, however, his relationship with Jim Pine involved much animosity over Sullivan's use of the well. In this narrative, limited water was the source of conflict. Bill McHaney's relationship with Jim Waterman illustrates the deep level of trust that was possible between settlers and Indians. The details of how that bond developed are unclear, but for thirty-five years McHaney reportedly dug where Waterman told him he would find gold. Like many of the stories found in these oral histories, without corroboration it is difficult to assess whether this narrative entails some exaggeration on Maud Russell's part, but it remains a story of trust possible between settler and native.

Of all of the relationships discussed above, Jim Fife's working cooperation with Fig Tree John might have the most independent corroborations and entail the highest level of trust. Their trade and labor agreements persisted for at least a decade and required an intense level of trust. Lost Horse Mine, after all, produced a significant amount of gold; the whole operation had to be kept secret lest someone attempt to rob the mine. The crew of Indians, and likely Mexicans or Mexican Americans as well, worked in close proximity to this vulnerable and prosperous operation. Whoever Fife and his partners would have hired to work at the mine, they would have to be confident that their workers would not attempt to steal or let others know about the location of the mine and its success. Likewise, Lost Horse Mine is at least fifty miles from the Torrez-Martinez

Reservation, a significant distance to travel through the mountains and across the desert at the turn of the century. In a time when there was much conflict between settlers and Indians, how could Chief Fig Tree John know that the workers he provided to Fife would be properly treated and that Fife would not, as Hester had claimed, "work the devil out of them and then when he got ready to pay them off...kill them and bury them instead of paying them off"? Fife's ongoing trade with Fig Tree John could perhaps account for the level of trust both sides must have had with each other in order for such an agreement to be made. As stated above, the nature of the interactions between the native laborers and the mine's owners remain unknown, although Hester's accusation of murder seems to be a fabrication. The incentive here, on both sides, is economic, but like many trade and labor agreements, it was built on mutual trust developed over time. Information on settler and native relations in the land now known as JTNP is preserved, to the extent that it is, because of the founding of the park. In the more populated areas of Southern California tribal labor often entailed domestic work. Settlers outside the present-day park boundaries faced the same challenges as those inside; likewise, dependence on Indian labor and knowledge would have been equally necessary for survival. But the relations outside JTNP are not systematically preserved in oral histories as they are inside the park. This case study provides a unique look at the kinds of relations and perceptions that likely occurred wherever natives worked for California settlers. In some places deep trust might have developed, like that between Fife and the Cahuilla, and between Jim Waterman and Bill McHaney. Admiration, like Keys's, can develop in these close relations, but prejudice, like Hester's, could also endure. Both inside and outside present-day park boundaries the income earned from native labor not only supported tribal populations as they became increasingly separated from their traditional mode of production but also fueled the growth of tribal activist organizations, including MIF. Before these activist organizations emerged, the Cahuilla actively resisted the paternalistic MIA, at times with deadly results.

The Cahuilla Uprising of 1907–12

As a result of native activism and efforts by their settler allies such as Helen Hunt Jackson, by the end of the nineteenth century the federal government recognized thirty-three reservations in Southern California, all of which were under the purview of the MIA. However, the additional protection of reservation land came at a cost: the MIA split oversight into separate subdivisions, each managed by a superintendent with the goal of assimilating tribal populations and minimizing native authority structures. Cahuilla political organization had continued to operate in accordance to their precontact structures of inherited ceremonial and political leadership positions with ultimate authority residing in the consent of the communities' constituent families in recognizing inherited authorities and with some adaptations to the Western politics in the form of elected village captains and regional generals. Until the end of the nineteenth century the MIA relied on these native authorities to fulfill goals of policing the reservations, and even recruited natives to serve on reservation police forces (Thorne 2004, 235). The early twentieth century witnessed an abrupt change in MIA policy: superintendents became increasingly dissatisfied with native authorities and attempted to undermine the native nations' democratically elected leaders. The MIA's new policy of asserting its authority above that of the tribal leadership led to a series of confrontations and ultimately to an uprising on the Cahuilla Reservation that led to the death of a superintendent.

Tanis Thorne (2005) provided a rich historical analysis of the events leading up to the superintendent's death. Presiding during the MIA's new suppression of tribal self-government, William Stanley (then only a reservation teacher but aspiring to become a superintendent) imposed settler authority even when it posed a direct threat to his safety. From the Spanish control to the American regime, Southern California native nations continued their annual gatherings for trade and communion, which became known as fiestas (precursors to today's powwows). Stanley was intent on eliminating these gatherings, which the MIA saw as bastions of drinking and gambling. In 1905, while still a teacher at the Soboba Reservation, Stanley sought to confiscate alcohol at the fiestas, culminating in a confrontation at Soboba's fiesta in 1907 where natives and Mexicans in attendance resisted. They succeeded in forcing Stanley and other MIA employees into the reservation jail (Thorne 2004, 240). Aware and wary of the MIA's attempts to usurp authority on other reservations, the relatively isolated Cahuilla Reservation in the San Jacinto Mountains elected Leonicio Lugo as captain in 1907. Inheritor of the *net* position and fierce critic of the MIA's new policies, Lugo fined settlers who trespassed on reservation land. Lugo wrote to government officials in Washington, DC, urging them to protect Cahuilla land and authority. Then-superintendent Francis Swayne ordered that Lugo stop issuing fines for trespassing settlers and withdraw from his position as captain. Lugo refused and encouraged his community to disobey all of Swayne's commands. When Lugo found out that Swayne had secret communications with federal government officials in Washington, DC, he successfully demanded that the MIA relieve Swayne of his position and hire a new superintendent that valued transparency. In 1911 MIA appointed Stanley as superintendent, hoping for a more cooperative relationship with the Cahuilla Reservation.

Stanley took a more conciliatory approach on the Cahuilla Reservation and did not attempt to impose his power until 1912 when his superiors in Washington, DC, ordered him to make the Cahuilla recognize his authority (Thorne 2004, 244). Cahuilla relations with Stanley were generally more positive than those with his predecessors. In May 1912 the Cahuilla extended an invitation for Stanley to attend a fiesta on their reservation. While on the reservation Stanley sought to intervene in a dispute between one tribal member, Cornelio Lubo, and his neighbors about whether a gate should be left shut to keep his cattle from escaping. Lubo requested that Lugo meet with Stanley in order to persuade him to let the issue of the gate be resolved internally, without the intervention of the MIA. Lubo and Lugo agreed that if the Cahuilla Reservation is to have any degree of self-determination, certainly they must be allowed to resolve minor disputes such as this without MIA intervention. The following day there was a contentious meeting at the reservation schoolhouse between Stanley, Lugo, and other Cahuilla with Stanley declaring that the reservation's cattle did not belong solely to the Cahuilla. Instead, Stanley claimed the cattle were jointly owned by the Cahuilla and the federal government. After the meeting Stanley sent his police officers to find Cornelio Lubo to discuss the issue involving his gate. When they arrived and sought to apprehend Cornelio, his brother, Francisco Lubo, attempted to intervene. One of the police officers, a native named Celso Serrano, drew his gun, prompting Ambrosio Apapas (godfather to Cornelio's children) to draw his. The officer and Apapas both fired shots and both Apapas and Francisco Lubo were wounded. Celso Serrano attempted to flee the scene while the wounded Apapas stormed toward the schoolhouse from which Stanley, Lugo, and others had witnessed the shooting from a distance. Witnesses reported Stanley ordered Apapas to "shoot that goddamn Indian" in reference to the fleeing Celso Serrano. Angry at Stanley's indifference toward Serrano, Apapas took aim at Stanley. Apapas fired, hitting Stanley in the back as he turned to flee. Stanley died within hours. Lugo drove Apapas to town and handed him to the local sheriff. The prosecutor charged nine members of the Cahuilla Reservation, including Lugo, with Stanley's murder. The defendants argued that the shooting was an act of self-defense and that Stanley and his police officers recklessly began the confrontation. The jury found Apapas, Lugo, Cornelio, and Francisco Lubo, along with two other Lubo relatives, guilty of second-degree murder (Thorne 2004, 247). This incident caused the MIA to double down on its agenda of destroying any tribal self-rule. However, the Cahuilla did not acquiesce. Instead, they joined with others to form a new coalition, MIF, to take nonviolent actions in order to strengthen native nation sovereignty.

The Mission Indian Federation

Growing out of frustration with the MIA's increasing encroachment on their rights and traditions, not the least of which were the incidents leading up to the death of Superintendent Stanley, Southern California native nations formed several alliances to challenge the federal government and restore their capacity for self-determination. One of many such groups, MIF gained measured successes through a grassroots effort that included an extensive fund-raising campaign on reservations across Southern California and the formation of partnerships with a few influential and sympathetic settlers. Founded in 1918 with the support of a white realtor named Jonathan Tibbetts, MIF provided a structure through which each reservation elected its own captain who was responsible for local leadership, including the administrative duties that the MIA was attempting to subsume. These captains worked to coordinate their resistance to MIA at both the local and federal levels (Costo and Costo 1995, 317). Adam Castillo from the Soboba Reservation, along with other volunteers, traveled to reservations across Southern California to gather support and collect donations for MIF. As noted in her chapter in *Handbook of North American Indians* (Shipek 1978, 613–14) Florence Shipek found that from the beginning MIF had its internal divisions, particularly between those who considered the most effective strategy would be to cooperate with the policies of the Bureau of Indian Affairs (BIA) in order to reform it and those who refused to cooperate and demanded the BIA be shut down. Despite these controversies, MIF strategies had a number of successes and laid the foundation for continued maintenance of tribal self-determination and their eventual revitalization.

At the local level one of MIF's priorities was to secure the titles of and self-determination on Indian lands and to remove white squatters who illegally leached off native resources. Trafzer (2002, 85) explained how MIF served the San Manuel Reservation: "Castillo and others within the Federation [MIF] encouraged the Mission Indian Agency [MIA] to clear up the title to the San Manuel Reservation, so that nonnatives could never again claim lands belonging to Indians. To this end, a United States District Attorney began the process to make null and void any possible claims by Smithline, Wiese or their heirs.... Still, the issue of boundaries surrounding the San Manuel Reservation had not been cleared. As a result, the Indian Office worked for years to ensure the exact location of the boundaries of section twenty." As suggested by the name of the organization, MIF operated as a federation of nations. By design MIF lacked central authority. Thus, MIF's structure reflected the organization of Cahuilla nations prior to contact. Each captain was independent, and MIF was the organization through which they coordinated their strategies. In this manner native nations learned from each other's experiences lobbying the MIA to clear up their reservation boundaries. Although the MIA did not recognize the authority of the native nation governments appointed by each nation, MIF provided an overarching structure that recognized and supported these tribally recognized authorities. For example, because the MIA appointed its own police officers to implement American laws and policies on native lands, each constituent nation of MIF appointed one or more of its own tribal police officers to enforce their own tribal laws. These MIF officers wore badges with the MIF seal, which, in effect, mirrored the MIA officials they opposed and sought to replace. In doing so, native nations continued to exercise political sovereignty. At the same time, and in a manner analogous to the interdependence of sibs prior to European contact, native nations united to coordinate their use of resources and ceremonial recognition of the tribally elected authorities from each native nation. MIF's work was both local and national, and often directly challenged the federal government. As described by Heiser (1978, 715), "At [MIF] meetings expressions of ill will or hostility to the [U.S.] government were occasionally heard. Grievances were aired and complaints, both legitimate and trivial, were uttered. As a result, and under orders of the Department of Justice, some 57 Indians were placed under arrest on the charge of conspiracy against the government. Upon arraignment they were dismissed without bail." No doubt the Department of Justice was still wary of Cahuilla resistance movements after the death of Superintendent Stanley. However, MIF was thoroughly committed to nonviolence and to using the U.S. political system as a venue for championing their rights. When its members were arrested for conspiracy, MIF provided legal counsel and succeeded at having the charges dropped.

One of MIF's most enduring, though incomplete, successes included its work to receive compensation for the land California native nations lost after the treaties went unratified. Writing about his father and her father-in-law, indigenous historians Rupert and Jeannette Costo (Cahuilla and Cherokee, respectively) described the beginning of Cahuilla and California legal action against the United States for theft of land:

> Early in the Twentieth Century Juan Marie Costo traveled by bus to the center of government. A leader of the Cahuilla Tribe, Costo headed the powerful family of Costakiktum, whose home is in the mountains near the town called Anza. Cahuilla tribal people collected funds from among their own members to send him to Washington. Returning to Anza, Juan Costo brought a proposal that the tribe unite with all those who had signed the unratified treaties, and file a lawsuit against the United States Government either for return of the land the tribes had ceded to the government, or payment for those lands as stipulated in the unratified treaties. This was the beginning of the first lawsuit brought by Indians in the State of California. Most of the treaty tribes agreed to the lawsuit, and Juan Costo next approached Earl Warren, then attorney general of the state, for help. (Costo and Costo 1995, 298)

Native labor such as at Lost Horse Mine, but also in settlers' homes and farms, provided for not only their subsistence but also for their resistance to the settler regime. However, natives first needed to establish their right to file suit against the federal government. The U.S. government maintains sovereign immunity, the legal principle that a sovereign entity cannot be sued without its consent. Since 1855 the federal government has operated the U.S. Court of Claims as a channel by which citizens can seek consent from the government to file suit against it. However, federal law explicitly prohibited native nations from filing in the Court of Claims, thereby preventing any native nation from suing the federal government. In order to gain permission to file suit, native nations across the country lobbied Congress to grant access to the Court of Claims. Congress responded by granting exemptions on a case-by-case basis; as the twentieth century progressed the number of exemptions increased significantly. In 1946 Congress created the Indian Claims Commission to handle the volume of native litigation requests and to serve as a designated channel for native nation suits against the United States (60 stat. 1049). Before 1946, though, Juan Costo, like leaders from native nations across the country, had recourse only through gaining an exemption to use the Court of Claims. To influence Congress, Juan Costo's first step was to lobby the California attorney general to file suit on the Cahuilla's behalf. In the 1920s MIF joined two other federations of California native nations, the Indian Board of Cooperation and the Indian Brotherhood, as well as other nonnative organizations including the Women's Christian Temperance Union, the Native Sons of the Golden West, the Common-wealth Club of San Francisco, and the Federated Women's Clubs. MIF and its allies succeeded, and in 1927 the California legislature passed "An Act to authorize the Attorney General, as guardian of the Indians of California, to bring suit against the United States in the Court of Claims in the event that the Congress of the United States authorize the same" (Assembly Bill No. 1215). However, with California's agreement to sue on behalf of its indigenous nations came state-imposed limits on any possible settlement. Passed in 1928 by the state legislature, the California Indian's Jurisdictional Act (45 stat. 602) limited the scope of any lawsuits related to the unratified treaties to $1.25 an acre. In 1929 the attorney general of California began the process of litigation in the Court of Claims and the state's native nations began the long and complex series of legal battles to earn recognition of and compensation for the loss of land taken after Congress failed to ratify the treaties.

California won the resulting lawsuit. Although the case was caught up in the court system for decades and the eventual payment of $150 each to 36,000 California Indians grossly undervalued the total value land of California (How could the entire state be worth only $5,400,000?), the win was a significant symbolic victory (Rawls 1984, 210). For the first time, the U.S. government officially acknowledged the theft of land that had resulted after the treaties were broken. The payment did nothing to make up for the loss, but the coalition of native nations and their settler supporters succeeded in ending the decades-long cover-up. The successes of MIF and other California Indian organizations resulted in part from the efforts of a few white benefactors. MIF was almost entirely organized and funded by Indians. Challenging the U.S. federal government through its own court system, a system historically rigged against natives, required no small amount of political and legal knowledge and strategy, which sympathetic settlers provided to strengthen the work of native coalitions.

Thus, here lies another historical paradox at the root of contemporary tribal revitalization: the wage labor of Indians employed by white settlers, including the work of those at Lost Horse Mine and elsewhere who destroyed the natural environment they held sacred while advancing the wealth of white settlers also provided the financial resources necessary for native nations to ultimately strengthen their sovereignty. In other words, while Indian labor directly supported the development of the settler society and the survival of Indian peoples, it also supported natives' activist efforts to disrupt settler colonialism. While the cost in some cases was painfully high, such as the intense labor destroying sacred trees in the Mojave Desert and elsewhere, this wage labor enabled these native communities to not only support themselves but also to represent themselves directly before Congress.

Romanticism of California's Past

As demonstrated above, in the first half of the twentieth century white settlers regularly employed California Indians while native nations worked together to pursue activism effectively at both the local and federal levels. Given the active role California Indians played in local economies and in both local and national politics, how could settlers have become decreasingly cognizant of their native neighbors? This cultural forgetting can be understood as the result of a combination of historical dissonance and the diminishing awareness of settlers of their native contemporaries. This section explores how popular media added to already existing pressures for settlers to assume that California's native nations had assimilated or faded long ago. Moreover, as new arrivals swarmed into California they easily adopted these narratives from popular media.

One of the most notable and failed attempts to increase settler awareness of the plight of their native neighbors was a novel by Helen Hunt Jackson, the settler activist discussed in the previous chapter. Jackson published *Ramona* in 1884 with the explicit goal of educating the public about the injustices suffered by California Indians, beginning with the mission era. The novel became a best seller, but not for the reasons Jackson intended. Set in the period after the Mexican–American war, its plot centers on the relationship between Ramona, a half-Indian and half-Scottish young woman who had been adopted by a wealthy Hispanic family, and Alessandro, a California Indian and the son of a chief. Ramona's adoptive family abuses her because of her Indian heritage and refuses to allow her to have a relationship with Alessandro because he is Indian. Ramona and Alessandro elope, have a child, and attempt to establish a series of homesteads, only to be driven from each by white settlers. The novel provides fictionalized accounts of California Indians forced off their land; like many at this time, Ramona and Alessandro settle in the San Bernardino Mountains. After Alessandro is murdered by a white settler, Ramona marries one of her siblings from her adoptive family and the novel concludes with the two leaving America to settle in relative peace in Mexico. The plot is one of California Indians suffering injustice after injustice at the hands of white settlers, with the protagonists able to survive only by fleeing the country. However, Jackson's intentions were lost on the novel's readers as it grew in popularity. Jackson outlined the goal of her work, which she likened to *Uncle Tom's Cabin*, in a letter to a newspaper editor: "I am at work on a story—which I hope will do something for the Indian cause: it is laid in So. California—and there is so much Mexican life in it, that I hope to get people so interested in it, before they suspect anything Indian, that they will keep on.—If I can do one hundredth part for the Indians that Mrs. Stowe did for the Negro, I will be thankful" (Cited from Castrovono 2012, 383). Jackson died the year after her novel was published. It took off in popularity, inspiring tourists from across California and the country to visit sites from her novel.

One of the most important factors at play in the widespread popularity and misinterpretation of *Ramona* is that, at the time of its publication, railroad companies had just laid tracks providing much easier and more-affordable access to Southern California from the rest of the country. Tourists and migrants were arriving in large numbers to Southern California at this time. Those seeking new homes in Southern California would have been largely unaware of the problems facing California Indians. Dydia DeLyser's (2003) analysis of the tourist practices that sprang up in response to *Ramona* provides insight into the cultural knowledge and values of the audience that so clearly interpreted the book against Jackson's intentions. DeLyser (886) argued that the images of Southern California presented in *Ramona* "creat[ed] not so much a false past for the region as a new social memory, one well suited to rapidly changing times and easily enfolded into tourists' itineraries." DeLyser (891) pointed out that the new settlers arriving in Southern California would have had little knowledge of California Indians, but they would have had substantial awareness of General Custer's 1876 defeat at Little Big Horn. These settlers also had exposure to the ongoing nationwide portrayal of American Indians as savages. While Jackson intended to lure readers with rich descriptions of the Hispanic heritage of Southern California, her portrait of this heritage became the source of the novel's popularity because, as DeLyser (891) argues, "Its widespread success lay in its presentation of places and people that had remained outside of—that had escaped—the urbanization and industrialization of the rest of the United States." While Jackson hoped that descriptions of a romanticized Spanish heritage would attract readers so that they could read her message about racial injustice, real estate developers and tourist attractions latched onto the romanticized Spanish heritage represented in the book. Developers named streets, created tourist sites such as the purported grave of the fictional Ramona, and cited passages from the novel in their pamphlets to advertise homes in the area (901). In an effort to draw tourists to the then-remote towns of Hemet and San Jacinto, these towns partnered in 1923 to establish the Ramona Pageant, a play based on the novel, which retains its popularity today. In fact, the popularity of the novel resulted in a city naming itself Ramona in hopes of attracting settlers lured by their perceived romantic view of the novel.

The romanticizing of California Indians grew at the same time as settlers increasingly came to fatalistically believe that their passing was imminent. Writing for the *Los Angeles Herald* in 1908, Amy Dudley offered a narrative entitled "Passing of the Mission Indians" that captures both the simplicity and the tacit racism of this perspective:

> The history of the North American Indian is much the same as that of the wild animals.... The fate of final extermination stares one and all in the face....
>
> An example...is the passing of the Mission Indians of California. In 1769, when the Franciscan friars set foot upon the shores of California, all unwittingly they sounded the first note of the death-knell of a race. The motives of the Franciscan missionaries were the purest that animates men....
>
> The history of the Mission Indians of California can be told in the story of those of San Bernardino valley.... Those now living in San Bernardino valley are of the Cahuilla and Serrano tribes....
>
> Had it not been for this spirit of docility among the Indians the history of California missions would have been a vastly different story from what it is.... In 1834, on account of the decree of

secularization, San Bernardino was abandoned and only a dilapi-dated adobe ruin marks the place where the buildings once stood.

The Indians, left to themselves, wandered around the valley for a few years. Then, under the Mexican grants...new task-masters came. The rancheros of that day had the gentle custom of rounding up the Indians exactly as they did cattle. *They would lasso them* [emphasis added], drag them to the ranchos and compel them to work.

The American colonists came in 1851. They found many Indi-ans in the valley, but their condition was bad and became rapidly worse.... The seductive red liquor of the white man appealed to the Indian as nothing else ever did. The simple-souled savage seemed to take naturally to all the vices, missing entirely the mild virtues of the white man....

So came the beginning of the end, and the end is not far removed. Of all this broad, fertile valley...the white man has gen-erously left him one square mile of land—the government reser-vation of San Manuel.

This reservation is situated about one mile north of the state insane asylum at Highland.... It appears utterly incapable of sustaining anything, even though San Manuel is called a "self-sustaining reservation." That means these Indians receive no annuity or supplies from the United States government.... Their houses are scattered here and there among the hills, and though poor and mean in appearance, the surroundings are remarkably clean. The men are sometimes employed as wood choppers on the mountains and by the ranchers as laborers in the valley. The women are able to obtain some work as washer-women. They also make a few baskets. These Indians are said to be perfectly honest. One rancher in the vicinity frequently loans them small amounts of money which, he says, are always repaid....

The inaccessibility and general undesirability of the land set aside for San Manuel reservation may prevent further encroach-ment by the white men, and allow the remnant of this race to at least sleep in undisturbed peace; but—quien sabe? (Dudley 1908, 5)

Dudley's (1908) first and most striking analogy, that "the history of the North American Indian is much the same as that of the wild ani-mals," continues the animal analogy that native people do not qualify as people at all and therefore, according to this logic, their demise is not as much a tragedy as it is a stepping-stone in the march toward progress. Her peculiar metaphor that the rancheros would "lasso them, drag them to the ranchos and compel them to work," further expands this analogy, suggesting that, like cattle, the natives could be rounded up without much resistance. Contradicting even her own accounts of raids against the missions, and the subsequent Garra uprising, Dudley declared that unlike natives elsewhere across North America, the California Indians "have quietly submitted to the inevitable from the beginning," presuming a passivity that lies in stark contrast to the then-well-known confrontations between settlers and natives in California. For Dudley, like the legions of tourists who flocked to the area after reading *Ramona*, the Spanish missions represent an idyllic, quaint, and naive past in which the "purest" motives were no match for the assumed inferiority of California Indians. Repeating the narrative of O. P. Fitzgerald and other fatalists, the principles of social Darwinism presumed the fate of California's Indians was sealed because, according to this theory, they never stood a chance of coexisting with Europeans. The best the Mission Indians could hope for, according to Dudley, was that the isolation of their reservations, such as San Manuel's, would allow "to at least sleep in undisturbed peace" as they approach their imminent demise. However, she did leave the door open for some alternative future, "but—*quien sabe?*," who knows? Dudley, like most of her contemporaries, could not fathom that the Cahuilla and Serrano, along with their fellow California native nations, were far from passive. Ironically, at the same time that she speculated on the demise of California's native nations, the Cahuilla and their allies (both native and nonnative) were at the early stages of mounting their activism for self-determination. These efforts led to the Cahuilla Uprising of 1907–12, the organization and successes of MIF, and ultimately to the transformation of the Serrano and Cahuilla nations into the epicenter of a multi-billion-dollar Indian casino movement.

Conclusion: Labor, Activism, and Ignorance

This chapter began with the paradox of the increasing activism of native nations in California at the same time that settler awareness of their native neighbors had begun to diminish. Those who employed California Indians, or lived near them, such as the settlers in the lands that now make up JTNP, were keenly aware of California Indians and the importance of the labor and knowledge they provided. The views of these settlers varied widely between the extremes of the noble and ignoble savage stereotypes. For settlers to locate water and gold required their cooperation with Indian communities, either informally through friendship or formally through business arrangements. These relations could be marked either by trust or by open hostility. The success of mining and cattle operations depended on labor provided by Indians, which often required a significant amount of trust on both parts. Those settlers with direct experience of and dependence on tribes had a substantial (albeit imperfect) knowledge of native life.

At the turn of the century, Indian labor supported the development of settler enterprises in Southern California, particularly those in locations on the fringe of settler society such as JTNP. That labor also provided native nations with the financial resources necessary to launch and maintain successful campaigns to reclaim their sovereignty. As stated above, MIF operated on cash donations from tribal members across Southern California. Indians earned the cash primarily through wage labor for the encroaching settler population. With these funds, MIF coordinated strategies for pursuing their rights locally and nationally. The successes of these collaborations had substantial impacts on local and national politics. Native nations strengthened the recognition of their borders and the federal government acknowledged its unjust treatment of these nations. Yet, other than the settlers who had direct experience of the native nations, settler awareness of their activities and plight was dim.

I suggest that three interrelated factors need to be taken into account in order to resolve the paradox of cultural forgetting amid political revitalization. First, at the turn of the century, settler wars with California Indians had concluded and their population was at its nadir. The population at this time was politically active but numerically small, especially given the swelling settler population. This meant that fewer settlers had direct experiences with native nations. Settler wars with these nations had already been fought, resulting in the loss of population and land when these nations were forced to relocate to the fringes of settler development. MIF and similar organizations pursued their goals through peaceful activism. While in many ways successful, the peaceful lobbying of these groups could not raise their visibility to settlers nearly as much as had the violent conflict that preceded them. Not only were there fewer Indians for settlers to interact with but also the interactions between Indians and settlers did not spur the headlines or hysteria of the conflicts of the 1860s.

Second, at this time the demographic makeup of Southern California was rapidly changing. The influx of immigrants from Asia and Mexico provided businesses with inexpensive labor; the growing population of these workers quickly swelled beyond the already diminished numbers of California Indians. Locations near reservations and on the outskirts of developed areas relied on Indian labor, but enterprises at the center of settler developments relied less and less on Indians. At the same time, the introduction of competing railroads to Southern California provided unprecedented access for settlers relocating from the East and the Midwest. These settlers came to Southern California without any knowledge or experience of California Indians. The absence of such knowledge, in addition to marketing strategies that linked real estate to the romanticized Hispanic images of *Ramona*, would have made it easy for these new arrivals to accept an almost mythic narrative of California's history. Receptive to the romantic images in *Ramona*, but not the injustice represented in the novel, this population of settlers brought with them simplistic knowledge of Indians based on what they would have read about the battles fought on the Great Plains.

Finally, forgetting was a way to resolve the historical dissonance between what settlers wanted to believe about the United States' commitment to democracy (and California's commitment to being a free state) and the early state's policies of enslaving and exterminating its indigenous population. It is not that settlers, whether the recent arrivals or those who migrated during the gold rush, were completely unaware that California had native inhabitants. In fact, as the wide interest in *Ramona* and Spanish missions demonstrates, people were quite aware that an indigenous population occupied California prior to colonization. Rather, the settler knowledge of California Indians at this time was centered on the Spanish missions and their assumed assimilation of Indians. To romanticize the mission era is to both acknowledge the presence of California Indians prior to contact and to glorify the missions' project of converting them to the Christian religion and "civilizing" them. Focusing on the Spanish period, with its emphasis on assimilating natives, drew focus away from the inherent contradictions between the extermination that took place and the self-professed values of the United States. With the native population in numerical decline, the need to justify the virtual enslavement of this population declined, as did the need to rationalize extermination of the Indians. The cultural forgetting that happened during the first half of the twentieth century was part of a process in which settlers, except the few who worked closely with native communities, had a diminishing need to discuss their native contemporaries and a need to resolve, through forgetting, historical dissonance. Only those who sympathized with Indians or employed them needed to develop and maintain working knowledge of this population. For the rest of the settler population, California Indians were part of the history of the missions. To most settlers, Indians existed only in the past, without any conceivable future. Of course, with the revitalization of native nations in the second half of the twentieth century, that assumption would prove to be untenable.

4

TERMINATION
AND REVITALIZATION

PUBLIC POLICIES can sometimes produce unintended results. There might be no greater example of this than the federal policies that sought to force American Indians to assimilate. These unintended results can especially be seen in the middle of the twentieth century, when Congress pursued an agenda that is now known as termination. Coupled with the attempt to assimilate native children by requiring them to attend boarding schools, termination only strengthened the resolve of native nations to retain their sovereignty. Policymakers wrongly assumed that if the federal government ceased its acknowledgment of tribal sovereignty, then it would disappear. Federal policies fomented a resurgence of tribal sovereignty that reaches into the present day, including the tribal gaming movement. This chapter examines the impacts of the termination policies and how the Cahuilla contributed to the larger movement of revitalizing sovereignty.

Termination

Around the middle of the twentieth century Congress began systematically repealing the Indian Reorganization Act, which had overturned the Dawes Act and encouraged limited forms of native nation self-determination. In August 1953 Congress passed House Concurrent Resolution 108 that asserted the federal government was to act "as rapidly as possible, to make the Indians...subject to the same laws and entitled to the same privileges and responsibilities as are applicable to other citizens...[and] to end their status as wards" (B132). Later that month Congress passed Public Law 280 (Pub.L. 83-280). (See chapter 5 for further discussion of the significant role Public Law 280 played in Cabazon's case before the Supreme Court.) Public Law 280 provided six states with criminal jurisdiction on Indian lands within those states, marking the first time since *Worcester v. Georgia* (1832) that the federal government granted states significant authority on tribal land; it now applies in sixteen states. However, Resolution 108 and Public Law 280 were just the beginning. From 1954 to 1964 Congress passed laws terminating the tribal status of more than 109 native nations. With termination, these native nations lost all external political sovereignty. The land of terminated native nations, which together totaled more than 1.3 million acres, came under the complete authority of state and local governments (Wilkinson 2005, 57). While some of their former reservations became the private property of individual members of the formerly recognized tribes, state and local governments sold much of the land to non-Indians for development. The termination policies (not unlike the Dawes Act), deconstructed tribal governments and put reservation land into privately held trusts and, thereby, enabled private developers and individuals to purchase it. These radical shifts from the Indian Reorganization Act reflect ongoing political and cultural shifts in settler society.

The philosophy underpinning the Indian Reorganization Act of 1934—namely that tribal governments can achieve what the private sphere cannot—was part of President Franklin Roosevelt's larger New Deal initiative. Like many aspects of the New Deal, these policies faced new challenges by mid-century. With the Cold War sparking suspicions of communist elements within the United States, an irrational fear of native collective land ownership gripped the public and, especially, elected officials. Although culturally and politically far from the Communist Party of the Soviet Union, Congress saw native nations and their practice of collective land ownership as a communist presence within the United States. For Congress, recognizing native nations' collective ownership was anathema to fighting communism. The Cold War created an atmosphere where both the public and the policymakers saw tribal sovereignty as at best obsolete, and at worst an insidious, existential threat.

There is no discounting the role that World War II played in profoundly altering American Indians communities and settler perceptions of them. Prior to U.S. entry in the war in 1941, only five thousand Indians served in the military. Four years later, at the end of the war, that number had increased nearly tenfold, to 44,500, as 12.5 percent of the entire Indian population joined the military (Rossum 2011, 67). During the war a roughly equal number of Indians left reservations to work in industries that supported the war. Though not the result of any explicit policy, World War II integrated Indians into settler society at a greater rate than ever before. The war changed native nations from both the inside and the outside. At the end of the war Indian veterans returned with new skills and connections valuable to settler society. Likewise, those who served the war effort through domestic industrial labor forged new connections with the wider settler society. At the turn of the century natives increasingly became invisible to settlers, who often fatalistically viewed tribes as on the verge of, or past, extinction. But Indians played critical roles in World War II, both as members of the general infantry and as the invaluable code talkers (Meadows 2002; Riseman 2012). Tales of the Indians' bravery circulated around settler society, sparking many settlers to think that Indians can and should integrate into the dominant society. This belief, coupled with the Cold War's mounting suspicion of communal living, informed Congress as representatives drafted the termination agenda. If the end of the nineteenth century was the demographic nadir of the California Indian population, the middle of the twentieth century served as a bottom for native nations' external political sovereignty. In the 1950s and 1960s Congress terminated tribal governments and relocated thousands of American Indians to cities (Fixico 1986; Wilkinson and Biggs 1977). By forcing the assimilation of tribal members and the appropriation of tribal resources, termination devastated tribes. But Congress could only extinguish the tribes' external political sovereignty, not their internal political and cultural sovereignty. Underestimating the strength of their internal sovereignty, Congress's attempts at extermination spurred American Indian activism on a scale never seen before.

Like the Dawes Act before it, the termination agenda only succeeded in ushering in its reverse. Termination failed to achieve any of its cultural or economic goals. Despite legislators' claims that it would raise natives' standard of living, termination plunged tribal communities deeper into poverty. Even relatively prosperous tribes, such as the Menominee Tribe of Wisconsin, experienced a great leap backward. The first terminated tribe, the Menominee, had operated the United States' first successful sustainable forestry operations (Beck 2005). The Menominee's collective ownership of reservation forests helped tribal members to open and operate a sawmill that invested its revenue into sustaining the Menominee community and its natural resources. By ending their external political sovereignty, converting their land into a county of Wisconsin and opening their land to purchase by settlers, termination destroyed the Menominee's most successful economic venture. Instead of encouraging Indian economic success through integration, termination made the newly formed Menominee County the poorest county in the state. The devastation of native nations occurred again and again as Congress pursued nearly two decades of termination. Once terminated, the federal government began removing natives from tribal lands. In total, more than 100,000 American Indians were bussed from native lands to major cities, including Los Angeles and San Francisco, where they were expected to integrate into the dominant society, leaving their native culture behind (Sorkin 1978). However, termination's cultural objectives failed even more tremendously than its economic objectives. The two sites of the greatest effort to force assimilation, Indian boarding schools and the cities that became home to those removed from their homeland, became crucibles of American Indian activism.

Cahuilla Under Termination

In the 1950s the specter of termination came to the Cahuilla nations. Though Congress never voted to terminate their reservations, under the Termination Doctrine it was only a matter of time before that would happen. Activist groups including the Mission Indian Federation (MIF) became divided on how to maintain their sovereignty. Heather Daly's (2009, 2012) research illuminates how termination policies sparked opposition and action among the Cahuilla nations. Opposing termination would retain federal recognition but also maintain the status quo, particularly the dysfunctional and paternalistic BIA. Supporting termination would end federal recognition along with the BIA and put tribal land ownership in jeopardy. Those who held this perspective supported termination not because they wanted to assimilate, but because they considered the federal government as an obstacle to sovereignty; they believed that they could better determine the course of their own future if the BIA got out of the way. Even without congressional action, political and corporate actors conspired to create a de facto termination on the Agua Caliente Reservation by means of guardianships.

Would termination bring an end to tribal sovereignty, or would it free native nations from the yoke of federal bureaucracy? Do native nations need federal recognition to maintain their internal sovereignty? Native nations across the United States wrestled with these questions, which proved to be especially divisive among the Cahuilla and the greater networks of activists in Southern California, including MIF. MIF had always opposed the BIA. It saw termination as an opportunity to finally bring an end to the BIA. Of course, this is not to say that MIF wanted an end to native nation self-determination, or home rule, as they called it. Throughout its life, MIF worked toward its singular goal, as defined in its constitution: "Secure...all the rights and benefits belonging to each Indian, both singly, and collectively" (MIF c. 1922, Art. I, Sec. 2). The constitution also established "Human Rights and Home Rule" as MIF's official slogan (Art. II, Sec. 1; home rule is another term for self-determination or sovereignty). Self-determination guided MIF's efforts to establish tribal authorities on each reservation to oppose the MIA. It guided MIF's pursuit of land claims against California; when termination presented the opportunity to dismantle the BIA, MIF's support for tribal sovereignty led it to support the forces for termination. This is how MIF came to support termination while maintaining its goal of self-determination, human rights, and home rule. But many native nations formerly united under MIF opposed termination, including the leadership of the Cahuilla nations of Los Coyotes and Torres-Martinez. Those who opposed termination formed their own group, Spokesmen and Committee, to counter termination. Support for MIF was strongest when it sought to initiate claims against the United States for the unratified treaties, but support eroded when it took a stance in favor of termination. Often, families themselves became divided and native nation politics became consumed with the question of whether to elect leaders in support of or against termination. There was no middle ground (Daly 2009).

In 1950 MIF sent representatives to Congress in order to urge termination, "[to] plead for the abolition of serfdom under the Bureau of Indian Affairs" and to be "relieved of the imposed slavery" (*San Diego Union*, February 21, 1950, quoted in Daly 2012, 105). It might seem that MIF was making strange bedfellows with the assimilationist Congress, but MIF's goal was to eliminate the BIA, not its own communities. Those Southern California native nations who opposed termination, of which there were many, created their own groups with their own lobbying efforts, including the Spokesmen and Committee. For these opposition groups, the BIA was far from perfect, but it was a known entity that, however flawed, preserved tribal land ownership to some degree. With termination, native nations would become liable for paying property taxes on their land. Moreover, they might have to repay the federal government for any improvements made to that land. Termination might have offered tribal members greater individual ownership and control over their land, but with debts accruing on that land and no means to pay, termination would ultimately mean forfeiting tribal land. The difference between MIF and termination opponents was, therefore, not a difference in ultimate goals, but in idealism versus pragmatism. Both wanted to preserve native communities, but at what cost? Termination would prevent any further federal encroachment on tribal life, but could native nations continue their way of life if they lost their land? Spokesmen and Committee reasoned that the potential for losing tribal land was too great. While these different approaches to termination divided native nations and families, both took the same activist strategies to reach their goals. Each side lobbied state and federal lawmakers to make their case.

Spokesmen and Committee found unlikely allies with the legislature of California. Termination would push federal obligations for natives onto the state budget. Welfare, education, and every other expense paid by the federal government for native nations would become the responsibility of state governments. Many in the California state legislature saw this as the federal government attempting to shirk its responsibilities and pass on a burden. Thus, California's policymakers partnered with Spokesmen and Committee. Like MIF's support of Congress's termination agenda, California's policymakers and Spokesmen and Committee worked together despite the differences in their motivations. Edmund Gerald "Pat" Brown, at the time attorney general of California and later governor, wrote, "In its present unworkable form California will have thrust upon it legal obligations which it simply cannot discharge because of the administrative preparation for the turnover on the part of the Interior Department" (State of California 1955, 17). California opposed termination, not because it supported tribal sovereignty, but because it refused to pay for what it saw as a federal responsibility. California's congressional representatives made certain that the state's concerns were known to Congress. One representative, Clair Engle, threatened a possible lawsuit:

> Do you think as a legal matter the Federal Government can hand the people of California the Indians and tell them to look after them when that has traditionally been the Federal obligation? It would occur to me that a bill like this might need an act from the State Legislature to prevent a lawsuit that would go to the Supreme Court of the United States. I just have grave doubts as to whether or not the Congress of the United States can walk up and toss this out the window, so to speak, hand this obligation to local taxpayers of the State. (State of California 1955, 25)

The wrangling within Congress and California native nations continued and, if anything, slowed the termination process. Only one reservation in Southern California was terminated, Mission Creek, which was uninhabited at the time. MIF may have been making gains in Congress, but it was losing support by the native nations it saw as its constituents. The work of the Spokesmen and Committee was part of a wider and ultimately successful movement in preventing the termination of any inhabited reservations in Southern California, while termination struck native nations across the United States. Ultimately, these delays lasted long enough for policymakers' and the public's attitudes to swing again, bringing a renewed, though limited, federal support for native nation self-determination. Termination never came directly to the Cahuilla, but the implications of Congress's fierce opposition to tribal sovereignty had devastating consequences.

The Guardianship Scandal

The Agua Caliente Band, located on a checkerboard reservation throughout the tourist hub of Palm Springs, became the center of one of the more insidious plots by settler institutions to usurp tribal land under the guise of helping tribes. The city of Palm Springs developed much later than other Southern California cities. The first settlers avoided the Coachella Valley, considering it to be a barren wasteland. However, by the turn of the century tourists began visiting the area's hot springs for their perceived health benefits. Within a few decades the remote desert town became a playground for Hollywood. Palm Springs' warm and sunny winters and its location a few hours' drive from Los Angeles became attractions for celebrities and wealthy tourists. Kray (2004) demonstrated how throughout the first half of the twentieth century city planners and developers sought to maximize the city's appeal to wealthy tourists at the expense of its working-class and minority populations. Developers targeted the Agua Caliente Band, with 6,500 acres of their 31,127-acre reservation laid out in checkerboard pattern across the city of Palm Springs and in particular one square mile, Section 14, in the town's center. Only a half mile from luxury hotels, Agua Caliente rented Section 14 to the city's service workers who were primarily African American and Hispanic. At the time Agua Caliente could extend only five-year leases to nonmembers, limiting the interest of any potential resort developers. Priced out of owning local real estate, the resorts' service workers could only afford to live on Section 14, which, as part of an Indian reservation, received neither infrastructural support from the city nor significant funding from the BIA to make improvements. Into the middle of the century Section 14's population had no indoor plumbing, limiting people to using outhouses only a short walk from the luxurious resorts where they labored.

For the developers and city planners, Section 14 posed both a challenge and an opportunity. The location could provide prime real estate for resort development, yielding fortunes in profit for developers and tax revenue for the city. But as it stood the slums marked the landscape, lowering the property values and tarnishing the image of the surrounding resorts. Nearby resorts found Section 14 to be a convenient location for dumping trash, further devaluing the area and increasing public health risks. Even if Agua Caliente could develop it, the city could not tax it. To reconcile this dilemma, developers and local authorities conspired to devise a plan to wrest control out of the hands of Agua Caliente and evict their impoverished tenants. Beginning in the 1920s city elites petitioned Congress to sell the reservation. At the same time, Agua Caliente lobbied Congress to allow the tribe to grant longer leases, a plan the city opposed as long as it could not collect revenue from reservation development. In 1948 the city believed it had found a solution with the help of the BIA's director for California, Walter Woehlke. Woehlke asserted that the city had the authority to impose its ordinances, especially sanitation and building codes, on the reservation, making way for local officials to condemn properties on Section 14 and evict its residents, serving the first notices in 1951 (Kray 2004).

By the middle of the decade Agua Caliente had succeeded in raising the length of its leases from five years to twenty-five. In 1959 the Indian Leasing Act further extended the length to ninety-nine years, making reservation land a viable location for private development. Also in 1959, Congress passed the Equalization Act, which required that revenue from land collectively owned by a tribe be distributed equally among its members. Congress passed the act for the ostensible purpose of protecting tribes from exploitation by developers, but it also allowed courts to appoint legal guardians and conservators to manage tribal real estate transactions. Palm Springs developers Floyd Odlum and Melvin Eaton, along with federal judge Hilton McCabe, lobbied for this clause in the Equalization Act. It enabled McCabe to declare tribal members incompetent and appoint his business partners, including Odlum and Eaton, as their guardians and conservators. These guardian and conservator appointments stripped tribal members of control over their land. In theory, tribal members should benefit financially from any actions taken by their guardians and conservators, but in practice they received nothing. The guardians and conservators charged excessive fees to those they were supposed to protect, benefiting themselves through both control of the land and the revenue generated by the land. By March 1961 Agua Caliente had lost effective control of Section 14 and the city gave eviction notices to the section's more than 2,500 households. The city began the processes of demolishing the section's dwellings, at times doing so without even notifying the occupants (Kray 2004, 108). Agua Caliente, joining with their tenants represented by the National Association for the Advancement of Colored People protested to the city and the BIA to no avail. The tribe's guardians and conservators could legally pursue the evictions. By the end of 1961, Section 14's population dwindled from more than 5,000 to 1,727 (109). The evictions and demolitions continued through the decade, against the protests of tribal members and residents.

In 1967 a local journalist, George Ringwald, began an independent investigation into the guardianships and conservators. Ringwald's investigation for the *Press Enterprise* revealed the depth of city elites' contempt for the tribe. He later recalled an exchange in which he asked Judge McCabe why the tribe could not control their property "the same as any other people," to which McCabe reportedly replied, "You call those things walking the streets people?" (Agua Caliente Cultural Museum 2011, 5). Responding to the investigations, President Lyndon Johnson ended the conservator and guardianships in 1968. The end of the guardianship scandal returned to the tribe its ability to manage its land, though it did not return the money siphoned away or return former tenants to their now-destroyed homes. Agua Caliente had vehemently protested the guardianship to local, state, and federal governments, but ultimately achieved its greatest success by cooperating with Ringwald to bring the story to the public outside of Palm Springs. In 1968 Ringwald was awarded a Pulitzer Prize for his investigative journalism. Though Agua Caliente never faced termination legislation, the guardianship scandal produced a de facto termination wherein the native nation lost its ability to determine future development on its land and the land went directly into the hands of private developers. The guardians and conservators could not have committed the damage they caused without the intervention of Congress, which accepted their guardian clause into the Equalization Act. Congress, while never officially terminating the tribe, provided the necessary legal guise for effective termination to take place anyway.

Like native responses to termination across the United States, Agua Caliente restored its sovereignty by appealing to the court of public opinion. In reaching out to the public through the *Press Enterprise* in 1967, Agua Caliente's activism converged with the wider American Indian activist movement. These public appeals for change, contributed to a nationwide change in public perceptions of tribal sovereignty. Ultimately, this activism led to the end of the termination era, restoring limited external sovereignty to native nations across the United States.

Revitalization

Intertribal American Indian Activism

The fallout from termination was exactly what the Spokesmen and Committee and other native activists had feared. Native nations plummeted deeper into economic and cultural crises. Yet Congress's assimilative strategies provoked the opposite of their intended goal. The policies designed to finally extinguish native identities—converting tribal lands to private ownership, removing parental control from education, and bussing natives to cities across the United States—each contributed in its own way to an emerging movement for tribal revitalization. In combination, these practices and the wider civil rights and countercultural movements of the 1960s created a resurgence of native identity, increased settler support for tribal sovereignty, and a new pan-tribal identity that transcended that of individual native nations. Whether paternalistic, self-serving, or earnest, there have always been settlers who sympathized with native nations. What was unique about settler perspectives at the end of the termination era was an unprecedented growth of settler concern for American Indians. For critics of the Vietnam War, U.S. military aggression against native nations was further evidence of an endemic American imperialism. In the romanticism of the counterculture, American Indians served the role of noble savage and foil to the excesses of industrial consumerism. These new settler perspectives were clearly simplistic, but these emerging public perceptions encouraged federal policymakers to swing from terminating to strengthening limited forms of native nations' self-determination.

Joanne Nagel's (1996) groundbreaking study of American Indian ethnic renewal demonstrated how termination caused the greatest resurgence of native identity in U.S. history by creating "an urban, intermarried, bicultural American Indian population [living] outside traditional American Indian geographic and cultural regions" (Nagel 1995, 948).

Nagel built on Barth's (1969) understanding of identity as a construction, emerging from relational processes of self-identification and identification by others. She pointed to the remarkable growth in the number of Americans who identify as American Indian on the census. In the decade between 1970 and 1980 the population who identify as American Indian grew by 72 percent, from 792,730 to 1,364,033 (Nagel, 951). Birth rates and immigration could not account for this growth. Instead, the growth came almost exclusively from ethnic switching, as Americans of mixed native heritage chose to deemphasize their other identities, most often the dominant white category, and emphasize their American Indian identity. Nagel found that these "new" natives more often than not lived in an urban area, were intermarried, and spoke English. This population was exactly what assimilationists had hoped to create through termination, boarding schools, and busing programs. But their cultural identity had not been lost—it had grown stronger. Urbanization meant natives from disparate and distant nations became neighbors in cities, often spending time in the same restaurants and bars, cultural centers, and occupations. In sharing these urban spaces together, they formed new communities centered on a common, intertribal American Indian identity. Boarding schools offered even more fertile grounds for intertribal networks to grow. Often conditions at these schools were horrific and humiliating for native children. Forbidden from speaking their language, practicing their religion, and being with their family, the distinctive cultural identities of each pupil retained their significance, while their shared experiences at the schools united native children from different nations who otherwise would have never met. They became unified in their opposition to settler society. These schools unintentionally incubated connections between native nations and future activists. The American Indian Movement (AIM) became one of the most publicly visible accomplishments of boarding school alumni.

The work of AIM and other activist groups effectively targeted public opinion, creating an environment for a renewal of American Indian identity and a surge in settler support for tribal sovereignty. The nineteen-month takeover of Alcatraz beginning in November 1969 and the Trail of Broken Treaties in late 1972 were just two of the groups' activities that captured the momentum of concurrent social justice movements. Broadcast across the country, these events caught the public's attention while other activist efforts, like those of Spokesmen and Committee, were less noticed but just as instrumental. In 1950 Rupert Costo from the Cahuilla

Reservation created the American Indian Historical Society for the purpose of disseminating scholarship and awareness of broken treaties. He founded the society in the Haight-Ashbury district of San Francisco before the neighborhood became the center for the late 1960s counterculture, though the location was fortuitous. While native activists held the nation's attention on Alcatraz Island in San Francisco Bay, Costo, not far away on the mainland, disseminated literature on broken treaties in the epicenter of the countercultural movement that celebrated, albeit simplistically, native identity.

Conclusion

At this point, returning to the distinctions between internal and external sovereignty, and cultural and political sovereignty, is useful for mapping the causes and outcomes of the activism for native nation self-determination. Termination threatened native external political sovereignty. Political pressure was necessary but not sufficient to restore tribal external political sovereignty. Activists needed to appeal to the public, as Ringwald did in his exposé of the Palm Springs guardianship scandal and AIM and other groups did nationwide. The shift in a significant proportion of settler perspectives signaled a strengthened external cultural sovereignty, more than at any time before settler society openly supported native self-determination. In the end, the federal government capitulated and repealed its termination policies. Many obstacles still remain, but American Indian activism, combined with strengthened public support, caused a cascade of new laws supporting tribal sovereignty. In 1973 President Richard Nixon repudiated the termination agenda when he signed a bill restoring federal recognition of the Menominee tribe (Kidwell 2001; Wilkins 2007, 122). Speaking to Congress in 1970, President Nixon asserted, "The first Americans—the Indians—are the most deprived and most isolated minority group in our nation. On virtually every scale of measurement—employment, income, education, health—the condition of the Indian ranks at the bottom. This condition is the heritage of centuries of injustice.... Even the federal programs which are intended to meet their needs have frequently proved to be ineffective and demeaning" (Nixon 1970, 248, 249). Termination's reversal continued through the 1970s; ultimately all but forty-four (Rossum 2011, 67) terminated native nations regained federal recognition. Following federal re-recognition, though they were still largely impoverished, tribes generally began to experience relative increases in economic development and prosperity because they were increasingly able to independently control tribal resources. In 1975

Congress passed the Indian Self-Determination and Education Assistance Act (Pub.L. 93-638), strengthening federal recognition of tribal sovereignty. This act ushered in an end to the termination policies of House Concurrent Resolution 108. With Public Law 93-638, federal policies now encouraged tribal self-governance. The education of native children became the right and responsibility of native people, with the support of the federal government. No longer could boarding schools usurp the rights of native parents to control the education of their children. This reversal of federal Indian policy served as the impetus for the tribal casino movement (Anders 1998).

During this new revival of external political sovereignty, Russell Bryan, an Ojibwe, bought a trailer for his family on the Leech Lake Reservation located in Minnesota. This seemingly mundane event triggered what would become a legal foundation for the tribal casino movement. The county where his trailer was located, attempting to impose its personal property taxes, sent Bryan a tax bill of $147.95 for the trailer. The Leech Lake Reservation contested the tax. In 1972 the matter ended up before the U.S. Supreme Court, which found that, as stated in the law itself, Public Law 280 provides the affected states, including Minnesota, only with criminal jurisdiction (*Bryan v. Itasca County*, 426 U.S. 373). The Supreme Court found that in passing Public Law 280, Congress has nothing "remotely resembling an intention to confer general state civil regulatory control over Indian reservations" (*Bryan v. Itasca County*, 1972, 385). To clarify the boundaries of Public Law 280, the Supreme Court made explicit what the law left implicit: it expands only state criminal laws to the reservation and native nations retain noncriminal jurisdiction—that is, regulatory and civil authority. The county could enforce criminal laws on the reservation, but asserting its civil and regulatory laws, such as its tax code, violated tribal sovereignty. In this case, the Supreme Court first applied the distinction between the criminal laws that are the purview of Public Law 280 and regulatory and civil laws, a distinction that became pivotal when the Cabazon Band of Cahuilla Indians entered the gaming industry. Noting the importance of the precedent set by *Bryan v. Itasca County*, Kevin Washburn (2008, 921) wrote, "While *Cabazon* is an important case, its primary significance is that it followed *Bryan's* holding that Congress, in granting Minnesota jurisdiction over the tribe under Public Law 280, never conferred 'general state civil regulatory control over Indian reservations.'"

THE CABAZON DECISION AND
ITS AFTERMATH

This chapter bridges the historical and contemporary analyses of this book. It traces the political and cultural processes entailed in native nation revitalization from mid-twentieth-century to the present-day Indian casino movement. It shows how the Cahuilla's activism continues to be at the forefront of native nation revitalization across North America. While chapter 6 focuses on contemporary representations and the distribution of assumptions among the settler population, this chapter takes a specifically political and economic focus for two reasons. First, the political and economic revitalization of native nations, including the myriad court cases and policy changes, is complex enough to warrant separate treatment. Second, one foundational premise in cognitive anthropology is that political–economic systems and cultural knowledge shape each other. The dynamic between these political–economic and shared cognitive (i.e., cultural) processes can best be understood by examining each separately before discussing their influences on each other.

Events that are as mundane as someone buying a trailer can have monumental consequences for native nations. This is because tribal political sovereignty is in some ways comparable to the sovereignty of state governments. Tribes, like states, can function as laboratories for testing public policy (both in judicial courts and in the court of public opinion). The tribal casino movement began from similar, seemingly trivial events, such as a bingo parlor opened by the Seminole Indians of Florida, and a poker club opened by the Cabazon Band of Cahuilla Indians. The tribal casino movement emerged from native nations working to develop new economic engines. Their efforts were mostly synchronous, sometimes coordinated, and always informed by each other. With the *Cabazon* decision, native nations regained a significant, though still limited, dimension of their external political sovereignty: their right to control economic development.

The Cabazon Band of Cahuilla Mission Indians' victory before the U.S. Supreme Court affirmed the right of native nations across the United States to operate gaming facilities. Their efforts could not have been possible without the efforts of other native nations. In fact, gaming was only the latest in a series of native economic activities that native nations pursued to strengthen their self-determination through economic self-reliance. In the 1970s, seeking to further their economic development and seeing their separation from state and local governments as a unique marketing opportunity, many native nations experimented with selling alcohol and tobacco products to non-Indians. Because state and local taxes do not apply on tribal lands, these tribes maintained that they could sell alcohol and tobacco to non-Indians free from state and local taxes. Settlers flocked to tribal lands to purchase alcohol and tobacco without the added taxes. However, both of these practices were short lived. In 1979 the Supreme Court of the United States sided with Washington state in Washington's lawsuit against the Confederated Tribes of the Colville Reservation for selling cigarettes without state tax stamps to non-Indians (*Washington v. Confederated Tribes of the Colville Reservation*, 439 U.S. 463). In 1983 California was victorious before the Supreme Court in applying its state liquor taxes on Indian reservations (*Rice v. Rehner*, 463 U.S. 713). In both cases, the Supreme Court ruled that the tribes were not exercising their sovereignty, but merely marketing it to avoid state taxes. With these Supreme Court decisions the native nation sale of alcohol and tobacco to non-Indians became subject to state and local taxes, closing these windows for economic development. While tobacco and alcohol sales failed, gaming ultimately succeeded before the Supreme Court.

Gaming emerged as a viable opportunity for economic development in the late 1970s and early 1980s as the federal government continued taking actions to strengthen tribal sovereignty. In the 1980s President Ronald Reagan cut the federal budget for tribal services and encouraged tribes to exercise their sovereignty by investing in tribally operated economic development projects, including bingo and gaming (Wilkins 2007, 122). This further encouraged a number of tribes to begin offering gaming activities to non-Indians.

In 1976 the Oneida Nation of Wisconsin was among the first to open a gaming facility (bingo) in order to promote economic self-reliance (Hoeft

2014). Three years later, the Seminole in Florida pursued a similar strategy. The Seminole's bingo parlor quickly became the focus of the first federal case to test the legal feasibility of gaming as a strategy for tribal self-reliance. At the time the tribe opened a bingo hall, Florida allowed only one form of gambling—bingo—and only charities could operate bingo games. Furthermore, the Seminole's jackpots exceeded the state level of $100 and paid the employees who operated the games, violating state law. The county sheriff attempted to shutter the operation, claiming that state bingo laws applied on tribal lands. In 1981 a federal appeals court ruled in favor of the Seminoles, arguing that, under Public Law 280 and under the precedent of *Bryan v. Itasca County*, Florida has criminal but not civil or regulatory jurisdiction on tribal land (*Seminole Tribe v. Butterworth*). This was the first case in which such a distinction was made for determining the application of Public Law 280. The *Seminole* decision set a new precedent. With this decision, the court found that if an activity is prohibited by the state, it is illegal on tribal lands. But if the activity is regulated by the state, tribes are free to develop their own regulations. Florida regulated bingo, therefore it was a regulated and not a criminal activity that Seminoles could pursue, too. The Seminoles directed bingo revenue to benefit the education and health of their members, making substantial improvements in their tribal community at a time when there were few opportunities for economic development and federal funds were drying up (Cattelino 2008). A handful of other tribes experimented with gaming in the late 1970s and early 1980s, each facing legal challenges. The Oneida Nation of Wisconsin and the Seminoles of Florida were among the first to market gaming activities to non-Indians, setting the stage for the Cabazon Band of Cahuilla Indians to initiate gaming and eventually take the issue to the U.S. Supreme Court.

Ambrose Lane's book *Return of the Buffalo* (1995) offers an up-close account of how Cabazon came to open their enterprise with his in-depth interviews with Cabazon's leadership shortly after the *Cabazon* decision. In an interview with Lane, tribal advisor John Paul Nichols explained,

> We started talking about doing it in August [of 1980], and it really was a very innocent process. We thought Bingo was too risqué [*sic*]; that's why we didn't get into Bingo.... We picked something we thought we could win with in California....
>
> About the time we were closing the cigarette business, a newspaper story came out in the *Daily News*. It said [Hall of Fame major

league baseball player] Leo Durocher and a guy named Rocco were trying to get a license in the City of Coachella for a California-style cardroom. And, in fact, City Council had passed an ordinance saying that they could legalize a cardroom. But the City fathers, the conservatives, forced a referendum, went directly to a vote, and the cardroom lost....

Out of the original article, my dad and I and [then-tribal chairman] Art Welmas were sitting around one day and said, "If they [the Indio City Council] can do it [vote to allow a cardroom] why can't we?"... The whole intent was to replicate what they were doing. Out of that, Dad or Art wrote a letter to the L.A. Dodgers... and we got a phone call a few days later and Leo said, "I want to bring this guy Rocco down. Let's get together." That's how the whole thing started. (Lane 1995, 60–61)

As described in the extract above, Cabazon's idea for opening their poker club came from observing state and local politics. California law allows local governments to legalize poker clubs, often called card rooms, where the players play against each other (as opposed to betting against the house). The tribe chose poker because California law made a more clear-cut legal basis for opening a poker enterprise than bingo. Fully aware of Public Law 280 and suffering from the closure of their smoke shop after the *Washington* decision, they had a legal basis to open their own gaming operation. When they contacted Leo Durocher about potentially hosting and financing the casinos, he agreed to support the operation and Cabazon began making plans to convert their smoke shop into a poker club.

Cabazon openly advertised their plans, hired employees, and bought ads. They were certain of their right to open a poker club, but it would take nearly a decade for the court system, at its highest level, to formally recognize this right. Not long after they began their preparations, the police chief for the City of Indio, Sam Cross, ordered Cabazon to stop. Tribal members met with Cross, along with the Riverside County sheriff, the County Council, and others to explain their plans. John Paul Nichols recalled from the meeting, "We asked Sam Cross, why can't we have a civil disagreement—why can't we just walk into court and say we have a difference and do this without having to play cops and robbers? Why can't we settle our differences in a civil manner? I remember him saying, 'The blue army never tells the red army.' Why we were the red army, I don't know. And he said that like 'This is a game. I'm the blue army; I got all the uniforms; and we will squash you'" (Lane 1995, 61). The Cabazon's leadership was incredulous. The city of Indio could take exception to their poker club, but Cabazon's federally recognized political sovereignty entitled the native nation to pursue activities that are legal in California. However, Cabazon was cautious not to involve any potential customers in any police raids, even if such raids were unjust. The tribe held a test game, playing cards on the tables of the new poker club before opening to the public. The police came and observed their game. The tribe had hoped for the police to take action during the test game, allowing the case to go to court without any customers becoming involved. But the police took no action and would step in only once non-Indians began playing. The poker club opened on October 15, 1980; it was an immediate success with more than a hundred patrons. Nothing occurred for the first few days. Then, on October 18, the city of Indio Police Department raided the club, complete with riot gear. They arrested the employees and many customers, and issued citations to others. With their leadership under arrest and poker tables and chips confiscated, the legal battle for Cabazon's casino began (61–62).

Cabazon's attorney, Glen Feldman, filed for a temporary restraining order (TRO) and a preliminary injunction in a maneuver to reopen the club. U.S. District Court Judge Laughlin Water granted the injunction but not the TRO, allowing the club to reopen with the case pending. Cabazon maintained that their reservation was outside the Indio city limits, meaning the Indio Police Department had no jurisdiction. In 1970 the city of Indio tried to annex a portion of the Cabazon Reservation, including the location that later included the poker club. However, the city failed to obtain Cabazon's consent for the annexation. Three years later the BIA informed Indio that the annexation was void because, as a sovereign nation, the Cabazon Reservation could not become a part of the city without its approval. Feldman made this argument before Judge Waters, but on May 18, 1981, Waters sided with the city of Indio and dismissed the injunction, requiring the club to close. Waters ruled that while the annexation was illegal, Cabazon had never contested it before and the statute of limitations had expired. This legally rendered the reservation to be part of the city, even though the native nation never consented. Feldman responded quickly on behalf of the tribe, petitioning for a stay pending an appeal. Waters accepted Cabazon's argument that the tribe would be severely harmed by the loss of income from the club's closure; he allowed it to stay open while the case moved to the Ninth

Circuit Court of Appeals. On December 14, 1982, the Ninth Circuit Court ruled in favor of Cabazon, finding the band never needed to contest the annexation because it was void from the beginning (*The Cabazon Band of Mission Indians v. The City of Indio, California,* 694 F.2d 634). With the reservation firmly outside Indio city limits, Cabazon was free to continue operating its poker club. Indio could no longer interfere, but a new fight was brewing.

One year later, on February 15, 1983, the Riverside County Sheriff's Department raided Cabazon's club. In an interview with Ambrose Lane (1995, 65), Brenda James Soulliere, tribal officer and member of the business committee, recalled what happened:

> I was in the [money] cage.... Then they were banging on the door to open the cage, and I didn't know whether I should or not. Finally, I opened the door. They came in and...they confiscated the money and the chips and, I believe, I had to sign something of what they were taking. I remember there was one of our customers; her name was Roth I believe. She was a survivor of Auschwitz, I believe it was, because she had the numbers tattooed on her wrist or hand or something. She thought it was happening all over again. She was yelling. She was an older lady....
>
> They took everything that wasn't nailed down. I think I was there when they started bringing everything back. So we just kind of went on. We did the best we could, put everything back together and went on about our way. That's when the lawsuit started. We said, "You know, we're not going to sit back and take this." (Lane 1995, 65)

Cabazon found itself in the same situation that it was in before, with the poker club closed pending a legal challenge, though this time it was with the county. Riverside County surmised that Cabazon might not be located in the city of Indio, but it is located in the county, which prohibited gambling.

Appearing again before Judge Waters, Cabazon argued, through their attorney Feldman, that Riverside County failed to understand the implications of Public Law 280, especially given the recent *Seminole* decision. The county had criminal jurisdiction on the Cabazon Reservation, but poker clubs are not criminalized under California law. Furthermore, while the county had an ordinance prohibiting poker clubs, another poker club already existed in the county. The county took no action against that club, so why did it target Cabazon? Feldman argued that by going after Cabazon but not going after others who violated the ordinance, Riverside County violated the equal protection clause of the Fourteenth Amendment (U.S. Const. amend. 14). On February 24 Judge Waters accepted Cabazon's request for a TRO, allowing the poker club to remain open as the case progressed. By this time the Morongo Band had also begun a bingo operation and faced the same threats from the county, which sought to shut down their bingo parlor. Morongo pleaded its case before Judge Waters, making the same argument as Cabazon had made. Judge Waters granted Morongo a TRO on May 20. He combined Morongo's case with Cabazon's on October 31. Cabazon's case took the lead because it had started first. Also that day, California's attorney general asked for and was granted the power to intervene and take over the case from Riverside County (Rossom 2011, 16–17). It was now the small, impoverished native nations of Morongo and Cabazon against the State of California. In December 1983 Judge Waters issued a permanent injunction preventing the state and the county from interfering with Cabazon's and Morongo's gaming operations. California appealed, meaning that 1984 would begin with a battle between Cabazon and California before the Ninth Circuit Court of Appeals. In 1986 the Ninth Circuit agreed with Judge Waters's permanent injunction. California appealed again and the U.S. Supreme Court agreed to hear the case.

California's case rested on a number of claims regarding its right to enforce Riverside County's gambling laws on federally recognized native nations within the state's boundaries. California argued that under Public Law 280 state gambling laws applied throughout the state, including in reservations lying within the state's boundaries. According to California, tribal gambling was no different from a tribe selling cigarettes and alcohol tax free. California claimed that like Colville and Rice, Cabazon and Morongo were marketing what amounted to an exception from state law. Furthermore, the state asserted that gambling attracts organized crime, therefore it was only a matter of time before Cabazon would become entangled in organized crime. California claimed that under the Organized Crime Control Act (OCCA; Pub.L. 91-452), passed by the U.S. Congress in 1970, it had the right and responsibility to shut down tribal gaming enterprises before they became involved in organized crime.

Cabazon responded that, as decided in *Bryan v. Itasca County* and *Seminole Tribe v. Butterworth*, Public Law 280 did not grant states regulatory jurisdiction on tribal lands. Because California legalized and regulated gambling, it was not a criminal but rather a regulatory matter. Feldman put forward that Cabazon's poker club was in no way analogous to tax-free alcohol and cigarette sales. In the *Colville* and *Rice* decisions, native nations took goods manufactured off the reservation and imported them to the reservation for the sole purpose of selling them tax free. In those cases, the court found that the goods of value were produced off the reservations and the tribes' only contribution was importing them for tax-free sale. But Feldman argued that Cabazon's poker club was an entertainment experience produced on the reservation. Cabazon did not move goods inside reservation boundaries to make them tax exempt: they offered an entertainment service that they created by themselves on the reservation. California countered that even if that was the case, the Cahuilla nations have no cultural history of gambling and Cabazon entered the gambling industry only because it could attract customers who otherwise would have gone to other poker clubs in the state. Anthropologist Lowell Bean, referring to the Cabazon traditional high-stakes game of *peon,* testified, "Traditional gambling techniques have continued among these people from time immemorial until the present. Gambling has at no time in the history of the Cahuilla peoples ceased as a significant activity, including today" (Rossum 2011, 91). (See chapter 1 for more discussion of the role of *peon* in the Cahuilla origin story.) Not only was Cabazon's poker club a service generating revenue on its reservation (as opposed to goods produced off the reservation) but it was also part of an ongoing traditional practice of inviting neighboring communities to their territory in order to partake in high-stakes gambling. The technology may be different, but the Cahuilla nations have always held the tradition of inviting non-Cahuilla to their territory for high-stakes games of chance.

California's claim regarding the occa was even weaker. Feldman asserted that because occa is a federal law, federal and not state authorities are responsible for enforcing it. Furthermore, California had no evidence of organized crime at Cabazon's poker club, so it could not intervene even if it had the authority to enforce the occa.

In a 6–3 decision the Supreme Court agreed with Cabazon on February 25, 1987. The decision found that California can enforce its criminal laws on the reservation; once it legalized and regulated an activity, however, federally recognized native nations within the state were free to regulate that activity as they see fit. Cabazon was not marketing an exception, but rather had launched its own revenue-generating entertainment service. Cabazon could invite nonmembers to participate in games of wager as it had done so since prehistory. Any economic development strategy would be doomed to failure if its participation would be limited to only tribal members. Finally, the Supreme Court found there were no grounds for California to enforce the OCCA. This decision came at a time when cash-strapped states across the country were legalizing state lotteries. The *Cabazon* decision meant that each state that had legalized a state lottery had, unknowingly, enabled any federally recognized native nation within its boundaries to pursue gambling too. The *Cabazon* decision opened the door for those native nations that are located in states that regulate any kind of gambling to establish their own gambling enterprises. For a brief moment, for those tribes located in states that had some form of legalized gambling, the potential for tribal gaming was relatively limitless.

Congress was already considering laws to regulate tribal gaming before the *Cabazon* decision. With the decision there was a new sense of urgency. If tribes could open poker clubs and bingo parlors, what else could they do? Could they open Las Vegas–style casinos without any interference from the surrounding state? In 1988 Congress passed the Indian Gaming Regulatory Act (IGRA). This created the National Indian Gaming Commission to provide federal oversight of tribal gaming. The IGRA also defined three classes of gaming and delegated each class to specific regulatory agents. Class 1 consists of traditional tribal games of chance played among tribal members, such as *peon*, a game still played today by the Cahuilla and their neighboring native nations. Only native nations regulate Class 1 gaming. Class 2 includes bingo and certain non-banked card games, such as poker, where players bet against each other but not against the house. Those tribes in states that regulate some form of gambling (today all states except Utah and Hawaii regulate some form of gambling) can operate Class 2, and the federal authority of the National Indian Gaming Commission oversees those operations along with tribal authorities. The most lucrative forms of gaming are in Class 3, which is loosely worded to include slot machines, table games, and other forms of Las Vegas–style gambling where the patron bets against the house. Class 3 is highly regulated, with three different levels of regulatory agencies. Like Class 2, Class 3 requires oversight by tribal governments and the National Indian Gaming Commission. However, in an unprecedented move the IGRA also requires native nations to negotiate a regulatory agreement, known as a compact, with the surrounding state government. With the IGRA came the first time the federal government delegated regulatory functions to the states that surround native nations. Public Law 280 limited *Worcester v. Georgia's* prohibition of state interventions on tribal lands by granting certain state governments criminal jurisdiction over native nations; now the IGRA permitted states to regulate Class 3 gaming on native nation lands. These compacts can mandate tribes to allocate revenue into funds that mitigate negative impacts of tribal casinos, such as construction projects to relieve traffic congestion and support services for individuals with gambling problems.

Compact Conflict in California

After the passage of the IGRA, native nations across the United States began negotiations with state governments to reach compacts for Class 3 gaming. Californian politics posed what appeared to be an insurmountable obstacle—the state's refusal to negotiate in good faith. Ultimately, California tribes, led by a coalition of Cahuilla, Serrano, Luiseño, and Kumeyaay nations, achieved compacts and in the process demonstrated the desire for the settler population to support tribal sovereignty, even when their elected officials did not. In 1988, when the IGRA came into effect, California native nations began discussions with Governor George Deukmejian. Negotiations were difficult during Deukmejian's time in office, and became even more challenging when Governor Pete Wilson, a vocal opponent of tribal gaming, took office on January 4, 1991. Three times—in 1993, 1995, and 1996—the California legislature passed compact agreements with native nations, only for Governor Wilson to veto them. During this time the number of tribal casinos in the state grew rapidly from eleven to forty (Marks and Spilde Contreras 2007, 2). Many of these tribes, none of which had a compact, began offering slot machines, which California law prohibited. Offering slot machines and other Class 3 gaming at this time was an act of civil disobedience against the state of California, but not against the federal government. Ultimately, it paid off. The federal Justice Department stated that it would not intervene with tribal gaming while compact negotiations were still taking place in California (Rossum 2011, 169). California native nations could continue their gaming operations, but they had to continue negotiating with a governor determined to hold them back. Governor Wilson insisted that he would never sign a compact with a native nation that was already violating California law, such as the forty that were already operating casinos.

In 1998 Governor Wilson thought he had a plan to successfully restrict tribal gaming. Wilson negotiated a compact with one tribe, the Pala Band of Mission Indians, in northern San Diego County, and insisted that any other native nations that wanted a compact needed to agree to the terms of the Pala Compact. Many of California's native nations chafed at Wilson's proposition, protesting that the terms of the compact were unfavorable and overly restrictive. Moreover, by mandating that all native nations must accept the Pala Compact or be shut out of gaming entirely, Wilson treated native nations as if they were interchangeable, lacking diversity and independence. The Pala Compact restricted tribes to 975 slot machines, would not permit many popular video machines like blackjack and poker, and mandated that tribes permit their employees to unionize. Moreover, the Pala Compact granted county governments the right to veto the development of any tribal casino in its boundaries. This move would have allowed Riverside County to finally achieve the agenda it began fifteen years before when it attempted to close Cabazon's poker club.

Like so many settlers before him, Wilson refused to acknowledge the diversity of California native nations and severely underestimated their capacity to assert their right to self-determination. Though eleven native nations did agree to the terms of the Pala Compact, a new coalition, led by the San Manuel, Morongo, Agua Caliente, Cabazon, Pechanga, Viejas, Soboba, and Barona nations, formed to appeal directly to the voters of California (California Voter Foundation 1998). The coalition launched a petition for a ballot initiative that would legalize slot machines on Indian land and require the state to negotiate in good faith. Having collected more than the necessary signatures, the initiative qualified for the November 1998 ballot, where it became Proposition 5. California voters passed Proposition 5 overwhelmingly with 62 percent of the vote. At the time, the campaign for the initiative was the most expensive in the history of the state. The opposition, led by casinos based in Las Vegas, spent $29 million. Proposition 5 proponents spent a record $63.2 million. One month after Proposition 5 passed, the state courts declared it unconstitutional. In 1984 California had passed a constitutional amendment to create the state lottery system. This amendment also outlawed slot machines. Because Proposition 5 was not an amendment to the state constitution, it could not end the state prohibition of slot machines. However, Proposition 5's success did demonstrate that California voters supported tribal gaming even if their governor did not. Recognizing that support, the state legislature passed a bill to bring the matter back before voters. The new ballot measure, Proposition 1A, contained all of the specifications of Proposition

5, with the important difference that 1A was a constitutional amendment. In 2000 Proposition 1A, also known as the Gambling on Tribal Lands Amendment, succeeded with 65 percent of the vote. Since then, more than fifty California tribes have begun operating casinos. As before, in the termination era during Juan Antonio's leadership and at countless other times, when public policy constrained native nation sovereignty the native nations appealed to the public to recognize their rights and pressure policymakers to expand tribal external political sovereignty.

Propositions 94–97

Despite the significant and positive economic impact that tribal casinos, especially the more prosperous ones, have on their neighboring communities, Indian gaming in California remains controversial and subject to ongoing legal and political challenges. In 2007 a number of tribes in Southern California sought to renegotiate their compacts to raise the number of slot machines allowed. Five tribes—San Manuel, Agua Caliente, Pechanga, Sycuan, and Morongo—began negotiating with then-governor Arnold Schwarzenegger to raise their limit of slot machines from 2,000 to 7,500 in exchange for sharing a higher amount of revenue with the state. As these tribes pursued negotiations, a coalition opposing Indian gaming, known as Stand Up for California and backed by a coalition between the horse racing industry and Las Vegas Sands, a commercial casino corporation, began a petition opposing the compacts. Normally, compacts are negotiated among the tribe, governor, and state legislature. Stand Up for California succeeded in its petition to make these compacts subject to statewide ballot initiatives. While one tribe, San Manuel, negotiated and signed its compact before the coalition collected the required number of signatures, the other four tribes did not complete negotiations in time. Their four compact negotiations came before voters on the February 2008 ballot as Propositions 94–97. Propositions 94–97 passed, with each compact receiving approximately 55 percent of the vote. But what is perhaps more telling is that the neighboring communities were often the strongest supporters of the propositions (Miller 2008). This pattern held true even for San Bernardino, a city that neighbors San Manuel, which already had the new compact in effect and therefore was unlike the four tribes directly impacted by Propositions 94–97, that could stand to lose revenue as the neighboring casinos at Pechanga, Agua Caliente, Sycuan, and Morongo expanded. In chapter 6 I further examine Propositions 94–97 and suggest some possible explanations for the greater support by neighboring communities, even when it may have been against their own economic self-interest.

Overall, California tribes that operate casinos and tribes without casinos have experienced sharp increases in living standards with the wealth from gaming enterprises. (In California, gaming compacts require tribes with prosperous casinos to share revenue with tribes that lack casinos or have small casinos; Marks and Spilde Contrares 2007.) The few tribes with reservations and gaming operations near major population centers receive the majority of tribal gaming revenue. Because of revenue-sharing agreements, however, all federally recognized tribes in California have received some benefit from tribal gaming. Over the past decade the per capita income on tribal reservations has outpaced income growth for the rest of the California population (Marks and Spilde Contrares 2007). Some tribes, like the San Manuel Band of Mission Indians, had an unemployment rate of 75 percent before tribal gaming; currently, revenue from the tribe's casino funds the per capita payments to individual tribe members, investment in reservation infrastructure, health care, educational scholarships, and tribal cultural projects (Trafzer 2002).

Political and Economic Impacts

Most tribal casinos operate on Indian lands that are in geographically isolated and economically undeveloped regions. As discussed in chapter 2, this was an intentional strategy, pursued as part of state and federal agendas to advance settler colonialism. In the late nineteenth century federal and state bureaucrats removed native nations to reservations they determined held the fewest natural resources; these forced migrations took place in California, as well as in the rest of the United States. The location of Indian reservations in often isolated, economically underdeveloped regions have two striking impacts for tribal casino development. First, the disparities within the tribal casino industry cannot be overstated. The National Indian Gaming Commission regularly compiles reports on the revenue generated by tribal gaming, which show vast differences in the revenue generated by different tribal casinos. Tribal identities and locations are removed from their data, so one cannot discern the extent of disparities between particular tribes or within any given state, but their reports do illustrate the extent of these disparities nationwide. In 2013 each of the twenty-six most successful tribal gaming operations (5.6 percent of total operations) earned at least $250 million in revenue. These top twenty-six tribal casinos earned more than 40 percent of total tribal gaming revenue that year. In contrast, each of 252 tribal casinos (approximately 56 percent of the total) that earned less than $25 million accounted for only 7.4 percent of total tribal gaming revenue for that year (National Indian Gaming Commission 2014). In other words, the top 5 percent of tribal casinos earn more than 40 percent of total tribal casino revenue, while the bottom half account for less than 10 percent. Clearly, gaming by itself is no silver bullet for the poverty that is endemic on many reservations. Often, location alone is enough to undermine the potential for a tribal casino to reap a major financial success. Being close to a major city certainly helps the prospects for a tribal casino, but most native nations are simply too far away from population centers to achieve the kind of revenue earned by the top twenty-six operations. For native nations that, due to location or a cultural prohibition of gambling, cannot earn substantive revenue from a casino, the greater opportunity for sustainable economic development lies in their capacity for self-determination; that opportunity, though, is constrained primarily by previous or current federal policies. The deliberate removal of native communities to small, isolated reservations shaped the present-day disparity between the few prosperous tribes located near metropolitan areas and the vast majority of tribes.

The second striking impact of the location of tribal casinos in underdeveloped regions is that those that do draw significant numbers of non-Indians can have a tremendous impact on the local settler economy. Mindy Marks and Kate Spilde Contrares (2007) found that between 1990 and 2000 the per capita income of households within ten miles of a gaming reservation in California grew 55 percent, significantly higher than the 33 percent average increase across the state during that time. This growth occurred when tribal casinos were still operating in a legal gray area without state compacts. This growth is due to the increased demand for local labor, goods, and services, as well as to the fact that tribal casinos must be located on Indian lands, which are located in the poorest areas of the state. Marks and Spilde Contrares found that tribal casinos drew patrons from wealthier parts of the state, especially patrons with disposable incomes, to some of the poorest parts of the state, thereby providing a much-needed jolt to local economies. The larger tribal casinos and resorts employ thousands from neighboring communities and those employees are predominantly non-Indian. When a tribal casino draws customers to an otherwise underdeveloped area, it draws money into both tribal and neighboring settler communities.

William Thompson (2014) uses what he calls "the bathtub model" to analyze the impact of a casino on the surrounding community. This model is especially useful for understanding how tribal casinos can have stronger impacts on local economies than their commercial casino counterparts. The premise is that a local economy is like a bathtub: it will be fuller (or grow) when more wealth flows into it than out of it. When a local economy produces goods and services that are purchased by outsiders, money flows in. Likewise, when members of the local economy purchase goods and services from outside that economy, money flows out. When a casino attracts visitors who spend money on entertainment (principally gambling, but also theater, concerts, etc.), food, drinks, and merchandise, water pours into the tub. When a casino is owned by a corporation that is not located in the local economy (as is now the case for many casinos located in Las Vegas and Atlantic City), some of the money that flows in through the casino leaves the local economy, to be returned as profit to the parent company. In turn, that profit may be distributed to shareholders who could live anywhere in the world. If most of a casino's patrons are from the local economy, and an outside company owns the casino, there could be even less money flowing into the community. Instead, money could flow out. Like a tub with only a little water dribbling in from a faucet while the plug is pulled, this scenario can quickly dry up an economy. This analogy is particularly useful when considering the differences between tribal and commercial casinos. The IGRA mandates that tribal casino revenue can flow only to the tribal government, where it may be used only for improvements to the tribal community or distributed evenly among tribal members. In other words, with commercial casinos, the revenue can be drained out of a community and flow to shareholders who live elsewhere. With tribal casinos, tribal sovereignty and federal regulations at least partially clog the drain, stemming the loss of revenue to outside investors. Tribal casinos are often managed by outside firms that are predominantly non-Indian. The IGRA prohibits these firms from charging more than 30 percent of casino revenue, however, putting a plug on the drain. As revenue stays within the tribal community, prosperity rises, especially when the casino draws primarily from non-Indians off the reservation. This scenario is common among many, but not all, tribal casinos in Southern California. In this case, much of the revenue that leaves the tribal community flows directly into the surrounding settler communities. For example, San Manuel has an adult population of slightly more than a hundred adult members, but a workforce of more than three thousand employees. With most of their employees coming from the surrounding communities, revenue flows into households in Riverside and San Bernardino Counties. Furthermore, their proximity to Los Angeles, which has poker clubs but lacks gaming of the variety and scale found at San Manuel, ensures a steady stream of revenue from Los Angeles not just to San Manuel, but also to the economically underdeveloped interior of Southern California.

Reservation Shopping

The settler colonial practice of removing native peoples from their land resulted in California having a few areas, like inland Southern California, that are home to many reservations, while most regions, especially the wealthiest, are devoid of Indian reservations. By the design of federal and state authorities, the regions with the most reservations tend to be among the poorest and most isolated regions in the state. Additionally, the remote location of many reservations provides little opportunity for substantive casino development. Because of these factors, many native nations have ancestral ties to locations that could be developed into successful casinos, but those nations have been removed to isolated areas where there is less opportunity. A few tribes have proposed a controversial solution to this problem: petition the Department of the Interior to have off-reservation land placed in trust in order to let the tribe develop a casino in an area away from their reservation but in their ancestral homeland. This process, known sometimes by its critics as reservation shopping, is often successful when the land to be put in trust is located within twenty-five miles of a tribe's reservation, but recent attempts to create in trust land farther away have not been successful. In 2006 the Big Lagoon Rancheria and the Los Coyotes Band of Cahuilla worked with casino developers and Barstow city politicians to create in trust land for the tribes near Barstow so the city could benefit from tribal casino operations. The proposed site was 150 miles from the Los Coyotes reservation and more than 750 miles from the Big Lagoon Rancheria, far from either's ancestral territory (Marquez 2006). To date Barstow and the tribes have been unsuccessful in bringing tribal gaming to Barstow, but their attempt concerned other tribes that trace ancestry to this land. While serving as tribal chairman of the San Manuel Band of Mission Indians, Deron Marquez wrote,

> The ancestral lands of my people...cover an area that includes Barstow.... San Manuel strongly supports the rights of tribes to

develop their ancestral lands as a basic and fundamental principle. To that end, we have made clear that we would not oppose a land acquisition by the Chemehuevi Tribe—even for gaming purposes—because the Chemehuevi also have ancestral ties to the Barstow area. However, we also very much support the basic and fundamental principle that an outside casino developer should not exploit a tribe's status and attempt to move that tribe hundreds of miles away to develop a casino on the ancestral land of another tribe. (Marquez 2006, 12)

For Marquez, reservation shopping would be an exploitation of a tribe's status if the tribe has no ancestral connection to the affected location. His support for a Chemehuevi casino, but not for one owned by Big Lagoon Rancheria, illustrates how his opposition is not primarily motivated by economics, but rather from cultural considerations. Big Lagoon Rancheria claimed that its connection to the Barstow area was spiritual and acknowledged the lack of any empirical archaeological or ethnohistorical connection. After much publicity and controversy surrounding reservation shopping cases in Barstow and other locations, the Bureau of Indian Affairs (BIA) clarified that it will not support tribal requests to annex land that is more than twenty-five miles from its reservation. Controversy and BIA limits aside, tribal gaming has prompted the modest expansion of some reservations in contrast to the history of native nations losing land to settlers.

The San Manuel *Decision*

Most federal laws do not specifically mention whether they apply to tribes. In 1960 the Supreme Court ruled that if a federal law does not specifically stipulate whether it applies to tribes, courts may interpret whether the law applies. When interpreting if such a law does apply to tribes, courts can consider whether the law would negatively impact tribal sovereignty (*Federal Power Commission v. Tuscarora Indian Nation*, 362 U.S. 99). Thus, when tribal governments participate in unprecedented activities like gaming, those activities become the subject of court battles over which federal laws apply. The recent interpretation of one federal law, the National Labor Relations Act (NLRA; Pub.L. 49-449, 1935), may be especially troubling for tribes engaged in gaming or any enterprise.

The NLRA limits the actions an employer can take in response to labor organizations and establishes regulations for how employees can collectively bargain with employers. The NLRA applies only to private sector employees, and not to government workers. The NLRA created the National Labor Relations Board (NLRB) as a judicial panel to hear cases regarding labor relations in the private sector. Two aspects of the NLRA are especially important for understanding how similarities and differences between the NLRA and the tribes' own labor relations ordinances. First, under the NLRA, if employees are to form a labor union they must file a petition with the NLRB that shows support from at least 30 percent of employees. The NLRB, upon receiving the petition, then holds a secret ballot election in which employees vote for or against union representation. If the union receives the majority of votes, the employer must recognize that union. Second, an employer is not allowed to influence which union will represent its employees. The NLRA does not specify whether it applies to tribal lands, but only that it applies to the private sector and not the public sector. Until recently, the NLRB asserted its jurisdiction on tribal lands only in cases where a private corporation leases tribal land. This precedent began in 1976, when the NLRB examined whether it had jurisdiction over the Fort Apache Timber Company (226 NLRB 503 1976). In this case, the White Mountain Apache tribe, based in Arizona, owned the company and determined all employment policies. The NLRB ruled that it did not have jurisdiction because the Fort Apache Timber Company was a tribal government entity operating on tribal land. The NLRB held this precedent until the development of tribal gaming.

This reversal originated from a labor union campaign to organize tribal casino workers. California included in its tribal gaming compacts that tribes must enact tribal labor laws (known as Tribal Labor Relations Ordinances) that permit labor relations similar to those in the NLRA. California negotiated a model Tribal Labor Relations Ordinance (TLRO) that the state requires that tribes adopt in order to have a gaming compact. Tribes may negotiate additions to the model TLRO, but the TLRO must allow employees to form unions through card-signing procedures similar to those outlined in the NLRA. (See Kamper 2010 for more on TLRO and tribal sovereignty.) Before state compacts created this model, the Viejas Band of Kumeyaay Indians voluntarily enacted its own labor relations policies. In 1998 Viejas, located outside San Diego, and the Communications Workers of America (CWA) signed a labor agreement. Speaking at the California Indian Gaming Summit, Viejas chairman Anthony Pico explained, "Some of this was driven by the tribe itself because we felt that the unions were natural allies with Native Americans" (DeArmond

2000). Pico also noted that the CWA supported Proposition 5, the first tribal casino compact ballot initiative. However, while Viejas and other tribal governments, including San Manuel, welcomed the CWA to unionize their employees, another union, the Hotel Employees and Restaurant Employees (HERE) did not receive the same welcome.[1]

Ultimately, San Manuel's decision to welcome the CWA but not HERE led to the NLRB reversing its decades-long precedent of not applying the NLRA to tribally owned corporations operating on tribal land. This dispute began in 1999 when HERE filed grievances with the NLRB, charging that San Manuel gave preferential treatment to the CWA. HERE asserted that San Manuel let the CWA place a trailer in the employee parking lot to solicit employees, while denying similar access to HERE organizers. This would be a violation of the NLRA because the NLRA forbids an employer from favoring one labor organization over another. The question at the center of this case was whether a casino owned by a tribal government and located on tribal lands is a government or a private enterprise. In 2004 the NLRB ruled that it has jurisdiction over the casino and ordered the tribe to give HERE access to employees at the casino. The tribe petitioned a federal court of appeals, arguing that under the *Fort Apache Timber* decision the NLRA did not apply to the casino. In 2007 the federal court of appeals sided with the NLRB (*San Manuel Band of Mission Indians v. NLRB*, D.C. 05-1392).

The court's decision reversed the thirty-year precedent. The U.S. Court of Appeals, District of Columbia Circuit, outlined a continuum of tribal activities where "many activities of a tribal government fall somewhere between a purely intramural act of reservation governance and an off-reservation commercial enterprise" (*San Manuel* Decision 12). According to the court, on this continuum the San Manuel Casino "was primarily commercial" (*San Manuel* Decision 15). In their reasoning, the casino is primarily commercial because "operation of a casino is not a traditional attribute of self-government" and "the vast majority of the Casino's employees and customers are not members of the Tribe, and they live off the reservation" (*San Manuel* Decision 16). Therefore, according to the *San Manuel* decision, the NLRA applies to tribal lands because the majority of casino employees and patrons are non-Indians. Moreover, the court found that the casino could not be a governmental enterprise because, in the court's view, governments do not traditionally operate casinos and the NLRA would not interfere with tribal sovereignty. It is important, and arguably problematic, that the court ruled that tribal sovereignty exists along a continuum. According to the ruling, a tribe's sovereignty is strongest when governing matters that affect only tribal members, and weakest when a tribe engages in economic activity that reaches beyond the reservation. In other words, the more a tribe engages in business with those outside the reservation, the more likely it is that courts will intervene to limit the tribe's abilities to become self-sufficient. This ruling could set a dangerous precedent. Similar to all nations, native nations cannot have economic development if they cannot trade with their neighbors and they can benefit tremendously from growing economically interdependent with their neighbors. After the *San Manuel* decision, the federal government can cease to acknowledge the sovereignty of any tribal enterprise that engages in commerce with nonmembers. This decision applies a newly emerging shared assumption about native nations, which misconstrues tribes as essentially for-profit, private corporations (see the next chapter for further discussion).

As of this writing the precedent set by the *San Manuel* decision is being upheld, but it is not without its challengers. Two recent rulings by the Sixth Circuit Court of Appeals, *NLRB v. Little River* and *Soaring Eagle v. NLRB*, demonstrate how the courts remain divided even as the precedent is upheld. Both involve union-organizing activities at tribal casinos and the question of whether the NLRA should apply to a tribal enterprise. Decided on June 9, 2015, *Little River* applied the new precedent from *San Manuel* in its finding that the NLRA does apply to a casino operated by the Little River Band of Ottawa Indians. Concurrent with the *Little River* case, the Sixth Circuit Court of Appeals heard *Soaring Eagle v. NLRB*. Although both cases involve the same circuit court, they each had a different panel of judges. On July 1, 2015, less than a month later, the court in the *Soaring Eagle* case found that "if writing on a clean slate, we would conclude that…the Tribe has an inherent sovereign right to control the terms of employment with nonmember employees at the Casino" (*Soaring Eagle* Decision 27). However, given the *Little River* ruling one month earlier, the court was not writing on a clean slate. In a decision that thoroughly critiques the logic of *San Manuel,* the court in *Soaring Eagle* argued that the earlier *Little River* ruling forced them to apply the NLRA to the Soaring Eagle Casino. In *Soaring Eagle* the court was reluctant to impose the NLRA for the following reasons: "(1) the fact that the Casino is on trust land and is considered a unit of the Tribe's government; (2) the importance of the Casino to tribes' governance and its ability to provide member services; and (3) that [employees] voluntarily entered into an employment relationship with the Tribe" (*Soaring Eagle* Decision 26). Moreover, the court asserted that,

> to the extent Congress already has acted with respect to Indian sovereignty and Indian gaming, it has shown a preference for protecting such sovereignty and placing authority over Indian gaming squarely in the hands of tribes. In the same year Congress enacted the NLRA, it also passed the Indian Reorganization Act of 1934 to move federal policy away from a goal of assimilation.... Thus, although Congress was silent regarding tribes in the NLRA, it was anything but silent regarding its contemporaneously-stated desire to expand tribal self-governance. (*Soaring Eagle* Decision 26)

The judges of the Sixth Circuit Court of Appeals are clearly divided on whether the NLRA should apply. While *Little River* applied *San Manuel*, *Soaring Eagle* showed that another court panel was troubled by *San Manuel*. The *Soaring Eagle* decision found that Congress did not intend to include tribal enterprises in the NLRA because the Indian Reorganization Act, which Congress had passed the same year, showed Congress's explicit intent to support tribal self-governance. Citing the divisions within the Sixth Circuit, both tribes tried to appeal their case to the Supreme Court. On June 27 the Supreme Court declined to hear their appeal, leaving *San Manuel* as the current precedent. A spokesperson for Saginaw Chippewa Indian Tribe responded, "The law in this area is—to put it charitably—a mess" (Iafolla 2016).

With the conflicted courts upholding *San Manuel* and the Supreme Court declining to hear appeals on the matter, the most direct avenue for reversing the *San Manuel* precedent might be through legislative action. On November 17, 2015, the House of Representatives passed the Tribal Labor Sovereignty Act (HR-511), that would amend the NLRA's definition of employers affected by the law so that the NLRA would specifically exclude "any Indian tribe, or any enterprise or institution owned and operated by an Indian tribe and located on its Indian lands" (HR-511 Section 2). The House of Representatives passed the act on November 17, 2015, and the Senate received it the following day. However, President Barack Obama threatened to veto the act unless it was amended to exempt from the NLRA only those tribes that have Tribal Labor Relations Ordinances that offer the same worker protections as the NLRA (Indianz.com 2015). Ultimately, this act never became law, but the potential exists for it, or something similar, to eventually become law. In the years to come, it will be important to watch the continued fallout from *San Manuel* because of its potential to impact more than just tribal labor relations and to impact the boundaries of native nations' capacities for self-determination.

Conclusion: The Return of Cahuilla External Sovereignty

In retrospect, the activism of organizations, such as MIF and Spokesmen and Committee, during the first half of the twentieth century was a harbinger of a coming tribal resurgence. In the middle of the twentieth century termination threatened tribal sovereignty across the United States, but this threat served only to strengthen the resolve of American Indian activists and to encourage them to unite in strategies to both lobby Congress and to appeal to the public to support policies that recognize and strengthen native nation sovereignty. Tribal gaming emerged as part of a nationwide movement to revitalize tribal sovereignty. In the 1970s and 1980s the Oneida Indian Reservation in Wisconsin, the Seminole Tribe of Florida, Cabazon, and Morongo, joined by others across the United States, began exploring new ways to raise revenue, even if it meant testing the boundaries of their external political sovereignty. As illustrated in this and the previous chapters, testing those boundaries with tribal gaming was part of a long history of Cahuilla nations working to strengthen their sovereignty. When Durocher's original plan for a poker club in the Coachella Valley failed to materialize, the Cabazon Band seized the opportunity, followed by the Morongo Band, to open their own poker clubs. While other native nations were pursuing this strategy, the repercussions of Cabazon's act of civil disobedience successfully challenged California's expectations about when states can intervene on Indian lands.

The present landscape of native nation political sovereignty is uneven and in flux. The success of any particular native nation's gaming operation depends on a variety of unpredictable factors, not the least of which are the wider economy and the constantly shifting landscape of laws and court rulings. Native nations across the United States now have wider range to exercise their sovereignty, yet only a few, including some Cahuilla nations, have attained significant wealth and political influence. Even among those few, as the *San Manuel* decision demonstrates, the legal frameworks that underpin their revitalization are under constant challenge. As in the past, native nations take the lead in their revitalization; their efforts can succeed in large part because they reach out to build alliances with members of the settler population. For example, when the governor of California refused to negotiate compacts directly with native nations, these nations, led in large part by a coalition of native nations in Southern California, organized to provide voters with the opportunity to override the governor. As tribal gaming has grown, so has the economic and political influence of native nations across the United States, and, in particular, in California. This growth has significant implications for the distribution and structure of cultural knowledge that, in turn, can impact the political and economic processes that underpin the success of tribal gaming. The next chapter explores how the growth of the tribal gaming industry impacts the sources and distribution of the different settler assumptions about their native neighbors.

Notes

1. In 2004 HERE merged with the Union of Needletrades, Industrial, and Textile Employees, and is now UNITE HERE.

6

CONTESTED KNOWLEDGE

THE CENTRAL ARGUMENT of this book is that native nations often strengthen their sovereignty by appealing directly to settlers. We see this strategy in Juan Antonio's speech to the county judge and in Santos Manuel leading his nation to live beside the settlement of San Bernardino. This strategy was also present when tribal activists resisted termination by embarking on public campaigns and when Agua Caliente collaborated with the *Press Enterprise* to expose the guardianship scandal. Today, the practice of appealing directly to settlers continues. In particular, those native nations that earn substantial revenue from casino enterprises have more opportunities than ever before to represent themselves directly to the public. Ad campaigns, powwows, television programs, museums, and even the casinos themselves are where those native nations with the resources can educate the public. Yet native nations are still far from being on an even playing field in the contest to shape settler knowledge. In particular, public education, media, and political ads continue to reinforce the tired stereotype that Indians are passive or incapable of governing themselves. With the advent of tribal gaming, settler knowledge of native nations is more contested than ever before. In the first part of this chapter I analyze the form and content of the various representations of native nations prevalent across Southern California to identify the consistencies and discrepancies in the information that residents of this area are commonly exposed to. In particular the first part looks at the ways the Cahuilla and other native nations represent themselves to the public to challenge common misconceptions. This part also examines the ways government officials and institutions (especially public education), along with opponents of tribal casinos, often disseminate simplistic representations of native history and culture. The second part of this chapter uses evidence from surveys of and interviews with nonnatives in order to examine the different kinds of settler knowledge of and assumptions about native nations. The data presented in the second part of this chapter suggest a wide variety in settler knowledge, which may correlate with the different kinds of experiences settlers have with native nations. I begin with public education, which is a widely shared experience that imprints children with a narrative that lays the foundation for their future conceptions—and misconceptions—of native nations.

Education

The California Department of Education establishes the required content for public schools across the state; until 2016 it sanctioned representations of California Indians that are a modern-day iteration of the mission nostalgia described in chapter 3. California's state history curriculum is described in full in *History—Social Framework* (California State Board of Education 2017); this document explains in detail what content students are to learn at each grade level. Individual school districts and teachers have some leeway to add local history to the state curriculum, while the state establishes the minimum requirements. Some schools have gone above and beyond the state requirements, but the state required content for California Indians has been shallow, partial, and often fallacious. In 2012 *Content Standards'* only state-required historical content about California Indians occurred in fourth grade, when students learned about tribes prior to and immediately after contact. In many schools the curricula centered on a project in which students construct dioramas of California missions, complete with representations of the missionaries and Indians working together (California State Board of Education 2012). Many teachers and schools included additional, and more accurate, information about the impact of the missions. However, any teachers who followed the state minimum would have swept aside the violence of the mission era. As described earlier in this book, the Spanish missions were sites of forced labor and religious conversion. Having students learn about these missions by constructing dioramas is not unlike requiring students to learn about slavery by making replicas of plantations, complete with slaves and masters. It romanticizes exploitation by making sites of brutality appear peaceful and quaint. Fortunately, in 2016 the California Board of Education made sweeping changes to the fourth-grade social studies curricula. The new standards require that "attention should focus on the daily experience of missions rather than the building structures themselves. Building missions from sugar cubes or popsicle sticks does not help students understand the period and is offensive to many" (California State Board of Education 2017, 13). Instead, the new framework suggests that instruction should focus on the ways missions disrupted the lives of many California Indians. While this is a change for the better, many students who took fourth grade before the new framework received instruction in romantic images of an idyllic past. Likewise, the new framework requires fourth-grade students to learn about "the different kinds of governments in California, including the state government structures in Sacramento, but also the governments of local cities and towns, Indian Rancherias and reservations" (California State Board of Education 2017, 35). Students who took fourth grade before 2017 have not had the benefit of these new guidelines. Thus, until 2017 (when the new framework was first implemented), public schools across the state taught a mostly fictional narrative about California Indians, focused on assimilation, with the Spanish peacefully converting natives to Christianity and teaching them European skills. The frequent television, radio, and outdoor ads promoting tribal casinos ensure that the students and graduates of this system are quite aware of the presence of tribes in present-day California. But until recently most Californians were educated according to state requirements that provided no link between the past and present lives of California Indians. It will take years to measure the impact of the new framework, but it at least signals a future where settlers in California will be exposed to more nuanced, and more accurate, information about the state's indigenous peoples.

Trafzer and Lorimer's (2014) analysis of California history textbooks demonstrates that publishers have refused to include California's history of genocide, even though the state educational board requires that students learn about genocide and textbook consultants have recommended California be included as a site of genocide. The California State Board of Education's *Model Curriculum for Human Rights and Genocide* (2000) mandates that social studies classes and their textbooks accurately and sensitively educate students about genocide. As a result of this policy, social studies curricula cover injustices suffered by populations across the world, including the Holocaust and the enslavement of Africans. The *Model Curriculum for Human Rights and Genocide* serves an important purpose: future generations need to learn from these atrocities. Yet the atrocity that occurred closest to home for Californians, the genocide of California Indians, has been notably absent from textbooks (though hopefully the new framework will address this shortfall). This absence continues in spite of the efforts of publishers' textbook consultants, including Clifford Trafzer (Trafzer and Lorimer, 68). Rather than focus on the state's culturally diverse native populations or on human rights abuses endured by many of these populations, California school curriculum, until recently, has consistently presented the colonial pioneer mythology of white settlers finding gold and developing the early state without any assistance, coerced or otherwise, from the California Indians. Trafzer and Lorimer found that in the few textbooks that include California Indians in the gold rush, Indians are represented as antagonists attacking settlers. As discussed in chapter 2, the settlers and natives raided each other, and the conflict was far from one sided, with state-funded settler militias seeking to indiscriminately exterminate all natives. Given that publishers are aware of the California genocide and that the state requires that genocide is included in social studies curricula, but continue to omit the atrocities endured by California Indians, Trafzer and Lorimer (80) conclude that this absence continues because "textbook publishers would lose sales if they presented the genocide. Politicians and government staff would have to acknowledge their shortcomings and might be forced to recognize that California Indians have legitimate claims against federal, state, and local governments." The false assimilative myth that fourth graders had to construct in their mission dioramas, and the omission of the gold rush genocide, serve a specific agenda. By erasing historical injustices, school curricula delegitimize attempts by native nations to seek justice. Fortunately, more and more individual public-school districts and teachers now work to provide a more inclusive history than the minimum required by the state.

Frustrated by the state's inability to reform its social studies curricula, many California native nations have taken it upon themselves to partner with local school districts to fill this gap in historical and cultural knowledge. One example includes San Manuel's annual California Native American Day activities hosted by California State University, San Bernardino. Since its inception in 1999, more than 45,000 students and other members of the public have attended their events, which include speakers and performers for elementary school students and conferences for teachers interested in providing a more accurate and inclusive education than the state's problematic curricula (California Native American Day 2015).

In Palm Springs, Agua Caliente is now partnering with the local school district to help students understand their native neighbors.

Beginning in the 2018–19 school year, the Palm Springs Unified School District will offer a Native American studies curriculum in partnership with the Agua Caliente Band of Cahuilla Indians. The purpose of the curriculum is to increase the local population's understanding of Agua Caliente's past and present. Tribal chairman Jeff Grubbe explained, "Since they go to school on our land [the school is on reservation land], we want to share our history" (Ung 2017). By reaching out to local public schools, both San Manuel and Agua Caliente are continuing a strategy repeated throughout their postcontact history: they are finding ways to build connections with their neighbors by educating them.

In the Casino

A few native nations now operate casinos that attract many non-Indians to reservation casinos; these casinos have a unique opportunity to capitalize on their increased visibility by presenting their history and culture to the public as they see fit. In *Casino and Museum*, Bodinger de Uriarte (2007, 33) analyzed the largest tribal casino in North America, the Foxwoods Casino and Resort, which is owned by the Mashantucket Pequot. He found that at Foxwoods, "while 'the Indian' plays a major role in Foxwoods design and thematics, this same popular notion is challenged at crucial points and in part by the very scale of the complex.... [Although these sites] resist simple categorization as counterhegemonic...Mashantucket projects of self-representation and industry reflect...oppositional responses to existing hegemonic orders." In Southern California many tribal casinos follow similar practices where self-representations in the casino challenge common assumptions. While casino patrons may visit just for the entertainment experience of gambling, they may also come home having seen, and perhaps having contemplated, representations that question settler colonialism. During my visits to these casinos from 2008 to 2012 I found a few that fully embrace the possibility of informing the public about their cultural history, and some that are, except for their location on a reservation, mostly indistinguishable from commercial casinos. Because decisions on whether to incorporate native themes into the casino décor are made by casino management, with oversight from the tribal government, the variations between casinos demonstrate, to a certain extent, the potential combinations of marketing and native self-representation strategies. The marketing and self-representational motives are not mutually exclusive yet might pose challenges for representing the native identity as authentic while marketing the casino as a site of entertainment. Below I describe in detail the format of three tribal casinos in Southern California. The casinos at the Sycuan, Rincon, and Pechanga Reservations take significantly different approaches to self-representation. I suggest that these casinos can be seen along a continuum with counter-narrative at one extreme, self-effacement at the other, and native aesthetic in the middle.

Sycuan: A Counter-Narrative

The Sycuan Casino in San Diego County is perhaps the strongest example in Southern California of a tribal casino's potential to challenge patrons' understandings of tribal culture and national history. In the bridge between the casino and the parking garage, the Sycuan Band of the Kumeyaay nations prominently display the Treaty of Santa Ysabel. When I observed the framed replica of this treaty in late 2010 it was posted with an interpretive sign that read,

> In 1851 through 1852 United States treaty commissioners negotiated a treaty with the various bands of the Kumeyaay nations. The treaty would have set aside a very large reservation for the Kumeyaay people.
>
> But under pressure from the state of California, the United States Senate did not ratify the treaty. It was hidden under an *"injunction of secrecy"* [emphasis in the original] until 1905.
>
> By treating with the Kumeyaay for land, the United States thereby acknowledged that the land rightfully belonged to the Kumeyaay. Because no Kumeyaay lands were ceded to the United States by an unratified treaty, all Kumeyaay lands presumably continue to be the rightful possession of the Kumeyaay nations....
>
> "...Critical to the status and rights of American Indians are treaties that were negotiated in good faith but were not ratified by the Senate. If Indian treaties have the same dignity—that is, legal standing—as the treaties of foreign nations, then the United States should not claim lands cited in treaties it formally rejected."
>
> —Vine Deloria Jr.

Across the hall from the treaty and interpretive sign hung a map of precontact Kumeyaay territory overlaid with the present-day cities of San Diego County and the federally recognized Kumeyaay reservations. Taken together, these displays directly confront casino patrons with a Kumeyaay perspective of history, backed by the historical facts of the treaty, the injunction of secrecy, the disparity between the United States' recognition of foreign and native nations, and the extent of Kumeyaay territory taken illegally by settlers. Through this display, Sycuan Casino is informing its patrons, many of whom live in the greater San Diego area, that they are not guests on an Indian reservation only when they visit a casino. Instead, they are visitors on Indian land even when they go about their daily life in San Diego County. Sycuan's display informs their patrons that the entirety of this area still belongs to the Kumeyaay, who assert that they have a right to exercise self-determination over it but have been denied the dignity to exercise this right.

Like Bodinger de Uriarte (2007), I see this strategy of in-casino self-representation as an explicit counter-narrative because it, as directly as possible, confronts patrons with claims that challenge the commonly held settler assumption that tribal lands are restricted to the reservation. I refer to this style of self-representation as counter-narrative in order to contrast it with other kinds of self-representation used by other tribes and their casinos. In the counter-narrative strategy, the patron is informed upfront, before entering the casino (and once again when leaving), that the Kumeyaay continue to claim ownership of most of San Diego County as well as the northernmost portion of Mexico's Baja de California. No doubt this territory includes the homes of most Sycuan patrons. The counter-narrative is straightforward: none of their land actually belongs to the United States. Of course, while these displays are ubiquitous, any patron intent on heading directly to the game of his or her choice will not be stopped and confronted with this counter-narrative. However, as discussed later in this chapter, many patrons do stop, read displays like these, and learn something.

Pechanga: Native Aesthetic

If the Sycuan Casino incorporates elements to directly challenge the commonly received perception of settlers, the Pechanga Casino, near Temecula in southwest Riverside County, subtly incorporates a native aesthetic that, in most cases, only an observer with knowledge of Luiseño culture and symbolism would recognize. To most patrons the Pechanga Casino has a pleasing abstract aesthetic décor, but without patterns in the motif that a person could identify with any particular cultural tradition. Katherine Spilde Contrares provided insight into the decision-making processes behind this strategy:

The tiles in the bathroom, for example, or the wall hangings in the entrance to the conference center, were inspired by petroglyph designs found in Temecula's surrounding mountains.... The mural above the hotel front desk was painted to portray the eagle's nest located on the Pechanga Reservation, and the baskets in the Cabaret Bar display the renowned basket weaving skills of the Luiseño women. The decision to incorporate but not emphasize tribal cultural elements derives from the tribe's philosophy that the Pechanga Hotel and Casino is a tribal business and not a political statement. "We don't need to prove we're Indian," said [tribal official Anthony] Miranda. "We know who we are. If you know our culture, you know that the snake design [on the floor of the hotel lobby] was part of our traditional puberty ceremony.... If you don't know that, it's just a cool-looking design," said Miranda. (Spilde Contrares 2006, 330)

These "cool-looking" designs hold significance for what must be only a small fraction of casino patrons. For tribal members, these designs are significant for Luiseño heritage of the casino. However, only a handful of non-Indians visiting, perhaps a native history buff or the occasional anthropologist, would know the significance. This is not to say that the casino is devoid of any widely recognizable markings of tribal ownership. Framed historic photographs of tribal ancestors decorate the walls in certain parts. A mural above the entrance to a conference area includes sketches of tribal ancestors against the night sky, as if they are looking down from the heavens. A central bar is located in a circle around a multistory, lighted representation of an oak tree, a tree sacred to the Luiseño. Yet none of these representations are accompanied by any interpretive displays to provide the patron with context and nothing directly challenges settler assumptions. The decorations appear "tribal," but only someone with intimate knowledge of Pechanga's history would recognize the individuals represented. As Miranda related to Spilde, this strategy was chosen, in part, because they saw no "need to prove we're Indian." From this perspective, there is no need to assert the authenticity of Pechanga's identity; attempting to assert authenticity might, in effect, normalize challenges to their identity. This is what I refer to as the native aesthetic strategy because the incorporation of designs significant to tribes separates the casino from commercial casinos, but there are no explicitly counter-narrative elements. For tribal members the Pechanga

Casino is not just any casino—it is uniquely Pechanga, with cultural significance on the walls, carpets, and the centerpiece to the central bar. For the vast majority of patrons, its motifs make it look different from a typical casino and the pictures of ancestors mark it as connected to a certain historical context, but that context is never provided. It is just a "cool-looking" and different style.

Rincon: Native-Effacing

At the time of my visit, from inside Harrah's Rincon Casino, there was no reason to suspect that it is a native-owned and native-operated casino located on an Indian reservation. There are no cultural or historical displays and there is no native aesthetic recognizable to the layperson or anthropologist. The gift shop does not sell Indian-related wares. This casino, managed by Harrah's, which lends its name to the establishment, has the lights, chandeliers, high ceilings, and décor common to commercial casinos, without any suggestion of the native context in which it operates. It is, in many ways, indistinguishable from a commercial casino. Of course, this is not to say that its patrons are unaware that they have traveled to an Indian reservation. The Rincon Reservation is located in a relatively remote section of the mountains of northern San Diego County. The winding road to the casino takes visitors past a sign welcoming them to the Rincon Reservation, and the tribally operated Rincon Tribal Fire Department sits across the street from the casino. This casino stands apart from the other tribal casinos discussed above because it has few, if any, representations of its tribal ownership. Its design lies on the opposite extreme from Sycuan's counter-narrative. I refer to the Rincon Casino as a native-effacing style because, compared to neighboring casinos that highlight, or at least hint at, their tribal affiliation, Harrah's Rincon (now known as Harrah's Resort Southern California) has an appearance that is closer to a glitzy, though generic, commercial casino. However, Harrah's Rincon Casino is the only casino in Southern California that is managed by Harrah's, and the only casino to include in its name the name of its management corporation. Harrah's Entertainment, a casino corporation that was bought by Caesars Entertainment Corporation in 2010 although it continues to lend its name to the casinos it owned or managed before 2010, has its own brand image. The native-effacing style of Harrah's Rincon might function to maintain a pure Harrah's brand image. Harrah's Rincon Casino is a rare case in which the image of the managing corporation is prominent while tribal affiliation is effaced.

The three strategies—counter-narrative, native-aesthetic, and native-effacing—provide a framework for understanding the range of strategies that tribal casinos have taken in their degree of representation of native identity. I chose Sycuan, Pechanga, and Rincon because they stand at three points along a continuum: the two ends and a middle ground, in the variety of self-representational approaches taken by tribal casinos. The remaining tribal casinos in Southern California can be seen as falling somewhere along this continuum, with most Cahuilla nations casinos taking the native aesthetic approach in common with Pechanga. From the perspective of casino managers and tribal officials, there are potential strengths and weaknesses associated with each approach. A counter-narrative may educate patrons and perhaps, as discussed later in this chapter, sway patrons to support specifically tribal casinos and native nation rights, at the risk of alienating patrons by challenging their worldview or, as is suggested by Anthony Miranda, imply to patrons that the tribe's identity is in question and needs to be proved. On the other end, a self-effacing casino does not communicate any message, either directly or through subtle native-aesthetics and portraits, that the casino is, in fact, a tribally owned and operated entity; this strategy could lend itself to the common misperception, further elaborated below, that native nations, especially those that operate casinos, are facades for corporate interests. There is no unified formula for self-representation in tribal casinos. Nor should one expect there to be such a formula because each native nation is independent and has its own unique cultural values and economic needs. Whether patrons see a counter-narrative or native-effacing décor depends on which casino they visit.

The Powwow

The powwow circuit in Southern California illustrates the capacity for native nations to both maintain practices that they were once persecuted for and to represent their sovereignty to other native nations and the broader public. In their influential volume on powwows, Ellis, Lassiter, and Dunham (2005, viii) wrote, "It's true that most powwows follow a common template that participants instantly recognize no matter where they are, but local customs and ways inevitably frame dances as events that are situated in specific contexts with particular meanings." This is perhaps nowhere truer than in Southern California, where much of the drumming and dancing styles found at powwows come from other cultural regions (especially the northern plains). At the same time, the powwows also provide a platform for the hosting nations to showcase traditional forms of song and dance and represent their capacity for self-determination. The powwow itself is a synchronism of two different strands of performance, one indigenous and the other a product of settler colonialism. Throughout much of its history the BIA sought to shut down native gatherings and dancing, which, according to Ellis (2005, 12), it saw "as lurid spectacles that promoted everything from sexual licentiousness to pagan worship." Like elsewhere in the United States, the Cahuilla faced these attempts, especially during the first few decades of the twentieth century, and yet continued them anyway. Their traditional gatherings became known as fiestas and the MIA sought to prohibit them entirely. At the same time that the BIA fought to suppress traditional forms of dancing, settler society celebrated native dance, but only in the limited context of so-called Wild West shows created by "Buffalo Bill" Cody. Ellis (13) traced the grand entry, where all performers enter while dancing in a circle, to the shows organized by Cody. Likewise, the competitive aspect of modern-day powwows, where dancers compete for cash prizes, has its roots in the auditions for Wild West shows, where those judged to be the best dancers received contracts for work (13–14). Ellis (18) argued that "twentieth-century warfare is the critical link in the revival of many dances and rituals from the prereservation period." When native veterans returned from the battlefields of World War I and World War II, tribes celebrated their return with their traditional singing and dancing rituals for welcoming returning warriors. Caught between their conflicting desires to both suppress these dances and promote American Indian military service, the BIA began to lay off suppression of some, though not all, forms of native dance. This laid the groundwork for traditional ways of dancing to combine with structures from Wild West shows to create the modern-day powwow circuit, with its elements of indigenous culture and approval by settler society. This circuit expanded to Southern California in the 1970s, where it grew out of the long-persecuted tradition of fiestas. Below I analyze two elements of the Southern California powwow circuit, the Grand Entry and Bird Song performances, where the hosting tribe can take center stage.

Grand Entries are held at the beginning of each session of the powwow, typically one each morning and one each afternoon of the powwow. During the Grand Entry the color guard enters, followed by every performer in the powwow dressed in full regalia, as all participants dance in a circle rotating around the arena. Color guards vary but always include at least the flag of the United States as well as the flag of the native nation hosting the powwow. Other flags often include the flag of the state of California and the flag for Prisoners of War/Missing in Actions (POW/ MIA). Here, fitting Ellis's (2005) connections between warrior and powwow culture, the POW/MIA flag functions as both a tribute to the sacrifice of those military servicemen and servicewomen held captive or missing in action, and as a means to inform the public that the hosting native nation strongly supports the armed services. A powwow hosted in late summer 2009 by the San Manuel of Mission Indians featured one particularly prominent display of sovereignty. Joining the color guard were members the San Manuel Fire Department, in full uniform and on horseback. The message was clear: San Manuel is a sovereign polity and, as such, has the hallmarks associated with other sovereigns including a fire department that has its own uniforms, rides on horseback (at least during ceremonies such as this), and deserves the same respect and deference as all fire departments. The Grand Entry, thus, can function as a means to represent the hosting nation to attendees as a government, with institutions and symbols that are both unique to that native nation and, on a more general level, shared by all governments. After the Grand Entry, a representative of the hosting nation addresses all participants and attendees. These addresses consist of a welcome and a prayer, and, at times, explicitly political statements.

At Southern Californian powwows, Bird Song performances are the primary representation of native Californian music and dance. These may take the form of either stand-alone performances in which groups from different reservations or communities come forward to sing, or as competitions between groups, as I observed at the Morongo powwows in late 2010 and 2011. As they were traditionally practiced, men sing the Bird Songs as women and girls dance. The powwow's master of ceremony explains to the audience that the Bird Songs recount aspects of the origin stories. This follows what Daniel Gelo (2005, 138) called the Emcee's "didactic chain" that "reminds the Indians present of their own ideals while also teaching the non-Indian onlookers." The Grand Entry and Bird Songs, taken together, represent both the political and the cultural dimensions of tribal sovereignty. They expose nonnative attendees to both the structural and ceremonial aspects of the native nation as a government and to spiritual and performance aspects of the native nation as a cultural entity that predates European colonialism.

The Media

The American Indian activists of the 1960s and 1970s challenged the settler narrative of the vanishing Indian. Today, the tribal casino industry further enables some native nations to use the media as a means of self-representation. But the same industry that offers some native nations the resources necessary to use the media to reach the public has also generated controversy, fomenting widespread misrepresentations in the media. In this section I first examine a *Time* article and a native response to it that exemplify common media misrepresentations of gaming. Then I discuss the political advertisements used by native nations and their challengers.

Time's cover article, "Indian Casinos: Wheel of Misfortune," illustrates how a misrepresentation of the cultural and political processes underpinning the Indian casino movement can be used to portray the movement as an unjust and existential threat to equality (Barlett and Steele 2002). The article begins, "Imagine if you will, Congress passing a bill to make Indian tribes more self-sufficient that gives billions of dollars to the white backers of Indian businesses—and nothing to hundreds of thousands of Native Americans living in poverty. Or a bill that gives hundreds of millions of dollars to one Indian tribe with a few dozen members—and not a penny to a tribe with hundreds of thousands of members.... Can't imagine Congress passing such a bill? It did" (Barlett and Steele, 44). Of course, Congress passed no such bill. On December 17, 2002, Ernest Stevens, then-president of the National Indian Gaming Association, sharply critiqued. In his open letter to *Time* Stevens wrote, in part,

> Your story is based on the false and offensive premise that "Washington" created Indian gaming as a "cheap way to wean tribes from government handouts." Indian Tribes use gaming first and foremost for tribal government programs, community infrastructure, charity, and aid to local governments. Where Indian Tribes have suffered the highest teen suicide rates in the country, Indian gaming has built schools, funded colleges scholarships, and given our children hope for a brighter future....
>
> Indian gaming not only works for Indian Country, it works for America.... Non-Indians hold 75% of the 300,000 jobs Indian gaming has created nationwide. Tribes have brought economic development to historically rural and undeveloped areas.... In addition, Tribes have numerous service agreements with state

and local governments to share revenues, contribute emergency service equipment, build roads and other infrastructure.... For example...the Agua Caliente Band of Cahuilla Indians purchased fire trucks for Palm Springs. (Stevens 2002)

Stevens began his letter with the fundamental flaw with *Time's* representation of Indian gaming as some kind of federal program, which of course it is not. (In the second part of this chapter I discuss in greater detail implications of the persistent settler assumption that Congress, and not native nations themselves, started the tribal casino movement.) Point by point Stevens unearthed the article's flaws, while implicitly, by virtue of his letter, challenging the stereotype of the passive Indian. However, efforts like Stevens's are an uphill battle because mass media frequently disseminates such myths and falsehoods about native nations.

The bulk of media representations of California Indians are found in political advertisements for and against the numerous tribal gaming ballot initiatives that have come before voters, starting with Proposition 5 in 1998. These representations are explicitly political and therefore highlight only those images that their creators foresee as having the potential to change public opinions. When Arnold Schwarzenegger ran for governor during the California recall election of 2004, a central component of his campaign was his promise to require gaming tribes to share a high rate of their revenue with the state government. In a slogan prominently featured in his advertisements and stump speech, Schwarzenegger repeatedly stated, "It is time for the Indians to pay their fair share." While Schwarzenegger was referring specifically to native nations that operate casinos, his use of the generic label "the Indians" without any further clarification denotes all American Indians. This slogan frames American Indians as two contrasting types of organizations. The generic "Indians" label denotes an ethnic or pan-ethnic group, not the sovereign polities that his proposed policies would impact. Second, "pay their fair share," in the context of Indian casinos is an analogy between those enterprises and private businesses that pay, or should pay, taxes to the state. Thus, then-candidate Schwarzenegger characterized native nations that operate casinos as both an ethnic group and as a class of private businesses, when legally and culturally they are neither. Later, this chapter shows how Schwarzenegger's statements could be feeding a common settler misconception that American Indians are exempt from taxes.

The landscape of political advertisements is full of contradicting statements that can bewilder settlers already misinformed about native nations. For example, here is the text from two television ads that ran before the 2008 Proposition 94–97 ballot measure. The first was sponsored by a past partnership primarily funded by Agua Caliente, Morongo, Pechanga, and Sycuan (Coalition to Protect California's Budget and Economy 2008): "Who's really behind the ads opposing Indian Gaming agreements? They're paid for by a Vegas casino owner and two racetracks. In fact, only two tribes oppose the agreements, while tribes statewide support an agreement, because the agreements share revenues with all tribes that don't have casinos to fund health care, schools and housing on reservations throughout California, benefiting over 70 tribes. Vote yes for California and California Indian tribes." During the ad, a list of all seventy of the California native nations that support the campaigns is shown, followed by the slogan "Support Indian Self-Reliance."

Another ad, sponsored by an organization that opposes the propositions, Californians Against Unfair Deals, featured John Gomez Sr., the director of the American Indian Rights and Resources Organization, an advocacy organization that focuses particularly on the rights of non-enrolled American Indians. In the ad Gomez explains, "As a leader of an Indian rights group, I am outraged at the deceptive ads for the gambling deals. The truth: Props 94–97 are for the benefit of just four of the state's 108 tribes. The rich tribes get richer, the poor tribes don't get a penny more. In the name of fairness, California Indian tribes urge you to send these deals back" (Californians Against Unfair Deals 2008). When viewed back to back, as they were often aired in the run-up to the vote on Propositions 94–97 measures, these ads directly contradict each other and potentially confuse viewers. Are four tribes greedily expanding and hoarding casino revenue for themselves, or do all but two tribes support these measures that will benefit all tribes? Of course, the situation was very complicated, and both campaigns had elements of truth. The measures, which passed, allowed four tribes to expand their number of slot machines in exchange for paying a higher share of revenue to the state, but also a smaller amount of revenue into a fund for tribes with no or only small-scale casino development. Seventy federally recognized native nations supported the propositions, and two opposed them.

But not all California Indians are members of federally recognized tribes. The first advertisement discussed above claimed that only two tribes oppose the propositions when in fact the number could be much higher when one considers tribes that are not federally recognized. The second ad asserted that the compacts are only for the benefit of four tribes. While the compacts pertained only to four tribes, other tribes could be hurt indirectly if these propositions had failed. If these propositions had failed, it could have set a precedent for ballot initiatives to intervene in future compact negotiations. The Gomez ad is even more misleading in its claim that "California Indian tribes urge you to send these deals back." Gomez's organization represents a segment of the native population, but no organization can unilaterally speak for all tribes. With the public already uninformed about tribal politics, these ads could only further contribute to confusing settler society's already limited cultural knowledge of native nations.

Some tribally sponsored advertisements send a clear political message without appearing to be advertisements at all, but rather educational public service announcements. The San Manuel Band of Mission Indians regularly runs such advertisements, which can be found on their website, sanmanuel-nsn.gov. In a May 2011 interview with the blog *Newspaper Rock*, Jacob Coin, San Manuel's director of public relations explained, "We do two to three of them [advertisements] a year, and we show them to focus groups, and what we've found is that people are really interested in the history. And I think it's important for me to point out that these are made by the tribal government side, not the gaming side. We know that the public would rather learn about history than see a casino ad, and we're proud of our history and the positive contributions we've made to the communities here in the San Bernardino Valley" ("San Manuel Band of Serrano Mission Indians Gets the Message Out with Television Advertising" 2011). As stated by Coin, these ads are created by consulting focus groups to establish what messages will be the most effective. Notably, the tribal government rather than the casino operation produces these educational commercials, and they make no direct references to the casino. Some of these ads link the contributions of San Manuel and other tribes to early California settlers to a tradition that continues today. For example, one ad informed viewers, "If you look in any direction you'll see an Indian trade route that once existed. California's first roads were started by its first inhabitants, including ancestors of the San Manuel Band of Mission Indians. These Indian trails established commercial routes, becoming the roads of today's economy, including the route for Interstate 10. San Manuel continues to contribute to the economy through job creation, buying from local businesses, and partnerships with local cities. Indian tribes and California: together, one community" (San Manuel Band of Mission Indians 2010). As the narrator recites that text, the commercial shows reenactments of settlers cross-ing trails through the desert, followed by an image of Interstate 10. The commercial concludes by showing trucks from local businesses unload-ing goods on the reservation. The ad correctly illustrates that the origin of Interstate 10, a route very familiar to the residents of Southern Cali-fornia, lies along a precontact Indian trade route. Early settlers, much like Californians today, depended on that route. As the advertisement asserts, the present-day partnerships between San Manuel and their neighboring communities are not new but rather part of a long tradition.

In another ad, San Manuel educates the public about the genocide they faced and how their ancestors overcame it. Rather than conclude the ad, as many settlers might suspect, by expressing resentment over the genocide, the ad concludes by illustrating the potential for Califor-nians to benefit from what it calls tribal self-reliance. "In 1866, during a 32-day battle to rid the San Bernardino Mountains of all Indian people, a heroic Indian leader named Santos Manuel led his people on a perilous journey to freedom. As Santos Manuel saved his tribe, his story inspires a culture of bravery, leadership, and overcoming great odds in the tribe now named after him. The story of Santos Manuel benefits all Ameri-cans. Tribal self-reliance makes Californians self-reliant" (San Manuel Band of Mission Indians 2009) During the ad, actors reenact a peaceful Serrano village interrupted by settlers who fire at the Indians and set their dwellings on fire. Then the story of Santos Manuel is connected to a self-representation of the tribe today as a "culture of bravery, leader-ship and overcoming odds." The statement "tribal self-reliance makes Californians self-reliant" has appeared in several of San Manuel's educa-tional ads. Self-reliance, when it applies to a community, dovetails with self-determination. The ability for a community to determine its own future requires, at least in part, that it is able to economically sustain itself. Thus, self-reliance entails both self-determination and the politi-cal and economic factors that underpin a polity's capacity to maintain its independence. As self-reliance is used in the above ad, where tribal and Californian self-reliance are explicitly linked, it highlights the con-nections between internal and external sovereignty. Increases in tribes' capacities for self-determination can help California strengthen its own self-determination. The ad frames tribes as both autonomous and inter-dependent with other sovereigns, like the interdependencies described in Cattelino (2008) and Kamper (2010). These ads challenge settlers' assumptions about California's history and ask them to consider the possibility that California has always benefited from native nations. However, advertisements like this may be too little and too late considering the overwhelming influence of California's public education system and its simplistic representations of California Indians.

Today, there is little opportunity for settlers to learn about their native neighbors. Many native nations use powwows, advertisements, and sometimes even their own casinos as media to represent their history and culture to the public. San Manuel and Agua Caliente now work with public schools to ensure that future generations will have a more accurate and nuanced understanding of neighboring native nations. These are important efforts, but the narratives told by settler institutions, especially education and the media, are ubiquitous. In school, until the year before this book's publication, children learned the myth that the missions successfully assimilated tribes. Outside of school, children and adults are exposed to media and political rhetoric that misrepresent tribal sovereignty. Tribal gaming provides new revenue and opportunities for tribal self-representation, but it is an uphill battle against the onslaught of the problematic cultural knowledge disseminated by settler institutions. The representations discussed in the first part of this chapter offer settlers only indirect and mediated experience of native nations. The next part of this chapter examines the different segments of settler society that have direct experience with native institutions and how their different experiences challenge the predominant settler narratives.

Emerging Constructions

As suggested earlier in this book, the recognition of sovereignty is, in part, a cognitive process distributed across a population. The different ways in which members of a population recognize or fail to recognize the sovereignty of a neighboring community reflect their experiences (or lack of experiences) with that community, in addition to the wider shared assumptions about the world and their perceptions of their role in it. This part of this chapter maps the distribution of settler cultural knowledge to demonstrate how tribal gaming impacts settler perceptions, especially external cultural sovereignty.

From 2010 to 2012 I conducted interviews and surveys among different segments of the settler population who live in the now largely developed ancestral territory of the Cahuilla nations (i.e., primarily in Riverside County) in order to establish patterns of settler cultural knowledge variance. I conducted in-depth interviews with tribal casino employees, patrons, and neighbors, and conducted two surveys with university students in the region. Interviews allow participants to provide in-depth descriptions of their perspectives and knowledge of tribal sovereignty, but time and other constraints limit the number of participants. Conversely, surveys capture a wider sample, and allow more-precise measurements of the congruence of perceptions between participants but limit the depth to which all participants can expand on their perceptions. When combined, the design of these instruments captures aspects of both the depth and the breadth of structures of divergent perceptions and can further establish whether specific cultural knowledge structures are shared. Because participants were not recruited through random sampling, these methods are not intended to measure the proportion of any population that may hold such views. Instead, they are designed to provide evidence that certain assumptions are shared by members of a population. To the extent that significant commonalities exist among individuals' perceptions and knowledge, these commonalities are not idiosyncratic. The methods and analysis applied in this study are designed to describe those commonalities. I begin with the survey results and then analyze the interviews. This chapter concludes with a discussion of how tribal gaming might impact these shared assumptions and how changes in settler cultural knowledge could, in turn, impact the future of tribal sovereignty.

Surveys

In addition to asking demographic questions, including the participant's residential proximity to native nations and frequency of visits to tribal reservations, each survey asked about the participants' perceptions of native nations. Both surveys were conducted in introductory anthropology classes at the University of California, Riverside, a public research university of more than 20,000 students, within a one-hour drive of the casinos at San Manuel, Morongo, Agua Caliente, and Pechanga. An overwhelming majority of students at the University of California, Riverside are California residents. While these surveys do not allow for a generalization to the rest of the settler population, they do suggest certain patterns among a subset of the settler population who, on average, might have no more experience or knowledge of native nations than the general public. Participants took the survey before their introductory course provided any material on native nations. The first survey included fifty-eight participants. This survey used multiple-choice and open-answer questions about the participants' perceptions and knowledge of tribal gaming. The second survey entailed a triad test, designed to measure the consensus among participants about the similarity between native nations and other social groups, including ethnicities, nation-states, nongovernmental organizations, and corporations. The triad test included sixty-six participants and was based on first methods outlined by Weller and Romney (1988) and further refined by Russell Bernard (2011). Selected questions from the first survey, shown in figures 6.1a–6.1f, suggest participants commonly lack knowledge about the native peoples of their state.

Significantly, a substantial majority (65.5 percent) responded to the third question that American Indians are not required to pay federal income tax, which is false. Note that while this was not a randomized sample, the results correspond with the findings of Eve Darian-Smith's (2004) randomized phone survey in Santa Barbara County. Her survey found that "nearly 66 percent of those interviewed incorrectly believe Native Americans do not pay taxes or are unsure whether they pay taxes" (37). In my survey the overwhelming number of "no," answers, especially when "don't know" is an available response, suggests that few respondents were uncertain of their answer. Those respondents who chose "no" might have been confident in their answer, because if not they could have chosen "don't know." These results suggest there is a widely shared assumption that American Indians as individuals (as opposed to native nations as polities that are recognized by the federal government) are exempt from specific federal laws because of their ethnic identity. Revenue from native nation's enterprises, such as casinos, are exempt from federal taxes in the same manner that revenue collected by state and local governments are exempt. In fact, tribal casino revenue could be described as 100-percent taxed because the tribal government collects the entirety of the revenue. The popular assumption that American Indians are exempt from federal income tax may result from a conflation of native nation sovereignty and individual American Indian identification. In other words, people might assume that because tribal governments (like state and local governments) are not taxed, individual tribal members are also not taxed.

The survey results indicate an absence of knowledge about the regulation of native nation casinos. A small minority of participants responded

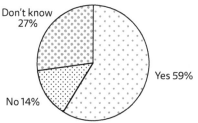

Figure 6.1a. Question 1:
Tribal reservations in California
were created by treaties.
(True/False)

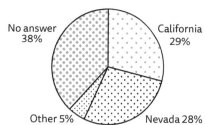

Figure 6.1b. Question 2:
Make your best guess at the location of
the first Indian reservation that offered
high-stakes gambling to the public.

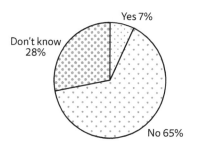

Figure 6.1c. Question 3:
Are American Indians required
to pay federal income tax?

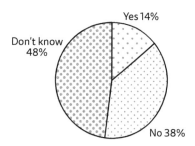

Figure 6.1d. Question 4:
Are tribally owned casinos
regulated by state law?

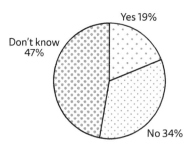

Figure 6.1e. Question 5:
Are tribally owned casinos
regulated by federal law?

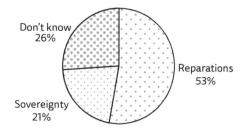

Figure 6.1f. Question 6:
What provides the legal basis for American
Indian tribes to operate casinos?

"yes" to questions 4 and 5 about state (13.7 percent) and federal (18.9 percent) regulation, which indicates that most are aware of the state and federal regulations of tribal casinos currently in place. Questions 1 and 2 were also designed to measure knowledge of California native nations and they both find high level of confusion. Treaties did not create tribal reservations in California, contrary to the answer from 53 percent of participants. Native nations did sign treaties, but these treaties were never ratified. Only 13.7 percent of respondents answered "no" to question 1, suggesting there might be little awareness of the failed treaty process and the devastation it caused. Question 2 was open-ended in order to elicit what the respondents saw as the most likely location for the origin of tribal gaming. Importantly, with Cabazon within a ninety-minute drive of the University of California, Riverside, the *Cabazon* decision was part of local history. However, a plurality of respondents (37.9 percent) left this section blank; 29 percent answered "California," but that answer nearly tied with "Nevada" at 27.5 percent. With the entire country to choose from, why did more than 25 percent choose to write in "Nevada"? Perhaps the prominence of the casino industry in Nevada informed their best guess. No answer mentioned other states that are home to tribes that played significant roles in the early years of the tribal gaming movement, including Wisconsin and Florida.

Likewise, the coded results for question 6, an open-ended question, found a majority (53.4 percent) of responses referred to reparations, or concepts closely associated with the concept of repayment for past injustices ("affirmative action," etc.). A minority (20.6 percent) of responses referred to native nations' capacity to govern their land, an aspect of native nation sovereignty (sovereignty itself was not specifically provided in any of the responses). Why might it be common for settlers to assume the federal government started the tribal casino industry? The answer might be because this explanation denies agency to native nations and positions gaming as a mechanism for redistributing wealth to the American Indians as the intended purpose of gaming. This sentiment—that the federal government intervened to give casinos to tribes—matched the misconception disseminated in the *Time* article discussed in the beginning of this chapter. Perhaps being exposed, generation after generation, to media and curricular narratives of American history that erase native histories could lead settlers to assume that native peoples could not have started tribal casinos by themselves.

The triad test offers a unique way to understand whether a population perceives certain concepts to be similar. There were eight concepts tested in this survey, presented to the participant in the format below:

1. American Indian tribe
2. Ethnic group
3. Racial group
4. Nation-state (e.g., the United States, Mexico, France)
5. State government (e.g., California, Rhode Island)
6. Local government (e.g., the city of Riverside, Orange County)
7. For-profit corporation (e.g., General Motors Corporation, Walmart)
8. Nonprofit organization (e.g., Red Cross, United Way, Planned Parenthood)

To prevent confusion, examples were given for five of the concepts. A triad is a set of three of the tested concepts. In this survey, I created a list of every possible triad, for a total of fifty-six triads. For example,

1. A. Racial group, B. Ethnic group, C. For-profit corporation
2. A. Nation-state, B. Local government, C. American Indian tribe
3. A. American Indian tribe, B. For-profit corporation, C. Ethnic group

Participants were instructed to read each triad and circle the concept that is the most different. By choosing the one that is the most different, the participants are implicitly indicating their perception that the remaining concepts are more similar to each other (relative to the one they chose as different). The results are then scored in a matrix to reveal how often each pair of concepts was ranked as relatively similar.

Table 6.1 represents the number of times each pair of terms was judged as similar by each participant. It can be read like a mileage chart on an atlas that represents the distance between destinations. However, instead of indicating the distance between places, the matrix in table 6.1 represents the degree of perceived similarity between concepts. And, like a map, it is possible to translate the relative similarities between these concepts onto a two-dimensional plane.

I ran a multidimensional scaling analysis (MSA) to produce the map shown in figure 6.2. This map illustrates the cultural constellation of these concepts. As can be seen, the resulting similarity scores yield three distinct bundles: (1) the racial and ethnic group, (2) the polities (local and state governments and nation-state), and (3) the for-profit and nonprofit private sectors. Tribe is positioned relatively closest to race/ethnic, second closest to the polities, and farthest from the for-profits

TABLE 6.1. Similarity Scores for Triad Test

	TRIBE	ETHNIC	RACE	NATION	STATE	LOCAL	FOR-PROFIT	NONPROFIT
TRIBE		286	242	79	77	100	41	59
ETHNIC	286		302	60	55	53	35	63
RACE	242	302		65	40	52	23	65
NATION	79	60	65		292	225	131	96
STATE	77	55	40	292		283	151	109
LOCAL	100	53	52	225	283		153	101
FOR-PROFIT	41	35	23	131	151	153		225
NONPROFIT	59	63	65	96	109	101	225	

and nonprofits. The stress score of the MSA, an indicator of the degree of fit between the similarity scores (in table 6.1) and the constellation produced through the MSA (figure 6.2), was less than 0.1, which indicates that the spatial arrangement of points on the MSA accurately reflect the ratios between similarity scores for the pairs. In other words, the MSA is an accurate spatial representation of the triad test results. A high degree of fit such as this is possible only where a strong consensus exists. The triad test results suggest a consensus among participants regarding the relative similarities between the tested concepts. Not surprisingly, the participants ranked race and ethnicity as the most similar. The three (nonnative) polities (local government, state government, and nation-state) formed a tight bundle, suggesting their perceived similarity. Tribe fell closest to race and ethnicity and second-closest to the other polities. Nonprofit and for-profit corporation were the farthest from tribe. These results indicate that, for the participants, tribes are most dissimilar from for-profit corporations. Though the participants might view tribes as similar to racial and ethnic groups, they indicated that tribes are much more congruent with polities than with private sector, especially for-profit, organizations.

In the first survey, the results indicate a high level of confusion about public policies that affect American Indians and native nations. In the triad test, contrary to the perspective offered by HERE, the NLRB, and the *San Manuel* decision (described in chapter 5), it appears that tribes may be commonly viewed as much closer to ethnic or racial groups, or as polities, than as members of the private sector. As discussed in the next section, in interviews tribal employees often compared their employer to

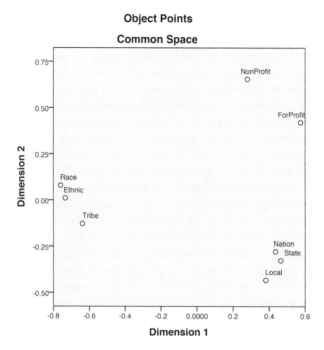

Figure 6.2. Multidimensional Scaling Analysis for Triad Test Similarity Scores

a corporation. The results of this survey suggest that the view that native nations are like corporations could be more common among employees of tribal casinos, while among the public there is a persistent and strong consensus regarding the dissimilarity between native nations and for-profit corporations. This suggests that some aspects of the experience of tribal casino employees may influence how they understand native nations relative to for-profit enterprises.

Interviews

In total, I conducted twenty-one in-depth interviews: six with tribal casino employees, eight with tribal casino patrons, and seven with neighbors of gaming reservations (which, for this study, are defined as individuals living within three miles of a gaming tribes in Riverside or San Bernardino Counties). To protect the identities of interview partici-pants, I have redacted all names. Additionally, I redacted the employer and job title of employee participants to further protect their identities. Each interview included questions about the participant's experiences with native nations as well as questions to elicit the participant's knowl-edge of the historical and cultural processes that underpin tribal gaming, especially tribal sovereignty. Afterward, each interview was coded for key terms and associated context in which participants used these terms. Interview results indicate that at least three constructions of tribal identity are commonly evoked in discussions of tribal revitalization and impacts (table 6.2). Each construction conveys different aspects of native nations and implies a different set of relations between native nations and the public. Variations in the experiences of participants correspond to the divergent constructions each referenced when discussing such experiences. Neighbors commonly used the polity construction while employees often favored the corporation. Patrons had a wider range of perceptions.

Six of the seven tribal neighbors that I interviewed expressed strong support for tribal revitalization. This corroborates Miller's (2008) analysis of election results that illustrates how the communities in San Bernardino and Riverside Counties that are nearest to tribal casinos showed the greatest support for tribal gaming expansion in the 2008 Proposition 94–97 referendum. A variety of factors influence their perceptions of native nations, including their previous knowledge of neighboring tribes as well as the economic, social, and political impacts of tribal revitalization. One neighbor, living two blocks from a tribal casino, explained, "I remember before [the casino] when they had nothing. They fought for that casino, they deserve it." Other neighbors echoed this refrain, that they knew of the reservation's living conditions prior to the casino and that they know that the casino developed as a result of tribes acting to determine their own future. This contrasts with the first survey results where most participants either did not know the basis for tribal gaming, or, similar to the article in *Time*, assumed the federal government intervened to give casinos to tribes.

Increased employment, economic development, entertainment, and charitable donations from the neighboring tribes were commonly cited as benefits to the local community. "Now people from [Los Angeles] come here for fun, that used to never happen," explained one interviewee. Another pointed out, "This area has been [economically] depressed for some time. With the casino, finally we have someone who's hiring." Local negative impacts cited included the increased traffic and crime associated with their neighborhood becoming an entertainment destination. One neighbor put it directly: "I get it, they [the tribe] needed the casino, they've [the tribe] put money back into the area, but the traffic all day, especially on weekends, is frustrating." Significantly, three tribal casino neighbor interviewees explained that powwows and other cultural events hosted by native nations influenced their views. One participant reported that her family goes every year. "It's a good cultural experience for [my children]," she said. As free events open to the public, these powwows enable families to experience native nations performing their sovereignty in an atmosphere that is educational, entertaining, and explicitly alcohol free and drug free. Thus, these events establish a community presence in addition to the casino, in marked contrast to the adult-oriented tribal casino gaming enterprise.

A recurring theme among interviewed employees, however, was that these experiences were often out of reach. One tribal casino employee laughed when asked if she attends her employer's powwow. She explained that "everyone is expected to work overtime" during the powwow, which is a busy time for the tribal casino, especially its hotel, restaurants, and other services. While all interviewed employees expressed an interest in attending their employers' powwow, five of the six tribal casino employees that I interviewed cited work or lack of available time as a reason for not attending. Each explained that during orientation as a new employee, human resources provided them with information on the history and sovereignty of their employer. When asked to compare their experiences as a tribal employee to their previous employers, and whether they perceive their experiences to be comparable to working for a nontribal government, all interviewees said their work environment is significantly different from what they had experienced, or would expect to experience, as an employee of a nontribal government. In other words, they reported that working for a tribal casino is not like working for a federal, state, or local government agency. As one employee who has worked at one tribal casino for more than ten years explained, working at a tribal casino is "like any other business.... The people I work for, management, they're all white. I don't know the [tribal] community. I don't get to be part of that."

There are a variety of factors that could influence the interviewed employees' perception of their employer as a private enterprise. First, all employees interviewed worked the floor of the casino in service or lower-level supervisor positions. Their daily work responsibilities, such as dealing poker under the supervision of a pit boss, were not too different from those of employees at commercial casinos, and were very different from what one would experience working for a federal, state, or local government. Moreover, given their employment positions, each interviewed

TABLE 6.2. Polity, Ethnic Group, and Corporation Constructions

1. POLITY

Key Terms	Nation, Sovereignty, Self-Determination, Government, Treaties
Context	Discussions of the independence and sovereignty of each native nation
Examples	"They are like their own government, they can come up with their own rules." "We signed treaties with them, that makes them independent." "That's what left of their land, they can do what they want with it."

2. ETHNIC GROUP

Key Terms	Race, Affirmative Action, Ancestry, Heritage
Context	Discussion of shared qualities among native nations, and American Indians outside of federally recognized native nations.
Examples	"Why don't they share with each other?" "They [American Indians] have all gotten rich now." "Does it benefit all Indians?"

3. CORPORATION

Key Terms	Corporation, Business, Company
Context	Taxes, profit, organizational structure, comparisons to Las Vegas
Examples	"They're just like any business." "Pay their fair share." "After working at a nonprofit, I think it [the tribal employer] is very corporate."

employee reported that interactions with tribal members were uncommon, except for two who were supervised directly by a tribal member. Three employees explained that they had provided services to tribal members who at times visit the casino, and that these interactions were, in the words of one interviewee, "brief" and "occasional." Thus, while they had been educated about the history and sovereignty of their employer during orientation, the interviewed employees did not experience the native nation as a community in a manner similar to how a government employee experiences the community of their employer: by either being a member of that community or by developing relations (outside of work) with community members. Both the polity and the corporation constructions were commonly referenced in employee interviews, and the corporation construction was especially prominent. These employees knew they worked for a sovereign government, but their work experiences more closely aligned with employment in the private sector. The perception among employees that their employer resembles a private corporation parallels the claims made by HERE and accepted by the NLRB and the Ninth Circuit Court of Appeals. When most of a tribal casino's patrons and employees are non-Indian, they might feed the perception among employees that the casino is a private, not a governmental, entity.

Fortunately, there are now tribally sponsored programs to provide culturally sensitive training for careers in tribal gaming. The Sycuan Institute on Tribal Gaming, at San Diego State University, now offers a bachelor of science in hospitality and tourism management with an emphasis in tribal gaming. This program, founded through an endowment by the Sycuan Band of the Kumeyaay nations, provides students with knowledge and skills necessary for success in careers working for tribally owned casinos (San Diego State University 2017). At Claremont Graduate University, employees of the San Manuel Band of Serrano Indians can earn a tribal administration certificate. In the coursework for the certificate they learn more about the history and culture of San Manuel, along with the skills necessary for working for a tribal government (Claremont Graduate University 2017). My interviews suggest that both of these programs work toward an important goal: to ensure that current and future tribal employees understand the significance and peculiarities of working for a tribal government.

The views of eight casino patron interviewees were more varied. For five of them, proximity was a determining factor in their choice between tribal and commercial casinos. One, a self-described frequent visitor, explained, "Why would we drive four hours to get to a casino [in Las Vegas]? There's slots right here." Three interviewees explained that they prefer tribal casinos because of their perceived impact on a tribal community. One, a San Bernardino resident and frequent tribal casino patron, reported, "It's good knowing that this [money spent at the casino] benefits a community." After describing the photographs, artifacts, and other displays she has seen at tribal casinos, she remarked, "I know most [people] don't, but I stop and look. I like learning about them." Another frequent patron and a Palm Desert resident who reported having visited at least ten tribal casinos explained that tribal reservation locations caused him to reflect on the historical challenges faced by native nations. He explained, "For almost all of them [tribal casinos], you have to drive out of the way and into the foothills [of local mountain ranges]. You can tell they were put there, where the land isn't worth much."

However, not all patrons learn from their experiences at tribal casinos. For some, visits strengthen their acceptance of stereotypes. One patron, a San Bernardino resident, shared how the visibility of prosperity at the reservation he frequents influenced his perception that all American Indians are now wealthy as a result of tribal gaming. He stated, "I can see their [the tribal members'] houses from the parking garage. The Indians are rich now." His generalization from observing a particular reservation to a broader category, "the Indians," mobilized the ethnicity construction by (quite erroneously) linking the attributes of one native nation to all American Indians. For this individual, not unlike the two who claimed to have learned more about tribes from their visits to tribal casinos, the casino visit provided them with new, albeit partial and limited, knowledge of native nations. Thus, in the interview sample there were differences in how the partial knowledge gained from their visits changed how each casino patron perceived tribes, and whether those changes led to uninformed generalizations about American Indians as a whole, or to a more nuanced understanding of the history of specific native nations. As noted in the Introduction to this book, both Philip Deloria (2004) and Jean Piaget (1953) offer convergent frameworks for understanding how new experiences can challenge or reinforce an individual's expectations or knowledge. While individual responses may vary, tribal casino décor can directly confront settler expectations. Conversely, some patrons might have had previous experiences that make them more likely to be receptive to these challenges. Others still may already have such predefined prejudice and expectations about native nations that the visibility of some wealth on some reservations reinforces their expectations.

Conclusions

The interviews discussed in this chapter suggest how direct experience can change how people think about native nations. The different experiences of being an employee, a neighbor, or a patron can lead to different perceptions. The greater support and knowledge of native nations among neighbors might be attributed to their proximity to and experiences of nearby native nations. Tribal casino employees, who have, by virtue of their employment, even greater experience of native nations, hold perspectives that could be significantly different from those of neighbors who are not employees. When describing their employer as more like a corporation than a government, these employees echoed the argument of HERE and the NLRB in the *San Manuel* decision. In the *San Manuel* decision employee perceptions that they work for a tribal enterprise fed into the legal argument that tribal casinos can be regulated as private for-profit enterprises. Intensive training programs, like those offered at San Diego State University and Claremont Graduate University, go well beyond the short-term employee orientations offered by some tribal casinos. In the future, programs like these could help counter the perception among some employees that their employer seems more like a corporation than a government.

Tribal casino patrons have a variety of reasons for visiting tribal casinos, ranging from the relative convenience of their locations (when compared to Las Vegas) to the preference that patronage at a tribal casino benefits a local community. Some visitors leave with a better understanding of a particular native culture and history, and others leave with generalizations about American Indians as a whole. Thus, tribal self-representations that highlight their sovereignty may succeed in challenging some patrons to rethink their assumptions about native nations.

Interviewees and survey participants noted experiences and perspectives of tribal gaming that reflect the patterns found by Marks and Spilde Contreras (2007). Participants noted that tribal casinos contribute to the local economy in addition to adding local entertainment and cultural venues. As Darian-Smith's (2004) research suggests, tribal gaming challenges non-Indians' preconceptions of American Indians. John Bodinger de Uriate's (2007) finding that tribal casinos and museums present against-the-grain representations of native nations is true of some tribal casinos in Southern California. While further research is necessary, these data suggest that certain individuals are more open to viewing representations of native nations in the casino environment and, therefore, could be more likely to have such representations alter their understanding of native nations. Unlike Darian-Smith's research in Santa Barbara, neighbors interviewed for this project did not list the attraction of working-class employees and patrons among the drawbacks of tribal casino development. The perceptions of employees and patrons reported by Santa Barbara area residents and those interviewed for this project may result from the relatively higher socioeconomic status of Santa Barbara–area residents (relative to San Bernardino, which has a population that overall has much lower incomes). Further research into this question is necessary to provide a more complete understanding of the relationship between the social and economic status of area residents and perceptions of tribal casino impacts. The perceptions that recurred among survey and interview participants (i.e., polity, ethnic group, and corporation) are among those listed by Steinman (2006) as popular representations of American Indian tribes that are often evoked by native nations themselves. This research suggests that these are representations, in addition to being popular in the media, of constructions that individuals apply when they communicate about tribes. Furthermore, the popularity of specific constructions among certain segments of the population (particularly tribal employees and neighbors) could be related to their experiences of native nations.

In terms of changing settler perceptions, tribal gaming may be a double-edged sword: it provides new opportunities for tribes to represent themselves to the public, and some patrons appreciate and learn from tribes. Others do not learn from their visits, and instead leave with their existing negative stereotypes reinforced. While casinos provided much-needed revenue for tribal governments and surrounding communities, their working conditions can create an environment that is fertile grounds for the emergence of a new perception—that tribal casinos are private, for-profit enterprises.

CONCLUSION

In his book *The Return of the Native*, Stephen Cornel (1990, 212) concluded, "The protection of sovereignty and treaty rights depends to some extent on public, non-Indian support. If Indian nations come to be viewed not as carriers of distinct ways of life, involuntarily put to risk by the larger society, but simply as anachronistic legal residues of an unfortunate past, that support may disappear. In a peculiar way, distinctiveness is a form of security." Tribal gaming might have forever altered the relations between settlers and native nations, but the patterns underlying their relations have stayed the same. One of the greatest tools for preserving tribal self-determination could be native nations' strategy of educating the public about native histories, cultures, and rights. This is particularly the case in the Cahuilla territory, the epicenter of the tribal gaming movement. Settlers differ in their sympathy and antipathy for native nations, but settler institutions, both private and public, covet tribal resources from land to casino revenue. Again and again, when settler desire of tribal resources turns into action against native nations, those nations respond by strategically challenging widely shared assumptions. The history of the Cahuilla nations illustrates how native nations can maintain their self-determination in large part by directly challenging settler misinformation in order to strengthen external cultural sovereignty. Of course, settler society and native nations are on an uneven playing field: settler institutions continue to be economically, politically, and culturally dominate. But by educating their settler neighbors, native nations can encourage positive external political changes and achieve significant results.

When he gave his speech at the home of a county judge in 1852, Juan Antonio executed this strategy well. As described in chapter 2, the judge accepted Antonio's plea and released the Cahuilla prisoner to Antonio, in acknowledgment that the Cahuilla should have authority over their own people. In 1866 Santos Manuel applied a similar strategy. He led his band of Serrano down from the mountains and into the foothills north of San Bernardino, where they were in closer contact with the society that was persecuting them. This led nearby settlers to better differentiate the Serrano from other tribes who they targeted. Under Santos Manuel's leadership, his band of Serrano made themselves visible as peaceful neighbors. Settlers still encroached on their land, but the Serrano avoided annihilation.

This strategy succeeded yet again in the early- to mid-twentieth century, when MIF and Spokesmen and Committee lobbied Congress. MIF's initial successes came by organizing its own resistance to the MIA and sending representatives to Congress, exposing treaties that Congress, decades earlier, had failed to ratify. While on opposite sides of the fight over the termination of external political tribal sovereignty and the closing of the BIA, MIF and Spokesmen and Committee both used the strategy of directly educating policymakers. This strategy was again present when Agua Caliente collaborated with Ringwald in his *Press Enterprise* exposé of the guardianship scandal. Tribal activism in the 1960s and 1970s fought to end termination by using demonstrations that attracted the media, broadcasting their appeal to settler society and challenging settler assumptions. The Indian gaming movement is no different. Not only did native nations create and lead the movement but also political challenges to the movement, such as Pete Wilson's refusal to negotiate tribal gaming compacts, became a site for native nations to directly inform and appeal to the public. One pattern recurs throughout settler and native relations: settler institutions covet native resources yet underestimate the strategies that native nations will use to protect their self-determination.

This book began with Audra Simpson's (2014, 177) observation that native nation sovereignty "fundamentally interrupts and casts into question the story that settler states tell themselves." As Philip Deloria (2004) noted, settler society has come to assume, or even to expect, a prescribed set of behaviors for Indians. Settler colonialism led to a set of expectations where even today many settlers cannot imagine natives engaged in modern activities. But when Indians appear in unexpected places they "resist...categorization and, thereby, question...expectation itself" (Deloria 2004, 11). With the aim of providing new tools for exploring how these expectations form and how they can be challenged, this book introduced theory and methods from cognitive anthropology. This approach leverages the decades of research conducted by psychology and the cognitive sciences in the ways humans acquire knowledge (or schemata), and how new experiences can reinforce (or assimilate to) existing knowledge. Alternatively, if an experience is new enough, under the right circumstances it can change existing knowledge.

One of the foundational discoveries in psychology is that holding two contradictory schemata can cause individuals to experience distress. Humans will rationalize, reject information, divert their attention, or employ any number of strategies to alleviate this cognitive dissonance. By bridging cognitive anthropology with Native American studies, cognitive dissonance can become a tool for understanding why settler society has had such poor understanding of native histories and cultures. When a settler society, such as the United States, assumes that its nation is founded on justice and democracy, native histories that expose injustices can cause what I refer to as historical dissonance (defined in chapter 3). Rejecting, omitting, or ignoring knowledge are all strategies for alleviating cognitive dissonance: in the case of North American historical dissonance, these strategies became widespread, enshrined in the media and school curricula. But native nations know how to challenge the underlying shared assumptions of settler society. When they confront settlers in ways that defy expectations, they can cause settlers to adapt their expectations. These adaptations can lead to better, though still imperfect, recognition of native nation rights.

Of course, neither cognitive anthropology nor developmental psychology first discovered their underlying premise that individuals learn from experience. These social sciences formalized methods for observing the dynamic between behavior and knowledge. However, that dynamic existed and others have understood much of its significance well before the invention of Western social science. Long before the emergence of cognitive anthropology, the native nations discussed in this book understood that they could challenge nonnatives' assumptions. By employing what is now cognitive anthropology's premise—a person's understanding of the world comes from that person's experience of it—native nations have often intervened in public discourse as a method to maintain their sovereignty. They continue to use direct action to revive external cultural sovereignty in order to pressure policymakers to restore their external political sovereignty. Since contact, native and settler nations have tried to anticipate how the other will respond to certain events, such as protests or termination. Settler society has often failed to correctly anticipate native responses, while native nations, such as the Cahuilla, have successfully predicted how their actions can change settler perceptions. The Cahuilla and other native nations thrive today, in spite of settler attempts to annihilate them, in large part because they have had a more sophisticated understanding of settler society while settlers often failed to grasp native society. Following the premise of feminist standpoint theory (Harding 2004), the very experience of subjugation provides native nations with distinct cultural knowledge about settler society and how to change it for the better.

When displacing native peoples, settler colonial regimes had the upper hand with guns and diseases that target indiscriminately. But settler institutions often failed because of their simplistic assumptions about native nations. Rather than assimilate native nations, boarding schools sowed the seeds of future native activism. Riverside County (and eventually the state of California) sought to shutter Cabazon's modest poker club based on their flawed, or absent, understanding of tribal sovereignty. Instead, California lost the case and set the precedent for the expansion of what has become a multi-billion-dollar industry. These and other unintended consequences produced the opposite of their intended goals because settler institutions underestimated the resiliency of tribal sovereignty.

What accounts for the Cahuilla and other native nations having such pragmatic understandings of settler society when settlers so often failed to understand their native neighbors? Why is settler society so often shortsighted in its expectations about the future of native nations? The difference may not have as much to do with any intrinsic difference between settlers and natives, but instead with their different experiences and goals. First, after the California gold rush the settler population quickly came to outnumber natives. This meant that while natives had to routinely interact with settlers, the larger the settler population became, the less often settlers had to interact with natives (with the exception of those few settlers who still employed natives). When policymakers have little knowledge of native nations, it should not be surprising that their policies can have devastating results but ultimately fail. On the other hand, native activists have developed strategies based on their experiences with settler institutions. They know how to make neighbors into allies by representing their culture and history in ways that challenge common settler perceptions. Moreover, native nations know foundational events in the history of the United States much better than most settlers. Tribes know, firsthand, that genocide enabled the expansion of the United States, and that tribal sovereignty has endured and continues to shape the settler economy. By knowing these and other parts of settler society better than most settlers themselves, native nations develop strategies to counter misconceptions and build interdependency.

Second, settler institutions and native nations often hold divergent goals. These goals shape their interactions. The goal of maintaining tribal sovereignty looks infinitely into the future, aspiring for perpetual self-determination. The settler colonial goal of resource extraction focuses more on returns in the immediate future. This might limit the foresight of settler institutions. The assumption that boarding schools could succeed in total assimilation, or that native land could be appropriated in totality without recourse, originated in a worldview that prizes present needs over the future. For example, consider the California gold rush: the discovery of gold meant the potential for immediate material success, leading settlers to pursue mining at all costs, both environmental and human. No wonder, then, that in the hurry toward native resource extraction so many settler institutions failed to account for the future. Each time, their sense of urgency led to ill-conceived and devastating public policies. These bad policies, in turn, created fertile ground for future native activism.

These missteps produce the arc of federal Indian policies, often described as a pendulum swinging from termination to supporting (however partially) tribal sovereignty. These swings may be changes in intensity but they are not changes in kind. Federal Indian policy at its most supportive of tribal sovereignty has only been tepid, with Congress and the president capable of returning to termination at any moment. What prompts these changes in intensity? Shortsighted settler goals and their constituent misconceptions account for this pattern. Faults inherent in those policies become their eventual undoing. The allotment created a crisis leading to reform. Termination spurred the intertribal native rights movement—providing the grounds for the tribal gaming movement. Even when the federal government responds to native activism with policies that support self-governance, these policies are crafted within the confines of settler colonialism and its need for resource extraction. Laws may change but the root cause of terminationist policies, the desire for settler institutions to extract native resources, has never withered.

Policymakers and private corporations in the United States may always have their eyes on tribal resources. Reforms made in the wake of termination have partially strengthened tribal sovereignty, but the threat of termination, in one form or another, remains (like the looming implications of the *San Manuel* decision, which may signal a shift toward future losses in external political sovereignty).

In the United States' long history of conflict with native nations, cultural knowledge is a key mechanism for change. Guns can be an effective tool for genocide, but people's misconceptions about their neighbors, coupled with fear or greed, can inspire them to participate or be complicit in genocide. As Cornel (1990, 212) argued, preserving tribal sovereignty requires maintaining distinctiveness in the eyes of the public (i.e., their external cultural sovereignty). In a society where generations have grown up exposed to media and schools that continue to prop up the myths of native assimilation and passivity, native self-representations run counter to most people's assumptions. The recent reforms in the California Board of Education's social studies framework are an important step toward ensuring that future generations understand the role their native neighbors have played and will continue to play in the state's political economy.

Fortunately, much of the emerging field of tribal gaming research challenges common preconceptions and gives tribal sovereignty the analytical weight that it deserves. The work of Katherine Spilde (1998), Eve Darian-Smith (2004), Jessica Cattelino (2008), and David Kamper (2010) demonstrate how tribal gaming derives from tribal sovereignty and leads to greater political and economic interdependency between tribal and settler society. By investigating the impacts of tribal gaming in Cahuilla territory, the epicenter of the movement, this book shows how the perception that tribes are corporations may be emerging in certain segments of settler society alongside their growing interdependence. As Kamper argued, "Indigenous rights within settler colonialism are certainly based on notions of distinction and difference...[but] this does not necessarily mean autonomy" (Kamper 2010, 12). By distinguishing between the internal and external dimensions of sovereignty, this book provides a framework for understanding how sovereignty can grow through mutual recognition and interdependence. Sovereignty itself emerges from internal beliefs about a collective and inherent right to self-determination. When the federal government sought to terminate tribal sovereignty, it devastated native nations but it did not undercut their own belief that they should have self-determination. Scholarship on tribal gaming correctly recognizes that tribal and settler societies can grow through interdependency. This book adds new evidence and a new theoretical perspective to this literature. By maintaining and acting on their beliefs in their right for self-determination, native activists enact their sovereignty (as limited as it is) even when settler society refuses to build interdependencies.

To the larger anthropological questions regarding the processes that influence how different populations understand each other, this research shows the role that direct experiences can have in limiting the distribution of specific assumptions. A population's cultural knowledge about its neighbors may be held in check by that population's direct experiences of their neighbors. For example, during the first decades of California's statehood, those settlers who lived near or worked with native people might have been less likely to accept simplistic views of native people.

Likewise, native nation orientations for casino employees that highlight tribes as nations can only have their intended impact when those characterizations match individuals' experiences. Extensive training programs, like those at San Diego State University and Claremont Graduate University, could help counter this. In other words, this research suggests that linguistic labels tend not to have the impact that direct experience can. During the gold rush it was easy for many settlers to imagine natives as pests, as long as those settlers had little direct experience with tribes. Increasing their experience, as Santos Manuel did, can challenge those characterizations. Likewise, despite tribal representations of their sovereignty, tribal employees may become skeptical if their work experience more closely matches the private sector.

This research also shows how the contradictions between what members of a society want to believe about themselves and their actual history can lead to a collective form of cognitive dissonance that I refer to as historical dissonance. While California settler society in the nineteenth century was quite aware of the area's indigenous populations (even if most of their beliefs were simplistic), by the early twentieth century, historical dissonance, along with demographic factors, suppressed settlers' awareness of the native population. A rapid change in one population—such as a significant influx of outsiders who quickly assimilate to that population, as was the case when migrants from the Midwest and Eastern United States settled in California during the turn of the century—could hasten the disappearance of that population's cultural knowledge of its neighbors. Likewise, the sudden loss of the perceived political and economic impact of a population may result in a drop in the cultural knowledge of that population, even in cases where the forgotten population continues to play a significant, but less visible role. The media and public education cannot by themselves cause a society to forget or misunderstand parts of its history, but they might function as a catalyst, hastening the forgetting processes. The development of Indian gaming can be understood as part of a tradition of native nation adaptation and self-determination, but a settler society that lacks knowledge of its history also lacks a framework for understanding its present. To the settler population, events like native nation revitalization can become unthinkable and result in ad hoc explanations of such events that reflect only the motives and assumptions of that population.

What happens when a society forgets its past? The answer is clear: Such a society cannot comprehend the present or make effective plans for the future. North American settler society must learn about the genocides in its past in order to empathize with those still suffering from this legacy of injustice. But settler societies must also learn from their history in order to create a future where it is safe to be native and where settlers and natives can work and grow together. Self-reliance does not have to be a zero-sum game. When neighboring nations recognize and work with each other, their interdependence makes each stronger. Consider how, ignorant of tribal sovereignty, Riverside County tried to crush Cabazon's modest casino. The county lost the case and now benefits significantly from being home to a multi-million-dollar tribal gaming industry. Imagine how much more native and settler societies would benefit from each other if settlers commonly understood the culture and history of their native neighbors. From genocide to gaming, the Cahuilla other native nations maintain their sovereignty by using a peaceful strategy of combating ignorance and violence with knowledge. Yet there is only so much that tribal self-representation can do when settler institutions, such as education and the media, perpetuate myths. Reforming these institutions to more accurately reflect our shared history can unlock the potential for native and settler societies to experience mutually beneficial, interdependent growth.

REFERENCES

Agua Caliente Cultural Museum. 2011. "George Ringwald and the Conservatorship Program." *The Spirit: Newsletter of Agua Caliente Cultural Museum* 15(4): 4–7.

Agua Caliente Cultural Museum. 2014. "In the Beginning." Agua Caliente Cultural Museum, Palm Springs, CA.

Alfred, Taiaiake. 2005. "Sovereignty." In Barker, *Sovereignty Matters*, 33–50.

Anders, G. C. 1998. "Indian Gaming: Financial and Regulatory Issues." *Annals of the American Academy of Political and Social Sciences* 556(1): 98–108.

Anderson, Benedict. 1983. *Imagined Communities: Reflections on the Origin and Spread of Nationalism*. New York: Verso.

Anonymous. 1855. "Editorial." *Sacramento Daily Union*, February 3.

Anonymous. 1872. "Indian Curiosity." *Daily Alta California*, August 9.

Anonymous. 1972. "Phil Sullivan, 1898." *Desert Trails*.

Barker, Joanne. 2005a. "For Whom Sovereignty Matters." In Barker, *Sovereignty Matters*, 1–32.

Barker, Joanne, ed. 2005b. *Sovereignty Matters: Locations of Contestation and Possibility in Indigenous Struggles for Self-Determination*. Lincoln: University of Nebraska Press.

Barlett, Donald L., and James B. Steele. 2002. "Indian Casinos: Wheel of Misfortune." *Time* 160(25): 44–48.

Barth, Fredrik. 1969. *Ethnic Groups and Boundaries: The Social Organization of Cultural Difference*. Bergen, Germany: Universitsforlaget.

Bean, Lowell John. 1972. *Mukat's People: The Cahuilla Indians of Southern California*. Berkeley: University of California Press.

Bean, Lowell John, and Sylvia Brakke Vane. 2002. *The Native American Ethnography and Ethnohistory of Joshua Tree National Park: An Overview*. Twentynine Palms, CA: Joshua Tree National Park.

Beck, David. 2005. *The Struggle for Self-Determination: History of the Minominee Indians since 1854*. Lincoln: University of Nebraska Press.

Bernard, Russell. 2011. *Research Methods in Anthropology*, 5th ed. Lanham, MD: AltaMira Press.

Blount, Benjamin. 2011. "A History of Cognitive Anthropology." In Kronefeld et al., *A Companion to Cognitive Anthropology*.

Bodinger de Uriate, John J. 2007. *Casino and Museum: Representing Mashantucket Pequot Identity*. Tucson: University of Arizona Press.

Bruyneel, Kevin. 2007. *The Third Space of Sovereignty: The Postcolonial Politics of U.S.-Indigenous Relations*. Minneapolis: University of Minnesota Press.

Buchowski, Michal, David B. Kronenfeld, William Peterman, and Lynn Thomas 1994. "Language, Nineteen Eighty-Four, and 1989." *Language in Society* 23, 555–78.

Bunnell, Lafayette. 1880. *Discovery of Yosemite and the Indian War of 1851*. Chicago: Fleming H. Revell.

California Native American Day. 2015. "Program Overview." California Native American Day, San Bernardino, CA. http://nativeamericanday.org/

Californians Against Unfair Deals. 2008. "Unfair Deals." January 14. https://www .youtube.com/watch?v=HmUbKQ9Fp4c

California State Board of Education. 2000. *Model Curriculum for Human Rights and Genocide*. Sacramento: Department of Education.

California State Board of Education. 2012. *History—Social Science Content Standards for California Public Schools, Kindergarten Through Grade Twelve*. Sacramento: Department of Education.

California State Board of Education. 2017. *History—Social Framework*. Sacramento: Department of Education.

California State Library. 2017. "State of the State Address, Peter Burnett, January 6, 1851." Governors' Gallery, California State Library, Sacramento. http://governors .library.ca.gov/addresses/s_01-Burnett2.html

California Voter Foundation. 1998. "Follow the Money: Top Ten Contributors—California Propositions." As of December 31, 1998. California Voter Foundation, Sacramento. http://www.calvoter.org/voter/elections/archive/98general/follow themoney/topten1.html#5S

Castrovono, Russ 2012. The Oxford Handbook of Nineteenth-Century American Literature. New York City: Oxford University Press.

Cattelino, Jessica. 2008. *High Stakes: Florida Seminole Gaming and Sovereignty*. Durham, NC: Duke University Press.

Chrisomalis, Stephen. 2016. "Diachronic Approaches to Cultural Models." Presentation at the Annual Conference of the Society for Anthropological Science, Vancouver, BC, Canada.

Claremont Graduate University. 2017. "Tribal Administration Certificate Program." Claremont Graduate University, Claremont, CA. https://research.cgu.edu/tribal -administration/

Coalition to Protect California's Budget and Economy. 2008. "Yes on Props 94–97: Two Tribes vs. Many." January 22. http://www.youtube.com/watch?v=wZ9RDg AymYQ

Cohen, Felix S. 1953. "The Erosion of Indian Rights, 1950–1953: A Case Study in Bureaucracy." *Yale Law Journal* 62: 348.

Comaroff, John, and Jean Comaroff. 2009. *Ethnicity Inc*. Chicago: University of Chicago Press.

Cook, Sherburne. 1976. *The Conflict Between the California Indian and White Civilization*. Berkeley: University of California Press.

Cornel, Stephen. 1990. *The Return of the Native: American Indian Political Resurgence*. Oxford, UK: Oxford University Press.

Costello, Jane, Alaattin Erkanli, William Copeland, and Adrian Angold. 2010. "Association of Family Income Supplements with Development of Psychiatric and

Substance Use Disorders in Adulthood Among an American Indian Population."
  Journal of the American Medical Association 303(19): 1954–60.
Costo, Rupert, and Jeannette Henry Costo. 1995. *Natives of the Golden State: The Cali-
  fornia Indians*. San Francisco: Indian Historian Press.
Coulthard, Glen Sean. 2014. *Red Skin, White Masks: Rejecting the Colonial Politics of
  Recognition*. Minneapolis: University of Minnesota Press.
Daly, Heather Marie. 2009. "Fractured Relations at Home: The 1953 Termination
  Act's Effect on Tribal Relations throughout Southern California Indian Country."
  American Indian Quarterly 33(4): 427–39.
Daly, Heather Marie. 2012. "American Indian Freedom Controversy: Political and
  Social Activism by Southern California Mission Indians, 1934–1958." Ph.D. diss.,
  University of California, Los Angeles.
D'Andrade, Roy. 1995. *The Development of Cognitive Anthropology*. Cambridge, UK:
  Cambridge University Press.
Darian-Smith, Eve. 2004. *New Capitalists: Law, Politics and Identity Surrounding
  Casino Gaming on Native American Land*. Independence, KY: Wadsworth.
DeArmond, Michelle. 2000. "First Tribe to Sign Labor Deal Hopes Union Will Be
  Good National Ally." *Las Vegas Sun*. March 21. https://lasvegassun.com/news
  /2000/mar/21/first-tribe-to-sign-labor-deal-hopes-union-will-be/
Deloria, Philip. 2004. *Indians in Unexpected Places*. Lawrence, KS: University Press of
  Kansas.
Deloria, Vine. 1969. *Custer Died for Your Sins: An Indian Manifesto*. Toronto, ON,
  Canada: Macmillan.
Deloria, Vine. 1979. "Self-Determination and the Concept of Sovereignty." In *Eco-
  nomic Development in American Indian Reservations*, edited by R. D. Ortiz, 33–38.
  Albuquerque: University of New Mexico Press.
DeLyser, Dydia. 2003. "Ramona Memories: Fiction, Tourist Practices, and Placing
  the Past in Southern California." In *Annals of the Association of American Geogra-
  phers* 93(4): 886–908.
Dudley, Amy. 1908. "Passing of the Mission Indians." *Los Angeles Herald*, June 1.
Eadington, W. R., and David Schwartz. 2012. "A History of the International Confer-
  ence on Gambling and Risk-Taking." *UNLV Gaming Research and Review Journal*,
  16(2).
Ellis, Clyde. 2005. "The Sound of the Drum Will Revive Them and Make Them
  Happy." In Ellis, Lassiter, and Dunham, *Powwow*.
Ellis, Clyde, Luke Eric Lassiter, and Gary Dunham, eds. 2005. *Powwow*. Lincoln:
  University of Nebraska Press.
Emboy, Elthea. 1905. "Young Women Are Learning to Cook." *Los Angeles Herald*,
  November 12.
Festinger, Leon. 1957. *A Theory of Cognitive Dissonance*. Stanford, CA: Stanford
  University Press.
Fife, Edward J., and Donald L. Fife. 1982. "Geology and History of the Lost Horse
  Gold Mine, Lost Horse Quadrangle, Riverside County, California." In *Geology and
  Mineral Wealth of the California Transverse Ranges*. Santa Ana, CA: South Coast
  Geological Society, 455-466.
Fitzgerald, O. P. 1878/1881. *California Sketches*. Nashville, TN: Southern Methodist.

Fixico, Donald Lee. 1986. *Termination and Relocation: Federal Indian Policy, 1945–1960.* Albuquerque: University of New Mexico Press.

Gelman, Susan. 2005. "Science Briefs: Essentialism in Everyday Thought." *Psychological Science Agenda* (May).

Gelo, Daniel. 2005. "Powwow Patter: Indian Emcee-Discourse on Power and Identity." In Ellis, Lassiter, and Dunham, *Powwow.*

Goodenough, Ward. 1957. "Cultural Anthropology and Linguistics." In *Report of the Seventh Annual Round Table Meeting on Linguistics and Language Study,* 167–173. Washington, DC: Georgetown University, Monograph Series on Language and Linguistics, No. 9.

Goodrich, Chauncey. 1926. "The Legal Status of the California Indian." *California Law Review* (March).

Greene, Linda. 1983. *Historic Resource Study: A History of Land Use in Joshua Tree National Monument.* Denver, CO: U.S. Department of the Interior National Park Service.

Handwerker, W. Penn. 2011. "Methods of Data Collection." In Kronefeld et al., *A Companion to Cognitive Anthropology.*

Harding, Sandra. 2004. *The Feminist Standpoint Theory Reader.* New York: Routledge.

Harmon-James, Eddie, and Judson Mills. 1999. "Cognitive Dissonance: Progress on a Pivotal Theory in Social Psychology." *Science Volume Series.* American Psychological Association, Washington, DC.

Heiser, Robert F. 1978. *Handbook of North American Indians,* vol. 8. Washington, DC: Smithsonian Institution.

Hirshberg, Diane, and Suzanne Sharp. 2005. *Thirty Years Later: The Long-Term Effect of Boarding Schools on Alaska Natives and Their Communities.* Anchorage: Institute of Social and Economic Research, University of Alaska.

Historic American Engineering Record (HAER). 1992. *Lost Horse Gold Mill.* Twentynine Palms, CA: Joshua Tree National Monument.

Hoeft, Mike. 2014. *The Bingo Queens of Oneida: How Two Moms Started Tribal Gaming in Wisconsin.* Madison: Wisconsin Historical Society Press.

Hoffman, Ogden. 1862. *Reports of Land Cases Determined by the United States District Court for the Northern District of California.* San Francisco: Numa Herbert.

Iafolla, Robert. 2016. "U.S. Top Court Won't Consider Labor Board Power over Indian Casinos." Reuters, June 27. https://www.reuters.com/article/usa-court -casinos-idUSL1N19E144.

Indianz.com. 2015. "White House Slams Tribal Labor Sovereignty Act." November 22. http://www.indianz.com/IndianGaming/2015/11/22/white-house-slams -tribal-labor.asp

Irwin, M. H., and S. Roll. 1995. "The Psychological Impact of Sexual Abuse of Native American Boarding-School Children." *Journal of the American Academy of Psychoanalysis* 23(3): 461–73.

Jackson, Helen Hunt. 1883. *A Century of Dishonor: A Sketch of the United States Government's Dealings with Some of the Indian Tribes.* New York: Harper.

Jackson, Helen Hunt. 1884. *Ramona: A Story.* Boston: Little, Brown and Company.

Joshua Tree National Park (JTNP). n.d. "Oral History Collection." Joshua Tree National Park, Twentynine Palms, CA.

Kamper, David. 2010. *The Work of Sovereignty: Tribal Labor Relations and Self-Determination at the Navajo Nation*. Santa Fe, NM: School for Advanced Research Press.

Kidwell, Clara Sue. 2001. "Ada Deer, Menominee." In *The New Warriors: Native American Leaders since 1900*, edited by R. David Edmunds, 239–60. Lincoln: University of Nebraska Press.

Kray, Ryan M. 2004. "The Path to Paradise: Expropriation, Exodus, and Exclusion in the Making of Palm Springs." *Pacific Historical Review* 73 (1): 75–126.

Kronenfeld, David. 1996. *Plastic Glasses and Church Fathers: Semantic Extension from the Ethnoscience Tradition*. New York: Oxford University Press.

Kronenfeld, David. 2008. *Culture, Society and Cognition: Collective Goals, Values, Action, and Knowledge*. Mouton Series in Pragmatics. Berlin: Mouton de Gruyer.

Kronenfeld, David. 2018. *Culture as a System: How We Know the Meaning and Significance of What We Do and Say*. New York: Routledge.

Kronenfeld, David, Giovanni Bennardo, Victor de Munck, and Michael Fischer, eds. 2011. *A Companion to Cognitive Anthropology*. Boston: Wiley-Blackwell.

"Labor the Great Necessity of Los Angeles." 1869. Editorial. *Los Angeles Daily News*, February 11.

Lane, Ambrose. 1995. *Return of the Buffalo: The Story Behind America's Indian Gaming Explosion*. Santa Barbara, CA: Praeger.

Lawson, S. S. 1878. "Lawson Correspondence to Commissioner of Indian Affairs and Others." Record Group 75, Special Cases 31. National Archives, Washington, DC.

Lawton, Harry, and Lowell Bean. 1968. "A Preliminary Reconstruction of Aboriginal Agricultural Technology Among the Cahuilla." *Indian Historian* 1(5): 18–24, 29.

Lindsay, Brendan C. 2012. *Murder State: California's Native American Genocide: 1846–1873*. Lincoln: University of Nebraska Press.

Marks, Mindy, and Kate Spilde-Contrares. 2007. "Land of Opportunity: Social and Economic Effects of Tribal Gaming on Localities." *Policy Matters: A Quarterly Publication of the University of California, Riverside* (Summer).

Marquez, Deron. 2006. "Reservation Shopping Has Far-Reaching Consequences." *Indian Gaming* (March): 12–13.

McKee, Redick, G. W. Barbour, and O. M. Wozencraft. 1851. *Annual Report of the Department of the Interior*, Vol. 2. Washington, DC: Department of the Interior. http://calindianhistory.org/wp-content/uploads/2015/09/05_15_1851.pdf

Meadows, William C. 2002. *The Comanche Code Talkers of World War II*. Austin: University of Texas Press.

Miller, Jim. 2008. "Casinos Scored Expansion Win with Help of Neighbors." *Press Enterprise*, March 10.

Ministry of Foreign Affairs, Republic of China [Taiwan]. 2016. "Diplomatic Allies." Ministry of Foreign Affairs, Taipei City, Taiwan (R.O.C.). https://www.mofa.gov.tw/en/AlliesIndex.aspx?n=DF6F8F246049F8D6&sms=A76B7230ADF29736

Mission Indian Federation (MIF). c. 1922. "Mission Indian Federation Constitution." National Archives and Records Administration, Washington, DC. https://www.archives.gov/exhibits/documented-rights/exhibit/section3/detail/mif-constitution-transcript.html

Montgomery, John B. 1846. "Proclamation to the Inhabitants of California." *Californian*, November 7.

Nagel, Joanne. 1995. "American Indian Ethnic Renewal: Politics and the Resurgence of Identity." *American Sociological Review* 60(6): 947–65.

Nagel, Joanne. 1996. *American Indian Ethnic Renewal: Red Power and the Resurgence of Identity and Culture*. New York: Oxford University Press.

National Indian Gaming Commission. 2014. *Tribal Gaming Revenues 2006–2013*. Washington, DC: U.S. Department of Interior.

National Indian Gaming Commission. 2017. *Gross Gaming Revenue Trending*. Washington, DC: U.S. Department of Interior.

Nixon, Richard. 1970. "Special Message on Indian Affairs to Congress." The American Presidency Project, Santa Barbara, CA. http://www.presidency.ucsb.edu/ws/?pid=2573

Park, Willard Z. 1938. *Shamanism in Western North America: A Study in Cultural Relationships*. Chicago: Northwestern University Press.

Parker, Patricia. 1980. "One Hundred Years of History in the California Desert: An Overview of Historic Archeological Resources at Joshua Tree National Monument." Tucson, AZ: Publications in Anthropology, No 13, Western Archeological Center, National Park Service.

Phillips, George Hardwood. 1975. *Chiefs and Challengers: Indian Resistance and Cooperation in Southern California*. Berkeley: University of California Press.

Phillips, George. 1997. *Indians and Indian Agents: Origins of the Reservation System in California, 1849–1852*. Norman: University of Oklahoma Press.

Phillips, George. 2010. *Vineyards and Vaqueros: Indian Labor and the Economic Expansion of Southern California, 1771–1877*. Norman, OK: Arthur H. Clark.

Piaget, Jean. 1953. *The Origin of Intelligence in the Child*. London: Routledge.

"Pioneer Society." 1898. *Los Angeles Herald*, March 2.

Pratt, Richard. 1892. *Official Report of the Nineteenth Annual Conference of Charities and Corrections*, 46–59. Reprinted in Pratt, "The Advantages of Mingling Indians with Whites," in *American Indians: Writings by the "Friends of the Indian" 1880–1900*, 260–71. Cambridge: Harvard University Press.

Rawls, James. 1984. *Indians of California: The Changing Image*. Norman: University of Oklahoma Press.

Rifkin, Mark. 2009. *Manifesting America: The Imperial Construction of U.S. National Space*. Oxford: Oxford University Press.

Riseman, Noah J. 2012. *Defending Whose Country? Indigenous Soldiers in the Pacific War*. Lincoln: University of Nebraska Press.

Rosen, Deborah. 2007. *American Indians and State Law: Sovereignty, Race and Citizenship, 1790–1880*. Lincoln: University of Nebraska Press.

Ross, Norbet, and Douglas Medin. 2011. "Culture and Cognition: The Role of Cognitive Anthropology in Anthropology and the Cognitive Sciences." In Kronefeld et al., *A Companion to Cognitive Anthropology*.

Rossum, Ralph A. 2011. *The Supreme Court and Tribal Gaming: California v. Cabazon Band of Mission Indians*. Lawrence: University Press of Kansas.

Russell, Maud Carrico. c. 1920. "The Yesterdays of Twenty-Nine Palms." Unpublished manuscript. Twenty-Nine Palms Historical Society, Twentynine Palms, CA.

San Diego State University. 2017. "B.S. in Hospitality & Tourism Management, with Emphasis in Tribal Gaming." L. Robert Payne School of Hospitality & Tourism Management, San Diego State University, San Diego. http://htm.sdsu.edu /degrees/htm/tribal-gaming

San Manuel Band of Mission Indians. 2009. "Santos Manuel." San Manuel Band of Mission Indians, Highland, CA. http://sanmanuel-nsn.gov/news-room

San Manuel Band of Mission Indians. 2010. "Roads." San Manuel Band of Mission Indians, Highland, CA. http://sanmanuel-nsn.gov/news-room

San Manuel Band of Mission Indians v. NLRB. 2007. D.C. 05-1392. https://www.gpo .gov/fdsys/pkg/USCOURTS-cadc-05-01392/pdf/USCOURTS-cadc-05-01392-0.pdf

"San Manuel Band of Serrano Mission Indians Gets the Message Out with Television Advertising." 2011. *Newspaper Rock* [blog]. http://newspaperrock.bluecorncomics .com/2011/05/san-manuels-pr-strategy.html

Saussure, Ferdinand de. 1916/1998. *Course in General Linguistics*. Chicago: Open Court Classics.

Schwartz, David G. 2013. *Roll the Bones: The History of Gambling: Casino Edition*. Las Vegas: Winchester Press.

Senate of California. 1852. *Journal of the Senate*, 3d session. Sacramento: Senate of California.

Senate of the United States. 1853. "Documents of the Senate of the United States: The Special Session Called March 4, 1853." Washington, DC: U.S. Government Printing [Publishing] Office.

Shipek, Florence. 1978. "Mission Indian Federation." In *Handbook of North American Indians*, vol. 8, *California*, edited by William C. Sturtevant (gen. ed.) and Robert F. Heizer (vol. ed.). Washington, DC: Smithsonian Institution.

Shipek, Florence. 1987. *Pushed into the Rocks: Southern California Indian Land Tenure 1769–1986*. Lincoln: University of Nebraska Press.

Simpson, Audra. 2014. *Mohawk Interruptus: Political Life across the Borders of Settler States*. Durham, NC: Duke University Press.

Sorkin, Alan L. 1978. *The Urban American Indian*. Lexington, MA: Lexington Books.

Spilde, Katherine. 1998. "Acts of Sovereignty, Acts of Identity: Negotiating Interdependence through Tribal Government Gaming on the White Earth Indian Reservation." Ph.D. diss., University of California, Santa Cruz.

Spilde Contrares, Katherine. 2006. "Cultivating New Opportunities: Tribal Government Gaming on the Pechanga Reservation." *American Behavioral Scientist* 50(3): 315–52.

"The Standard on Indians." 1860. *Daily Alta California*, March 17.

State of California. 1955. *Progress Report to the Legislature by the Senate Interim Committee on Indian Affairs*. State of California, Sacramento.

Steinman, Erich. 2006. "(Mixed) Perceptions of Tribal Nations' Status: Implications for Indian Gaming." *American Behavioral Scientist* 50 (3): 296–314.

Stevens, Ernest 2002." Replacing *Time* Magazine's Falsehoods with Facts." *Indian*

Country Today. December 17. https://indiancountrymedianetwork.com/news
/replacing-time-magazines-falsehoods-with-facts/

Strong, William Duncan. 1929. *Aboriginal Society in Southern California*. Berkeley: University of California Publications.

Taber, Cornelia. 1911. *California and Her Indian Children*. San Jose: Northern California Indian Association.

Tharoor, Ishaan. 2014. "Map: The Countries That Recognize Palestine as a State." *Washington Post*, November 7. https://www.washingtonpost.com/news/world views/wp/2014/11/07/map-the-countries-that-recognize-palestine-as-a-state /?utm_term=.a7c91f63d96c

Thompson, William N. 2014. "Casinos in Las Vegas: Where Impacts Are Not the Issue." In *Legalized Casino Gaming in the United States: The Economic and Social Impact*, edited by Cathy H. C. Hsu. New York: Routledge.

Thorne, Tanis. 2004. "The Death of Superintendent Stanley and the Cahuilla Uprising of 1907–1912." *Journal of California and Great Basin Anthropology* 24(2): 233–58.

Thorne, Tanis. 2005. "The Mixed Legacy of Mission Indian Agent S. S. Lawson, 1878–1883." *Journal of California and Great Basin Anthropology* 25(2): 147–68.

Trafzer, Clifford. 2002. *The People of San Manuel*. Patton, CA: San Manuel Band of Mission Indians.

Trafzer, Clifford, and Joel Hyer. 1999. *Exterminate Them! Written Accounts of the Murder, Rape, and Enslavement of Native Americans during the California Gold Rush*. East Lansing: Michigan State University Press.

Trafzer, Clifford, and Michelle Lorimer. 2014. Silencing California Indian Genocide in Social Studies Texts. *American Behavioral Scientist* 58(1): 64–82.

Trafzer, Clifford, Luke Madrigal, and Anthony Madrigal. 1997. *Chemehuevi People of the Coachella Valley: A Short History of the Sovereign Nation of the Twentynine Palms Band of Mission Indians*. Coachella, CA: Chemehuevi Press.

Trouillot, Michel-Rolph. 1995. *Silencing the Past: Power and the Production of History*. Boston: Beacon Press.

Ung, Jenny. 2017. "Native American Studies Coming to Palm Springs Unified in Collaboration with Agua Caliente Tribe." *Desert Sun*, November 6. https://www .desertsun.com/story/news/2017/11/06/palm-springs-unified-works-tribe-start -native-american-studies-program-next-year/827595001/

United Nations. 1948. "Convention on the Prevention and Punishment of the Crime of Genocide." United Nations Human Rights Office of the High Commissioner, Geneva. http://www.ohchr.org/EN/ProfessionalInterest/Pages/CrimeOf Genocide.aspx

Unratified California Treaty K (or Treaty of Temecula). 1852. Washington, DC: U.S. Government Printing [Publishing] Office. http://nmai.si.edu/static/nationto nation/pdf/Unratified-California-Treaty-K-1852.pdf

Upham, Samuel. 1878. *Notes of a Voyage to California via Cape Horn*. Philadelphia: Self-published.

Washburn, Kevin. 2008 "The Legacy of Bryan v. Itasca County: How an Erroneous $147 County Tax Notice Helped Bring Tribes $200 Billion in Indian Gaming Revenue." *Minnesota Law Review* 92: 919–70.

Washington, George. 1783. "Letter to James Duane, September 7." Washington

Papers, National Archives, Washington, DC. https://founders.archives.gov/docu ments/Washington/99-01-02-11798

Wassman, Jurg, Christian Klug, and Dominik Albrecht. 2011. "The Cognitive Context of Cognitive Anthropology." In Kronefeld et al., *A Companion to Cognitive Anthropology*.

Weller, Susan, and Kimball Romney. 1988. *Systematic Data Collection*. Thousand Oaks, CA: Sage.

Wilkins, David. 2007. *American Indian Politics and the American Political System*. New York: Rowman and Littlefield.

Wilkins, David, and K. Tsianina Lomawaima. 2001. *Uneven Ground: American Indian Sovereignty and Federal Law*. Norman: University of Oklahoma Press.

Wilkinson, Charles. 2005. *Blood Struggle: The Rise of Modern Indian Nations. New York*. New York: W. W. Norton.

Wilkinson, Charles F., and Eric R. Biggs. 1977. "Evolution of Termination Policy" *American Indian Law Review* 5(1):139-184.

Wolfe, Patrick. 1998. *Settler Colonialism and the Transformation of Anthropology: The Politics and Poetics of an Ethnographic Event*. New York: Cassell.

INDEX

Act for the Government and Protection of Indians (California; 1850), 46–47, 58

Act for the Relief of Mission Indians in the State of California (1890), 69

activism. *See* native activism

"Acts of Sovereignty" (Spilde), 17

Agua Caliente Band of Cahuilla Indians, 110-13, 127, 128, 143–44, 154, 173

Agua Caliente Reservation, 107

Alcatraz Island occupation, 114

alcohol selling, 118

Alfred, Taiaiake, 7

Alta California, 37, 38

American Indian Historical Society, 115

American Indian Movement (AIM), 113

American Indian Rights and Resources Organization, 154

American Indians. *See* native nations

Anderson, Benedict, 5, 6

Antonio, Juan, 40, 41, 48, 49–50, 70, 74, 172–73

Anza, 94

Apapas, Ambrosio, 91–92

asistencias, 38

assimilation: Indian boarding schools and, 70–73; settler advocates of, 62–63

Bachert, Max, 65

Banning Pass, 80

Barker, Joanne, 6

Barona Band of Mission Indians, 127

Barstow, 132–33

Barth, Fredrick, 23, 114

bathtub model, 131–32

Bautista de Anza, Juan, 37–8

Beale, Edward Fitzgerald, 53

Bean, Lowell John, 35, 124

BIA. *See* Bureau of Indian Affairs

Big Lagoon Rancheria, 132–133

bingo, 14–15, 118–19, 123, 125

Bird Song performances, 151–52

boarding schools. *See* Indian boarding schools

Bodinger de Uriarte, John, 144, 146, 170

Boniface, Captain Jim, 83

British colonialism, 43

Broward County (Florida), 14–15

Brown, Edmund Gerald ("Pat"), 109

Bruyneel, Kevin, 15

Bryan, Russell, 116

Bryan v. Itasca County, 116, 119, 123

"bucks," 56, 57

Bunnell, Lafayette, 64

Bureau of Indian Affairs (BIA): Agua Caliente Band and the guardianship scandal, 111; Indian Reorganization Act and, 14; Mission Indian Federation and, 92; powwows and, 150; ruling on reservation shopping, 129; ruling on the Indio annexation of Cabazon Reservation, 121; termination controversy and, 107, 108

Burnett, Peter, 55–56

Cabazon Band of Mission Indians, 1, 10, 33, 116, 118, 119–125, 127. *See also* California v. Cabazon Band of Mission Indians

The Cabazon Band of Mission Indians v. The City of Indio, California, 122

ABOUT THE AUTHOR

THEODOR P. GORDON was born in Allentown, Pennsylvania, and earned his bachelor of arts cum laude in anthropology with honors from Muhlenberg College. In 2013 he earned his doctorate in sociocultural anthropology from the University of California, Riverside.

Cahuilla Nation Activism and the Tribal Casino Movement is Gordon's first book. This research was made possible by grants from the Sycuan Institute on Tribal Gaming Research at San Diego State University and the Labor and Employment Research Association at the University of California, Los Angeles. His research was also supported by the Gaming Research Fellowship (now the Eadington Fellowship) at the Center for Gaming Research, University of Nevada, Las Vegas. He has served as an ethnographic intern and a research consultant for Joshua Tree National Park. Since 2013 he has taught at the College of Saint Benedict/Saint John's University; these are two, single-sex, residential liberal arts colleges in Central Minnesota that share one academic program. At these schools he teaches courses in anthropology, education, and the honors and first-year seminar programs. In addition to his research on American Indian activism, he serves on the Board of Directors of the Central Minnesota Community Empowerment Organization, a nonprofit dedicated to serving immigrants and refugees in need. He currently lives in Saint Joseph, Minnesota.

Professor Gordon will donate all of his royalties from this book to the Native American Rights Fund.

CPSIA information can be obtained
at www.ICGtesting.com
Printed in the USA
LVHW092057081118
596491LV00001B/4/P